The Political Economy of the Middle East

Series Editor
Ashraf Mishrif
Humanities Research Centre
Sultan Qaboos University
Al Khaud, Oman

This series explores the nature of Middle Eastern political regimes and their approaches to economic development. In light of the region's distinctive political, social and economic structures and the dramatic changes that took place in the wake of the Arab spring, this series puts forward a critical body of high-quality, research-based scholarship that reflects current political and economic transitions across the Middle East. It offers original research and new insights on the causes and consequences of the Arab uprisings; economic reforms and liberalization; political institutions and governance; regional and sub-regional integration arrangements; foreign trade and investment; political economy of energy, water and food security; finance and Islamic finance; and the politics of welfare, labor market and human development. Other themes of interest include the role of the private sector in economic development, economic diversification, entrepreneurship and innovation; state-business relationships; and the capacity of regimes and public institutions to lead the development process.

The book series is Scopus Indexed.

Nadia Naim • Alhanoof AlDebasi
David Price
Editors

Intellectual Property and Innovation

Contemporary Developments in the GCC Member States

palgrave
macmillan

Editors
Nadia Naim
Associate Dean
International, Law and Social Sciences
Aston University
Birmingham, UK

David Price
Emeritus Professor
School of Law
Charles Darwin University
Casuarina, NT, Australia

Alhanoof AlDebasi
Executive Director of Copyrights
and Designs
Saudi Authority for Intellectual
Property
Riyadh, Saudi Arabia

ISSN 2522-8854 ISSN 2522-8862 (electronic)
The Political Economy of the Middle East
ISBN 978-981-96-4019-5 ISBN 978-981-96-4020-1 (eBook)
https://doi.org/10.1007/978-981-96-4020-1

This Palgrave Macmillan imprint is published by the registered company Springer Nature Singapore Pte Ltd.
The registered company address is: 152 Beach Road, #21-01/04 Gateway East, Singapore 189721, Singapore

Foreword

On a cloudy November day in 2024, I got an email from Nadia Naim, one of the editing trio of this book, in which she inquired whether I could write a foreword for the volume that the respected reader currently holds in hand. Based on my academic history in the field of intellectual property law, she rightly expected that I will have *interest* in accepting her invitation. What I doubt is—as that is less visible on an international level—that she was aware of the fact that I also teach comparative law for my students in Hungary. As such, she might have been unable to foresee how *deep interest* I will have commending this publication.

I was not present at the "Innovation and Development of Knowledge Societies – Transformational Impact of IP on Knowledge based Economic Growth with Focus on Frontier Technologies, Artificial Intelligence and IP Financing" workshop, held in the scenic Cambridge in July 2023, that formed the basis of the present edited book. But based on the words of David Price in his introduction (Chap. 1), I could immediately feel the vibe of this event and imagine the fruitful conversations of participants from the written versions of the presentations.

Let me list three further personal reasons for happily volunteering to write this short foreword.

First, as a professor of a Central-Eastern European university, I regularly feel the reality that the intellectual property (IP) system of smaller or marginal countries is of secondary importance compared to those of the leading Global North nations. This, coupled with the constant pressure to publish on globally relevant questions, oftentimes leads to the decrease in interest to publish on "local" issues. This feeling might be relevant for some authors from GCC countries, too. Overall, putting the IP regime of Gulf countries in the spotlight via this book is highly appreciated.

Second, as a comparative law professor, I constantly assign Marieke Oderkirk's seminal paper[1] on the ups and downs of selecting target countries for a comparative research. Oderkirk listed various reasons that can ruin the success of any comparisons, from which at least two arguments seem to be directly relevant for the purposes of this foreword. Sources on the GCC countries' IP regime are at most scarce, and there is plausibly a gap among the GCC countries' official languages and the language capabilities of the vast majority of IP researchers. As English has clearly become the *lingua franca* of science these days, we are in a dire need for high-quality publications on local experiences in certain topics on this language. The present volume fills that void.

Third, and that might be the most unique reason of mine, the operation of Shariah as well as any other religious laws in the modern world is a gold mine for comparative lawyers. One of the recurring subjects of any such analysis is related to the modern Islamic finance law. The present book serves the interests of the geek comparative IP lawyers, as its second part includes three chapters on the interplay of Shariah, financing and IP law.

Let me return for a second to Nadia's marvellous foresight. She could have perfectly known that one of my major fields of interest within (comparative) copyright law is related to frontier technologies—topics that are in the focus of this volume. These are especially decentralization through blockchain technology; artificial intelligence and its effects on IP law; the metaverse, innovative and decentralized financing. Topics like these are of vital importance to any researcher around the world, especially since these frontier technologies never stop at the frontiers—they are inherently cross-border due to their born-digital nature. Presenting the experiences from the GCC countries is therefore timely and relevant.

[1] Marieke Oderkirk: The Importance of Context: Selecting Legal Systems in Comparative Legal Research, 48(3) Netherlands International Law Review, December 2001, p. 293–318.

Overall, I am convinced that the importance of this volume will become clear to any and all researchers and practitioners of comparative IP and IT law.

Professor of Law, Faculty of Law and Political Sciences Péter Mezei
University of Szeged, Szeged, Hungary
December 6, 2024

Contents

Notes on Contributors

Alhanoof AlDebasi is the Executive Director of Copyrights and Designs at the Saudi Authority for Intellectual Property (SAIP), Saudi Arabia. She plays a pivotal role in shaping the landscape of intellectual property (IP) in the Kingdom of Saudi Arabia. Her multifaceted responsibilities span the domains of copyrights, related rights, industrial designs, and layout circuits. As a distinguished representative of Saudi Arabia, she actively participates in both national and international forums, and conferences. Also, she has served as a special member of committees and boards. AlDebasi focuses on the significance of intangible IP assets within the creative industries—ranging from music and film to the arts. Additionally, she explores the complex interplay between IP and emerging technologies, and the role of collective management organizations (CMOs) in nurturing creative economies.

AlDebasi has an extensive professional legal background. She has held positions as director of the Innovation Department, legal IP policy advisor, and legal consultant. Furthermore, she often serves as a senior advisor to various Saudi governmental entities, offering valuable insights on crucial IP matters. Her academic journey began as one of the pioneering women to graduate with a Bachelor in Law in Saudi Arabia. Her educational background also includes an LLM from the University of Pittsburgh and an SJD (PhD) in IP from the American University Washington College of Law in the United States, as well as a number of executive education programs from International Institute for Management Development (IMD) and Harvard Business School. Her unwavering commitment to advancing IP rights underscores her invaluable contributions to the field.

Muhanna Hamed Al Zuheimi is an Intellectual Property expert in Oman. His academic qualifications include a Master of Laws in Intellectual Property and a Bachelor of Science in Information Technology Security. With over ten years of experience, he has significantly contributed to organizations like Infoshield LLC, The Research Council, and the Ministry of Higher Education, Research, and Innovation. He is instrumental in solving intellectual property issues and creating compliance frameworks to support Oman's innovation goals. He organizes workshops and develops educational materials to equip individuals with the skills necessary for future technological development. His strategic insights and collaborative teamwork are pivotal in shaping policies, encouraging innovation, and supporting new creators in Oman. His deep knowledge and influence make him an important figure in the intellectual property field, instilling confidence in the future of Intellectual Property in Oman's growing innovation landscape and inspiring others to contribute to this exciting field.

Ida Madieha Abdul Ghani Azmi obtained her LLB from International Islamic University Malaysia (IIUM), LLM from University of Cambridge, and PhD in 1995 from University of London. Ida has authored and presented extensively on various issues on intellectual property and cyber law. She is currently a professor at the Ahmad Ibrahim Kulliyyah of Laws and the former dean of Center for Postgraduate Studies, IIUM, Malaysia.

She was the lead consultant for the Drafting of National Guidelines on Intellectual Property and Competition (2017–2018). She served as the consultant to WIPO for the drafting of IP modules for MyIPO (2017), the IP policy for Kathmandu University (2016), and IP curriculum and syllabus in Bangladesh (2014). She has assisted WIPO to design a database of copyright law and policy for ASEAN countries (2022), a model curriculum on copyright for arts and culture schools in developing countries (UG and PG) (2022), and serve as a resource person for WIPO training programs. She led the consultancy project to draft the Malaysian Cybersecurity Act 2024 and the Data Sharing Bill which is awaiting to be tabled to the Parliament in December 2024.

Mahyuddin Daud obtained his PhD in Cyber Law (Internet Content Regulation) from the International Islamic University Malaysia (IIUM), Malaysia. He actively writes for academic journals and teaches information technology, contracts, and tort laws in the Department of Civil Law at

Ahmad Ibrahim Kulliyyah of Laws, IIUM. He holds professional memberships for Inns of Court Malaysia (ICM), Malaysian Consumer and Family Economics Association (MACFEA), and Global Internet Governance Academic Network (GigaNet), and other various academic positions such as editor for *IIUM Law Journal*. Mahyuddin has presented academic papers in local and international conferences around the region. He was a former deputy dean (Student Affairs) and is currently the director of the Sports Development Centre. He is a member of the IIUM UNESCO Chair of Future Studies—Sound Future Legal System.

Zaid Hamzah is an artificial intelligence (AI) and data practitioner and intellectual property strategist who specializes in AI in law and finance, AI and data governance, and AI in information security. He is currently an Executive Education Fellow at the National University of Singapore (NUS) School of Computing's Advanced Computing for Executives center, where he runs programs on AI innovation management, intellectual property rights in AI innovation, and commercialization of AI innovation. Zaid has over 35 years of professional experience. He has previously served as (1) Microsoft's director for intellectual property and commercial software; (2) senior legal advisor to Singtel's joint venture with Warner Bros. and Sony Pictures; (3) Chief Regulatory Legal & Compliance Officer at listed Telekom Malaysia; (4) associate at KhattarWong & Partners (Singapore law firm); and (5) Singapore Government service. Zaid is the author of nine books spanning law, technology, and intellectual property including the book entitled *Islamic Private Equity and Venture Capital: Principles and Practices* published by IBFIM, Malaysia. Zaid is a board member of NIE1 International, which is wholly owned by Nanyang Technological University. He has a law degree from (NUS) and completed his Masters in International Relations from the Fletcher School of Law and Diplomacy, Tufts University, on a Fulbright scholarship.

Dina Widyaputri Kariodimedjo is an expert in business law and commercial law, technology, international commercial law, drafting, agreements in the WTO, intellectual property rights and drafting commercial contracts. Her research publications include "Intellectual Property Rights Issues on Foreign Investment—Southeast Asian Investment into Africa." She is a Lecturer at the Faculty of Law, Gadjah Mada University, Indonesia.

Noor Suhaida Kasri is a senior research fellow and deputy director of Research Development and Innovation Department at ISRA Research Management Centre, INCEIF (International Center for Education in

Islamic Finance) University, Malaysia. Prior to this, she was an experienced Malaysian advocate and solicitors as well as a Syarie lawyer. During her legal practice, she was appointed as one of the members of Malaysia's Investigating Tribunal Panel, Advocates & Solicitors Disciplinary Board and headed the Shariah Legal Clinic of Kuala Lumpur Bar Legal Aid Centre. Noor received her PhD in Islamic Banking Finance and Management from the University of Gloucestershire (in collaboration with Markfield Institute of Higher Education), UK, under the sponsorship of ISRA (International Shari'ah Research Academy for Islamic Finance). She completed her LLM from King's College of London and was awarded the British Chevening Scholarship. Her Bachelor of Laws and Diploma in Shariah Legal Practice were from the International Islamic University Malaysia. She has written a number of research papers, textbook chapters, and articles and presented in conferences locally and globally.

Nadia Naim is the Associate Dean International for Law and Social Sciences at Aston University, Birmingham, UK. She is a qualified barrister and fellow of the HEA. She has written many scholarly articles in the areas of international intellectual property law, Islamic finance, intangible asset financing, artificial intelligence and development, comparative law, and international law. She completed her Ph.D. in Intellectual Property Rights and Islamic Finance on the GCC titled, "The Intellectual Property Regimes in the Gulf Co-operation Council (GCC): Recommendations to Develop an Integrated Approach to Intellectual Property Rights." She has authored books in the intellectual property field and specializes in emerging areas of international development. Her most recent publications are *Islamic Legal Principles and Intellectual Property Rights in the Gulf* with Gerlach Press and *Developments in Intellectual Property Strategy* with Palgrave Macmillan. Nadia advises policymakers on intellectual property and Islamic finance principles.

Anthony O'Dwyer lectures in law & technology, AI, music law, and copyright at South East Technological University, UK. Anthony's current research with the Turing Institute on AI and music focuses on how cultural products—art and music—evidence a social transition that precedes the "next horizon," the next great change in humanities' social and cultural existence.

Shaista Peerzada is currently studying her MBA at the University Canada West, BC, Canada. She also works as an Associate Professor at Ajeenkya D.Y. Patil University, Pune, India, to supervise PhD students and specializes in teaching intellectual property laws, science, innovation and technology laws, cyber laws, commercial laws, etc. She holds a PhD in Intellectual Property and Information Technology from Shri Venkateshwara University, India, and a Master's degree focusing on innovation, technology, and intellectual property laws from Symbiosis International University. She has been in the WIPO Summer School at the Franklin Pierce Center for Intellectual Property, University of New Hampshire, USA. She has researched and delivered presentations at the WIPO-WTO Colloquium for IP teachers and researchers in Asia and at many other conferences on innovation in business and IPRs, information technology laws, and commercial laws.

David Price is Emeritus Professor of Public International Law and Intellectual Property Law in the School of Law at Charles Darwin University, Australia. His primary research area is the intersection of public international law, international trade agreements, and intellectual property law. This work has extended to the settlement of disputes encompassing the application of investor–state dispute settlement causes and outcomes. He has written and published extensively in these areas, focusing upon the GCC, ASEAN, Indonesia, and Australia as exemplars. David has worked, consulted, and researched in institutions in Australia, Indonesia, the UK, Europe, and the Middle East, and held visiting professorships in Indonesia and China.

Mas Rahmah is the director of the Intellectual Property Study Center at the Faculty of Law, Airlangga University, Indonesia. A Surabaya-Indonesia expert on IP, she is a Professor of Intellectual Property since March 2022. She is also the director of Innovation Business Development and Cooperation at BPBRIN (the Board of Innovation Business Development and Incubation), Airlangga University. She has more than two and a half decades of experience on government policies, trainings, seminars, researches, and publications on IP.

Sangeeta Verma is an experienced legal educator with a strong focus on contract law, corporate law, corporate governance, and other key areas of law. Her interest is in the field of academics and research. She has completed her Master's in Business Law from The Maharaja Sayajirao

University of Baroda, Vadodara, Gujarat, India, and completed her law degree from Mumbai University and is currently pursuing her PhD at Ajeenkya D.Y. Patil University, Pune, India. She has completed the UN Certification course on "RIO+25: UN Water Action Decade International Short-Term Course" organized by the United Nations with A Grad. She is a member of the Eudoxia Research Centre in the USA. She has written many research papers and attended various national and international conferences.

Zi Yang is a Lecturer in Law & Technology at Queen's University Belfast, UK. Using transparency as the keyword, Zi's work explores the intricate dynamics between law, economics, and societal impacts. She studies financial regulation and financial technology innovations through a socio-legal and historical lens. Currently, her research focuses on online trading and smart contract.

List of Tables

CHAPTER 1

Intellectual Property and Innovation: Opportunities and Challenges in the GCC Member States: A Preliminary Introduction

David Price

1 Introduction

The chapters offered in this volume explore the role of intellectual capital and property as a catalyst for change with respect to the emergence and development of knowledge-based societies and economies amongst the member States of the Gulf Cooperation Council (GCC). The chapters also reflect a particular focus on an assessment of the opportunity and need for the States to embrace new directions in intellectual property in order to capitalise upon the shift away from hydrocarbon dependencies in favour of establishing broader-based economies and developing new knowledge societies. The contributors collectively endeavour to provide an appreciation of progress made by the States, namely the Kingdom of

D. Price (✉)
Emeritus Professor, School of Law, Charles Darwin University, Casuarina, NT, Australia
e-mail: david.price@cdu.edu.au

N. Naim et al. (eds.), *Intellectual Property and Innovation*, The Political Economy of the Middle East,
https://doi.org/10.1007/978-981-96-4020-1_1

Bahrain, the State of Kuwait, the Sultanate of Oman, the State of Qatar, the Kingdom of Saudi Arabia and the United Arab Emirates in this regard. They also offer indications of the impact upon their respective economies and societies, as well as offering possible trajectories and options for future developments across the broad spectrum of intellectual property regimes. Indeed, technological development and adoption has been both rapid and pervasive, and the States may benefit from reflection and assessment of their respective intellectual property regimes at this critical juncture.

A common theme across these contributions is an examination of the emergence of artificial intelligence, including associated applications, such as ChatGPT, and the role of these technological developments in shaping and influencing the respective intellectual property regimes and, ultimately, society within the GCC member States. Other noteworthy subthemes reflected in this volume include technological development, intellectual property valuation and financing, theories of legal personality, cryptocurrencies and economics.

This transformational phase for the GCC member States was the subject of examination by presentations by practitioners, business leaders and academics at the Workshop conducted as part of the Gulf Research Council's 13th International Meeting at the University of Cambridge in 2023. The chapters that follow arise from those presentations by individuals and by collaborating authors with subject matter expertise from a wide range of nationalities from Middle East countries, Europe, Australia, South East Asian countries and the United Kingdom.

The overarching theme of the Workshop and the inspiration for the following research chapters were *Innovation and Development of Knowledge Societies – Transformational Impact of IP on Knowledge based Economic Growth with focus on Frontier Technologies, Artificial Intelligence and IP Financing*. Underpinning this theme was the consideration of the primacy of Islam, specifically Shariah, as well as the importance of principles of Islamic finance, in shaping this transformation and societal change. The Workshop reached a general consensus having identified that directions in intellectual property are likely to have a profound impact upon society and well-being in the GCC member States, and provided an opportunity to further explore these linkages and outcomes. A central tenet guiding Workshop presentations and discussion was the concept of innovation as an agent for metamorphosis in the pursuit of modern knowledge-based societies and economies in the context of the six States. This was an ambitious task given the diversity of the economic position of the States, the rich tapestry of their respective societies and the occasional fractious nature of the union. Nevertheless, the golden thread linking all the research was the opportunity for economic growth and society more generally if the States are able to effectively promote technological advancement within the context of their respective intellectual property regimes for the purpose of emerging as better societies.

A particular focus of the Workshop and the research presented therein was the complex interdependencies between the cultivation and regulation of intellectual property, innovation, economic growth and society. It was found that these factors are inextricably linked and that the GCC member States stand to benefit from the careful alignment of the protection and promotion of intellectual property with the development of societies. In short, it was generally agreed that regulatory regimes will be fundamental in the States achieving their stated goals as reflected in their respective vision plans and that this shift will not be without significant challenges, including but not limited to the need for increased investment in innovation, regulatory change and the preservation of traditional knowledge.

2 Shifting Sands: Economic Diversification and the Pursuit of New Technologies

The GCC member States have demonstrated an intention to undertake a significant programme of economic diversification and pursue instead knowledge-based economies and ultimately emerge as enhanced knowledge societies. Critically, within the GCC itself, there is significant variation in culture, society and economic integration as well as wealth. Over the last decade or so, each State has developed and published national strategic and economic development plans or 'Vision Statements', documenting their respective approaches and objectives with respect to the future during their periods of profound reform. A common element underpinning the respective vision statements is the goal of harnessing innovation for economic benefit. The espoused policy objectives in these widely promoted vision statements herald the pursuit of knowledge, economic diversification and consolidation, and social advancement. However, at the same time, they generally pay respect to the past and present by giving equal prominence to their respective cultural heritages. Within the various statements, declarations are made along the lines of "ensuring a balance between the legacy of the [nation's] civilisation and identity on the one hand, and the optimal exploitation of technical developments on the other hand to nurture pride within the society" are also present (*Moving Forward with Confidence: Oman Vision 2040*, 2019, p. 24).

The national vision statements also make reference to the supremacy of Islam. There is by clear inference where not otherwise stated that any pursuit of knowledge and intellectual property development, utilization of frontier technologies and adoption of certain forms of artificial intelligence adoption must be in accordance with the Shariah. The Saudi vison statement, for example, concludes with the declaration "May Allah Bless Us And Guide Us To The Right Path" (Saudi Arabia, *Vision 2030*, 2016, 84).

The impact of artificial intelligence on intellectual property rights is a complex and evolving topic, with both opportunities and challenges. Artificial intelligence technologies can enhance creativity by generating new and innovative content and material across various domains, streamline and improve intellectual property processes and enhance its further generation. But at the same time challenges and threats arise encompassing, for example, ownership and authorship issues, overlapping intellectual property rights and their new frontiers, potential bias and ethical concerns, and legal and regulatory gaps and uncertainties. It may be possible to mitigate the threats by clarifying legal definitions and adapting frameworks to clearly define ownership, authorship and the protectability of artificial intelligence-generated or -impacted intellectual property. Such steps would require implementing ethical guidelines and practices in AI development that can help mitigate bias and ensure responsible use of AI technologies. As Klaus Schwab asserts throughout his Fourth Industrial Revolution thesis, the challenges and threats are more legal, regulatory and ethical than technical (Schwab, 2016).

The evolving relationship between intellectual property rights and artificial intelligence necessitates a careful re-examination of existing frameworks and a proactive approach to address emerging challenges by the GCC members States, both individually and, where appropriate and beneficial, collectively. While artificial intelligence brings about transformative possibilities, it also generates a requisite rethinking of traditional concepts of authorship, inventorship and data ownership. A key factor will be development and enforcement of necessary, enabling and effective laws in each country. Furthermore, the States must restart working in harmony in regard to both regional relationships and regional and international commerce. By fostering collaboration, implementing legal reforms and embracing technological solutions, the States and their societies can harness the potential of artificial intelligence while safeguarding the rights of creators and innovators. The journey towards a harmonious coexistence of intellectual property rights and artificial intelligence requires a thoughtful and adaptive approach, recognising the dynamic nature of both technological progress and legal frameworks. It is suggested that the objective or destination should not be contrarian control of one form over the other but sound management that allows the positive aspects of both to emerge and flourish for the benefit of society in its multiple guises.

3 "The Future Ain't What It Used to Be"

In the Introduction to his ground-breaking seminal work on what he termed the "Fourth Industrial Revolution", Klaus Schwab (2016), founder and Chairman of the World Economic Forum, wrote that:

> Of the many diverse and fascinating challenges that we face today, the most intense and important is how to understand and shape the new technology revolution, which entails nothing less than a transformation of humankind. We are at the beginning of a revolution that is fundamentally changing the way we live, work, and relate to one another. In its scale, scope and complexity, what I consider to be the fourth industrial revolution is unlike anything humankind has experienced before.

American baseball legend and popular cultural icon Yogi Berra had expressed a similar sentiment many years earlier when he stated in a much simpler but equally effective way, "The future ain't what it used to be" ("Yogisms", Yogi Berra Museum, (n.d.)), and inadvertently summed up the contemporary context of dynamic change with a certain degree of unpredictability. The selection of chapters proffered in this volume reflect these two sentiments in many respects. The chapters collectively explore new directions in the application of selected aspects of the broad spectrum of intellectual property rights shaped by emerging technologies and artificial intelligence in the context of the GCC member states. While the chapters generally examine the application of their respective principles within the GCC context, they may also have application in the global context. The frontier technology elements of intellectual property growth are gaining increasing attention, and there are important lessons to be learnt from and by both Muslim and non-Muslim economies.

The chapters presented in this volume could lay claim to constituting expressions of confidence in intellectual property and artificial intelligence applications moving in new directions, either within the individual GCC member States or having potential for region adoption or modification. They have been rather loosely categorized into three groups. In the first group of three chapters, the reader is presented with an assessment of the current status of intellectual property regulatory frameworks amongst the States and an introduction to some potential future projects with an intellectual property/artificial interface. The second chapter examines the nature of the metaverse and the penetration of at least one of its elements, namely ChatGPT, amongst the respective States, and offers a state-by-state risk analysis of that penetration and its uncertain relationship with the prevailing intellectual property regime. The third chapter evaluates the commitment of the Sultanate of Oman to promoting technological advancement while safeguarding intellectual property rights by detailing government initiatives to foster innovation and growth.

The second group of chapters then turn to the specific subject of artificial intelligence systems and intellectual property financing under principles of Islamic law. The first chapter examines the potential role for artificial intelligence in the development of audit and valuation methods to expand the current market limitations on ascertaining the most accurate value of intellectual property assets and creating more opportunities for its financing and technology. The second chapter examines intellectual property securitization as one financing model for new alternative support and the prospect of securitization as a financial technique to turn intellectual property assets into marketable securities such as bonds, or *Sukuk*. The third chapter provides a case study of initiatives by the Malaysian government to build a sustainable intellectual property sector that encompasses Islamic financing products and conventional financing regimes because of the dual nature of the existing intellectual property industry.

The third group of chapters includes perspectives on differing aspects of commercialization in an artificial intelligence and intellectual property context. The first chapter examines the economies of the GCC member States in a shifting global market and considers whether they are positioning their economies in a new global landscape to address the challenges and prospects of driving artificial intelligence innovation and related intellectual property in the GCC economies. The second chapter offers an intriguing examination of artificial intelligence and intellectual property performing in the world of music. It proposes a possible alternative strategy to the conventional collective management agency strategy for artists from the States to promote and benefit from their creative outputs through an artificial intelligence-generated distributed ledger technology, to allow greater control over their work. The third chapter further explores the intellectual property and finance theme from a rather different and novel perspective by examining cryptocurrency in the global landscape, and its potential as a new method for conducting intellectual property-related financial transactions, in a digital environment.

The final contribution continues on with this future scenario on the intellectual property and artificial intelligence relationship but at the same retains in the foreground both an Islamic context and a fundamental precept of Shariah as the foundational core of the Gulf societies. In so doing, it also raises key questions on possible limitations to the extent and nature of that relationship.

3.1 The Brave New Worlds of Intellectual Property Application

Alhanoof AlDebasi and David Price provide the opening chapter to this volume and introduce some core theme across the chapters that follow. As demonstrated by its title, *Intellectual Property, Artificial Intelligence and Economic Development: Sport and the Saudi Arabia Exemplar*, they explore the role of intellectual property and capital as a catalyst for change with respect to the emergence and development of societies and economies amongst the GCC member States. They also reflect on an assessment of the opportunity and imperative for the States to embrace new directions in intellectual property to contribute to, and capitalise upon, the shift away from hydrocarbon dependencies in favour of developing broader-based economies. They do so by considering three related and mutually supporting 'pillars', namely intellectual property, artificial intelligence as representative of the digital environment, and the associated potential for positive contribution to national economic development. It utilises as the vehicle for this analysis a broad spectrum of activity which is deeply embedded in the psyche, history and custom of all States and their societies, as well as the world in general, namely sport. While this analysis includes frequent reference to all GCC member States with respect to the nature of their perspectives and commitments to promotion of sports activities, it focusses primarily on the experience of Saudi Arabia as arguably the regional exemplar of the utilization of intellectual property and artificial intelligence and economic development for mutual national, societal and individual benefit.

Dina W. Kariodimedjo, in her chapter *Intellectual Property in the Metaverse and Artificial Intelligence: ChatGPT in the GCC Member States*, analyses the current status of metaverse recognition and application of at least one of its elements, namely artificial intelligence, across the GCC member States. In so doing she focusses on the artificial intelligence-based software ChatGPT, and the uncertainty of its relationship with the prevailing intellectual property regime. Hence the question arises as to how society in general and educational actors specifically should behave regarding the use of artificial intelligence in various sectors, especially in terms of intellectual property rights.

Her discussion on aspects of the metaverse environment and potential in Indonesia, as the largest Muslim-based nation, the largest economy in South East Asia, as well as the author's home state, provides an international perspective on the metaverse and a basis for comparison with the States.

Kariodimedjo suggests that the metaverse is an immensely mounted and interoperable web of simultaneous extracted three-dimensional simulated worlds that can be practised in a synchronous and persistent way by a virtually unlimited number of users with an individual sense of presence. The metaverse has the potential to not only be as big as the real world, but also as diverse. It also supports the full transferability of data and digital assets, and thus positions e-commerce to become a dominant instrument. This has particular reference to, and potential impact upon, the States in light of the significant level of digital connectivity and social media penetration that already exists amongst their populations.

In order for the metaverse to function, it needs a vision for the future of the Internet, which is defined as web 3.0, the third phase or the smartest of the Internet. Web 3.0 will assist the metaverse's function using sophisticated technologies, for example AI, natural language processing, decentralized autonomous organization, decentralized finance, machine learning and blockchain.

Kariodimedjo argues that, from the main objective of intellectual property and the aspect of metaverse as a parallel connection between the digital to the physical world, it can be concluded that the metaverse user is obliged to respect the creator's, inventor's or owner's intellectual property rights. But the rights regime recognizes property specific to human creations, not the output of ChatGPT or any other artificial intelligence.

Accordingly, there are challenges to face by the creator, inventor or owner. Kariodimedjo discusses the regulatory and policy developments, as well as the legal issues concerning the metaverse and ChatGPT in respect of intellectual property rights, its challenges and to propose solutions, focusing in particular on the Gulf countries. However, the use of artificial intelligence has yet to show clear legal consequences, and the requisite legal sanctions. The author suggests that the concept of originality should be the approach that intellectual property rights offer for this issue.

Kariodimedjo concludes by acknowledging that the development of metaverse and artificial intelligence software in the GCC member States varies. While most have made efforts and improvements to utilise metaverse and artificial intelligence in areas which accommodate societal needs, especially in economic and socio-cultural sectors, the absence of specific law and regulation is a key element of concern. The confronting challenge is to enact laws and devise policies that will be able to anticipate practices in metaverse and AI but at the same time will be understood by industry, society and the individual, and thus accepted and enforceable.

Muhanna Hamed Al Zuheimi, in his chapter titled *Development of New Technologies and Intellectual Property Regulations in the Sultanate of Oman*, provides his analysis of the commitment by Oman to promoting technological advancement while safeguarding intellectual property rights. He asserts that Oman has made significant strides in creating a robust regulatory framework for intellectual property by actively participating in international agreements and conventions, by enacting laws, and by fostering an environment conducive to innovation. He details various government initiatives to foster innovation and growth, such as establishing research and development centres, building science and technology parks, and facilitating technology transfer from global entities.

Zuheimi argues that Oman has emerged as a significant player in global trade, utilizing its strategic geographic location and rich natural resources. Acknowledging the pivotal role of new technologies in facilitating trade and enhancing its competitive advantage, it has invested in research and development activities to diversify its economy, reduce oil dependency and facilitate sustainable economic growth. He examines development of new technologies in Oman in the areas of infrastructure development, information and communication technology, healthcare, and renewable energy and sustainability. He then comments on Oman's short-, medium- and long-term economic plans before moving on to the role of the industry establishment in supporting economic growth, and the role of local communities in technology development. He promotes the importance of an integrated approach to innovative development that encompasses the government, industry and academe.

Oman recognizes that effective utilization of new technologies is essential to diversify its trade portfolio and reduce reliance on oil exports. By embracing digitalization, it has expanded its export base and increased its competitiveness in non-oil sectors such as manufacturing, information technology and tourism.

Zuheimi promotes the importance of Oman safeguarding intellectual property as a top priority. He reviews the current status of the country's intellectual property regime and acknowledges the substantial economic advantages of protecting its rights to enhance the country's position in global trade, to stimulate economic development, promote innovation and attract foreign investment. He also suggests that further enhancement of the regime will attract foreign direct investment, boost investor confidence, enable business to safeguard assets, and contribute to nurturing international collaborations and partnerships.

Zuheimi offers a number of strategies aimed at leveraging technology to drive economic growth and enhance trade competitiveness through advanced technology for consideration. These include encouraging investment by providing government funding, partnering with universities and research institutions, tax incentives to encourage private sector investment, promoting entrepreneurship and start-ups, supporting digital transformation, and establishing digital infrastructure such as high-speed Internet connectivity. He also suggests that strengthening the intellectual property framework is essential to protect innovations and incentivize research and development. Robust laws and enforcement mechanisms give domestic and foreign investors confidence in Oman's technology sector.

3.2 Harmonising Intellectual Property and Islamic Finance Principles

In her chapter *A Framework Proposal for Islamic Finance-Based Intellectual Property Rights Audit Valuation,* **Nadia Naim** examines the role that artificial intelligence systems can play in intellectual property financing whilst considering Islamic law for the GCC member States. She analyses the potential role for artificial intelligence in the development of audit and valuation methods to expand the current market limitations on ascertaining the most accurate value of intellectual property assets and creating more opportunities for intellectual property financing and technology whilst considering issues around artificial intelligence trustworthiness and ethics. She suggests that this is relevant to the States as they embark on significant economic and business transformations.

Naim suggests that, as the artificial intelligence-inhabited space continues to grow and transcend aspects of intellectual property creation, there is opportunity for artificial intelligence-assisted and -generated systems to add to the audit and due diligence methods. Main emerging technologies can assist with both auditing and valuation systems and can be developed to enhance intellectual property valuation, overcoming buyer and seller disincentives. For the seller, the sale of core assets or intellectual property rights to another party can raise concerns over the worth of the remaining assets or even the worth of the business. Alternatively, concerns can arise for a buyer over the sustainability of those assets or the reliance on specialist teams when it is difficult to determine asset values without comparable transactions or other data. Hence, such audits can be very insightful and relevant to a company's financial forecast and value. The audits establish whether the appropriate policies and procedures are in place and what intellectual property rights a company has. The more detailed and accurate, the more reliable the audit is, in terms of validity and status. The audit aims to identify the most valuable rights as core assets. Due diligence is critical for identifying and verifying intellectual property assets and liabilities, in relation to a transaction.

Naim offers lessons that can be learnt from the United Kingdom because of its strong intellectual property regime, and its position as the leading European country for Islamic finance. She proposes a tailored approach for the GCC that can take into account intellectual property audit processes and practices for successful valuation whilst actively creating an Islamic law-compliant model.

In closing, Naim suggests that the GCC can develop a regulatory framework that defines and mitigates for the different levels of risk for artificial intelligence systems that are in compliance with Islamic law to develop a first of its kind set of related laws and regulations for intellectual property.

Although continuing on the general theme of IP and Islamic financing, **Mas Rahmah** nevertheless provides a rather different perspective on the subject. Within *Intellectual Property Financing for Innovation: Structuring Intellectual Property Securitisation for Issuance of Islamic Financial*

Instrument "Sukuk" she examines intellectual property securitization as one financing model dedicated to accelerating new alternative financial support for the development of creativity and productivity in an innovation world. She analyses the prospect of such securitization as a financial technique to turn an intellectual property asset (including royalties or receivables) into marketable securities such as bonds, or *Sukuk*.

Rahmah argues that, since *Sukuk* is an Islamic financial instrument, its issuance under intellectual property securitization might spark challenges at the doctrinal, normative and practical levels. At the doctrinal level, the main challenges are fundamental issues related to Shariah compliance in structuring securitization for *Sukuk*. At the normative level, the absence of regulation may affect the validity of securitization. At the practical level, the absence of the system and infrastructure leads to clumsy and unconfident practices of securitization as it involves complex procedures, interdisciplinary laws and professionals, and complicated asset valuation. The intrinsic risks of intellectual property assets with uncertainty of revenues or royalties, the small intellectual property market, and the problem of transferability also expose the securitization challenge. She considers how it might be possible to structure *Sukuk* issuance under such securitization provided it complies with Shariah requirements.

Rahmah contends that intellectual property securitization is needed to encourage *Sukuk* for financing creativity and innovation development since the securitization plays the significant roles of providing new financing alternatives and financial support for developing and strengthening creativity and innovation development. The use of intellectual property assets to back *Sukuk* warrants promotion since challenges to provide tangibles for underlying assets persist. Although it is possible to structure securitization for *Sukuk* and it has promising prospects, it is very important to address the set of challenges from the doctrinal/Shariah perspective, and the regulatory and practical level. From the Shariah doctrinal perspective, intellectual property assets as intangible objects, especially in the form of claims/royalties, cannot be used as underlying assets for *Sukuk*. However, the practice in Malaysia, Indonesia and several other countries is to allow intangibles as underlying assets for *Sukuk*, and thus the intellectual property intangible asset can be used to back *Sukuk*. From a legal perspective, most jurisdictions still do not offer adequate legal means for financing intangible assets, including securitization for *Sukuk* issuance. The issuance of the "Bowie Bond" in 1997, which transformed David Bowie's music copyright, is analysed as an exemplar of intellectual property asset monetization by transformation into financial securities and thus creating capital from the securitization.

Rahmah suggests that securitization for *Sukuk* issuance can be structured if such securitization complies with Shariah requirements which entail that transactions are based on sale of assets or their usage as underlying assets, that they are devoid of interest, and function on the basis of profit or loss from a sale/purchase. Such securitization can be an attractive financing mechanism for intellectual property owners or innovation industries seeking financing for their operation and further innovation development. She contends that the securitization is an attractive financing option to support creative and innovation development as *Sukuk* has a widespread appeal and marketability in Muslim, non-Muslim and Western countries.

Noor Suhaida Kasri returns more to the mainstream of intellectual property and Islamic financing, but offers valuable insights into the Malaysian context and relevance to the Gulf experience. *Tapping Malaysian Intellectual Property Islamic Financing* addresses a number of critical initiatives and infrastructures deployed by the Government of Malaysia towards building a resilient and sustainable intellectual property sector. While the chapter covers specifically Islamic financing and its financing products, it also provides a description of conventional financing regimes because of the dual nature of the existing initiatives offered to the intellectual property industry.

Kasri contends that the growth of the intellectual property sector is supported by the emergence of innovative start-ups and small and medium-size enterprises. However, funding/financing for intellectual property is a perennial problem, particularly in emerging economies. Despite it being a proven primary contributor to business value and wealth creation, many developing economies have yet to grasp its importance and relevance, since intellectual property issues, to a large extent, are still not well understood. Recognizing that there exists a funding gap as a paramount hindrance to the growth of the intellectual property sector, the Malaysian Government and relevant stakeholders have launched initiatives offering tailored-made funding/financing to related enterprises. Critical supporting infrastructure has been placed to overcome barriers for the more effective use of intellectual property assets in financing considerations. Kasri introduces a number of these initiatives and then considers Malaysia's standing in relevant global rankings, such as the World Intellectual Property Organisation's Global Innovation Index.

As Kasri points out, traditional debt-based financing funded by financial institutions better suits enterprises with regular repayments and well-understood risks. However, reliance on this type of financing alone may not be appropriate for start-ups or scale-ups engaged in new growth ventures or business transformation exercises. Perceived lack of tangible collateral, a common profile of such firms, and valuation mechanisms are also key challenges to intellectual property being accepted as collateral, with many financial institutions lacking the necessary experience, expertise or capability to assess its viability and value as collateral.

The chapter then showcases studies on existing Malaysian intellectual property financing initiatives which examine the two main categories of financing models for the sector, namely the traditional financing model represented by debt-based financing and the alternative financing model reflected by equity-based funding and innovative funding. These schemes share one common feature, namely, the provision of funding/finance for innovative start-ups and small/medium enterprises in the intellectual property sector. To facilitate these funding/financing initiatives, the Malaysian Government has established critical supporting financing enablers that help in enhancing the creditworthiness of intellectual property businesses and eliminating or minimizing the risk associated with them. This initiative addresses the funding gap that beleaguers the sector and helps to instil resilience and sustainability in the ecosystem in the long term.

Kasri concludes that the examination of these case studies is timely as the global economy is searching for exemplary financing/funding models including alternative financing models for the intellectual property industry. There is no one-size-fits-all solution because each economy has its own set of preferences, needs and ecosystems. However, the case studies exhibit practical lessons and perhaps could be the genesis of their search for the appropriate real-economy-based financing and investment models for the nation.

3.3 Specific Commercialization Opportunities for IP Applications

Zaid Hamzah continues with an economic perspective but offers a different pathway in his chapter, entitled *AI Innovation, Intellectual Property Commercialization, and the Rise of the Intellectual Capital Economy: Challenges and Prospects for GCC Economies*, in which he examines the economies of the GCC member States in a shifting global market. He asserts that in the era of the 'fourth industrial revolution', intellectual capital has emerged as a critical driver of economic value.

Hamzah questions how the States are positioning their economies in this new global landscape and addresses the challenges and prospects of driving artificial intelligence innovation and the commercialization of related intellectual property in the GCC economies. He argues that the economies face challenges across two fronts. Firstly, how to accelerate the pace of innovation, especially in the area of artificial intelligence development, and secondly, how to leverage intellectual property as the new value driver through more effective commercialization. In the current environment, innovation is increasingly dictated by the value of artificial intelligence contribution in research and development. According to the Stanford University AI Index 2020, China and the United States are leading the world in its development, with the United States at the top of the ranking in research and China leading in adoption. In contrast, the GCC member States lag far behind.

To catch up, the GCC member States need to leapfrog by choosing niche sectors to innovate, as they cannot compete across too broad a front with larger economies such as the United States and China. Innovation in new areas is critical. The States need to leverage their unique strengths and opportunities to innovate in niche areas, such as renewable energy, agro-technology in harsh hot climates and smart cities. Even more important is to build capabilities to commercialize and extract economic value. Owning assets is not as critical as the ability to commercialize such assets. This requires investment in the development of human capital, building robust innovation ecosystems, and fostering an enabling regulatory environment.

The GCC member States may find useful lessons from smaller but high-value economies such as Singapore, which relies solely on people and the creation of intellectual capital to drive commercial value. Hamzah suggests that a niche approach is probably the best way for their economies. It is important to build the "soft" infrastructure and the capabilities to commercialize and extract economic value.

The author concludes with the assertion that the States have long recognized the need to shift from an over-dependence on oil revenue. They recognize the value of intellectual capital, including knowledge assets, intellectual property and other forms of intangible assets. The transition to the emerging intellectual capital economy, however, will not be an easy one, with challenges to face on multiple fronts. To succeed, they need to focus and excel in niche areas while building capabilities to commercialize and extract economic value. The Singapore example may provide a useful blueprint for how this can be achieved.

Zi Yang and Anthony O'Dwyer move away from the mainstream discourse on intellectual property and artificial intelligence interaction by offering an intriguing examination of artificial intelligence in the GCC world of music. In *Distributed Ledger Technology as an Innovative Collective Management Tool for the GCC Music Industry*, Yang and Dwyer propose an alternative to the conventional strategy for artists from the GCC member States to promote and benefit from their creative outputs. They argue that the continued development of the small but growing Gulf music industry is crucial for both the well-being of creators and the social and cultural fabric of the region. They propose using distributed ledger technology as a possible alternative to traditional collective management organization structures which currently allow artists to license their work, manage their revenue, and promote the ethno-musicological importance of the region.

The authors describe collective management organizations as authorized to manage the copyright and related rights of rights-holders. Authors assign their copyright and, in return, the organizations collect revenues from the exploitation of the work in jurisdictions around the world. They suggest, however, that these organizations face criticisms for a perceived lack of transparency, high transaction costs and a failure in certain situations to pay artists, which may provide scope for technical and structural improvement via distributed ledger technology. This technology has been described as a '… technical protocol to create a secure, transparent ledger that reports transactions to everyone within the network'. In this decentralized system, information is shared across the system in real time and verified by users. A public distributed ledger could resolve many of the claimed organization issues, foremost the transparency and cost elements via self-executing smart contracts which are controlled by the rights-holder rather than the organization.

The authors suggest that the distributed ledger technology is well fitted to address this perceived need for the following reasons. Firstly, it shares decision-making power with artists. Instead of using an intermediary, they can generate and monitor 'proof-of-work' via the peer-support network, where information is shared publicly in real time. Secondly, through smart contracts, they can better distribute and manage their own creative work. Together, these technologies have the potential to benefit creatives by reducing transaction costs inherent in the current model and in turn divert more royalties to artists.

However, the authors also warn that the technology is far from perfect. In addition to being extremely energy consuming, it has also been used for online scamming purposes and dubious speculations. Notwithstanding its shortcomings they argue that in music management it still offers a way to make the technology innovation meaningful. Furthermore, they argue that the GCC is better placed to mitigate some of the above shortcomings as a region governed by Islamic finance principles, which in turn has potential benefit for the GCC through pioneering knowledge society developments and web 3.0 innovations.

Again, from a somewhat different perspective, **Shaista Peerzada** and **Sangeeta Verma** in their contribution, *Synergising IP and Cryptocurrency: A Roadmap for Knowledge-Based Economic Growth*, continue the exploration of the intellectual property and finance themes from a rather different and novel perspective. They examine the explosion of cryptocurrency onto the global financial landscape, providing a new method for conducting transactions, storing value and investing. They submit that synergizing intellectual property and cryptocurrency has the potential to promote knowledge-based economic growth in a rapidly evolving digital economy. This synergy can open new opportunities for innovation, entrepreneurship and economic development. However, it presents intellectual property challenges associated with technology, business practices and regulatory compliance. They argue that it is necessary to comprehend and address these challenges to maintain a competitive advantage, manage risk, and comply with ever-changing legal and regulatory frameworks. Innovation in cryptocurrency trading frequently entails the creation of new technolo gies or novel applications of existing ones; patenting these innovations can be difficult due to the technical nature of the innovations and the varying patent laws in different jurisdictions. Cryptocurrency relies significantly on software, which is typically copyright-protected; however, open-source software is prevalent in the cryptocurrency world.

The authors provide a concise synopsis on the background to cryptocurrency and recent developments of cryptocurrency trading. They also offer a number of cases of trading that demonstrate the risks that can occur in an environment of inadequate regulation or safeguards. They contend that the GCC and its member States could leverage the power of intellectual property and cryptocurrency to drive knowledge-based economic growth. The required strategic approach would encompass an understanding of the economic landscape, placing an emphasis on intellectual property protection, fostering innovation and research and development, and promoting cryptocurrency and blockchain technology. It could also include launching a GCC-backed cryptocurrency or token, establishing technology hubs and incubators, providing regulatory clarity, strengthening cybersecurity and data privacy measures, as well as a number of other measures. By integrating protection and cryptocurrency into a comprehensive strategy, the GCC could harness the power of innovation and digital assets to drive economic growth and position themselves as leaders in the knowledge-based economy.

The intersection of intellectual property and cryptocurrency is likely to become even more significant as blockchain technology continues to evolve and proliferate. However, such intersection is not without its challenges and concerns. The tension between the anonymous nature of many cryptocurrencies and the requirement to identify parties to enforce rights will continue to present challenges. Issues of jurisdiction and international cooperation in enforcement will be increasingly important. New mechanisms for dispute resolution may evolve to address conflicts in the decentralized and pseudonymous context of blockchain and cryptocurrency. Cybersecurity will become increasingly important as cryptocurrency and blockchain technologies become central to intellectual property strategy.

The authors acknowledge that the proper management of regional cryptocurrency faces challenges, such as uncertainty in regulatory policies, risks of fraud and security, lack of awareness and education, cross-border transactions, market volatility and technological hurdles. However, the opportunities include an innovative ecosystem, financial inclusion, blockchain use cases, a digital economy, IP protection and monetization, environmentally friendly and sustainable cryptocurrency, international collaboration, and fintech hubs. Investing in these areas can attract investment and foster innovation.

3.4 Addressing the Intellectual Property/Artificial Intelligence Interface Conundrum

The presentations then move to the thorny and challenging issue of regulation and control of the intellectual property and artificial intelligence interface—or as some critics might suggest the 'IP and AI face-off'.

The research team of **Ida Madieha Abdul Ghani Azmi, Suzi Fadhilah Ismail, Nazli Ismail Nawang, Ani Munirah Mohamad, Mahyuddin**

Daud, Faiz Naqib Amirul Ramli and **Inshirah Amin** return the debate to some first principles in the interface, as well as the cultural context in which the debate commenced this journey of discovery, namely: Can there be an interface at all? In their chapter entitled *Liability Gap, Personhood Theories and Effective AI Legal Framework in the GCC Countries: Shariah as the Thread That Binds,* they provide a specific Islamic perspective on the question of the status of artificial intelligence in the intellectual property context but also the more crucial issue of where artificial intelligence stands in respect of Shariah. Their contribution, which will no doubt generate fresh grounds for further academic and research exchange, examines the very fundamentals of this interface, and is an appropriate point to draw this volume to a close (albeit, just for the time being).

The authors posit that the GCC member States are embarking on ambitious plans to take full advantage of artificial intelligence and emerging technologies in transforming their economic industries. They assert that such rapid transformation is predicted to have substantial pitfalls for the States, one of which involves the use of artificial intelligence-driven technologies. Given that their deployment necessitates a supportive and comprehensive legal framework, the legal status of artificial intelligence as an artificial person requires considered attention. Where these technologies are considered as mere tools for human consumption, the issue of recognition as separate legal entities entitled to their own rights and responsibilities does not arise. With the ability of these platforms to match humans with excellence, as well as the development of human-like sentient artificial intelligence, there is a fresh call for their legal status to be revisited.

The chapter begins with an examination of the ontological status of personhood in contemporary discourse. It then explores the notion of 'personhood' within the Muslim scholarship discourse. Core to the issue is the question of the context in which rights and obligations arising from artificial intelligence activities and transactions would be recognized under Shariah. It offers the proposition that granting human personhood entails a number of consequences, most importantly in terms of rights and responsibilities. Despite the compelling normative arguments in favour of passive rights or from the angle of a bundle of rights, with respect, those theories do not explore incidence of rights, privileges and responsibilities in their full ecosystem. In Islam, rights and responsibilities arise as a result of human interaction with others as well as accountability to one's ultimate Creator. The chapter pursues this argument further by considering the legal status of artificial intelligence under Islam, as well as exploring the notion of non-persons.

The chapter concludes by suggesting that a focus in this debate should be more on responsibility and accountability rather than full legal status as legal personhood would generate a compelling argument for Muslims and the GCC member States countries to shift from the traditional conception of personhood. Through this shift, there would be weaker legal obstacles to fully adopting artificial intelligence. The authors assert that, as Shariah is the golden thread that binds, the articulation of the Shariah perspective would be beneficial to countries aiming to build their economy based on artificial intelligence products and services.

4 Conclusion

The societal and cultural character of the Gulf region and its member communities are currently confronting the challenging questions relating to the application of frontier and emerging technologies. They include the broader issues of understanding, grasping and utilising artificial intelligence in its various and seemingly ever-increasing forms. But they also include specifics, such as exploiting the emerging methods of identifying, valuing and financing intellectual property commercial transactions, blockchain and cryptocurrencies, risk sharing and equitable reward. With frontier and emerging technologies and artificial intelligence come new opportunities and challenges for the GCC and its member States to expand their innovation capabilities.

References

Oman 2040: Moving Forward with Confidence. (2019, September 11). *Sultanate of Oman*. https://www.oman2040.om/?lang=en

Schwab, K. (2016). *The Fourth Industrial Revolution*. World Economic Forum. www.weforum.org

Vision 2030. (2016). *Kingdom of Saudi Arabia*. https://www.vision2030.gov.sa/en/

Yogisms. (n.d.). Yogi Berra Museum and Learning Center. https://yogiberramuseum.org/about-yogi/yogisms/

CHAPTER 2

Intellectual Property, Artificial Intelligence and Economic Development: Sport and the Saudi Arabia Exemplar

Alhanoof AlDebasi and David Price

1 Introduction: Sport in the Gulf

Intellectual property (IP) serves as the bedrock for innovation, creativity and economic growth across diverse sectors. In the GCC member States, nations rapidly advancing in various industries, understanding and harnessing IP rights are critical. In an era of rapid technological advancements and global interconnectedness, IP stands as a cornerstone for innovation, creativity and economic prosperity.

The GCC member States, having long recognised the need to diversify, have adopted a range of strategies, including non-energy mining,

A. AlDebasi
Executive Director of Copyrights and Designs, Saudi Authority for Intellectual Property, Riyadh, Saudi Arabia

D. Price (✉)
Emeritus Professor, School of Law, Charles Darwin University, Casuarina, NT, Australia
e-mail: david.price@cdu.edu.au

N. Naim et al. (eds.), *Intellectual Property and Innovation*, The Political Economy of the Middle East,
https://doi.org/10.1007/978-981-96-4020-1_2

production industries, trade infrastructure and facilitation, hospitality and tourism, and international financial and banking. One area which has attracted support right across the region amongst all the States and which has seen dramatic growth is sport in its multitude of forms. This chapter examines the impact of this sport involvement upon the national and economic development of the States and its contribution to their respective campaigns to broaden their economies and make progress in reducing current dependence on oil and gas industries.

Adoption of sport as a strategy for broadening the national economic base and for development generally has much to commend it. Sport across its broad spectrum of forms constitutes a pursuit that can be enjoyed in active (participatory) or passive (observational) form. It is also a pursuit that is universal, exists in a myriad of forms, occurs at the most elite global level or at the unseen and unnoticed local level, and can be non-ageist. It can be competitive or recreational. It can bring physical, mental and commercial benefits, and can be a potent tool in positive individual development, societal harmony and national pride. It can be extremely complex in infrastructure and organisation or extremely simple. The key performance indicators can be strategised in short-term, medium-term and long-term plans with outcomes that can have very public, promotional and political value. And in sport, one can observe IP, artificial intelligence (AI) and economic development interacting with, and mutually contributing to and benefitting from, each other.

Sports enthusiasts, commentators and the media argue incessantly as to which might be the most popular, rewarding (financially), watched and supported global sporting events, and the best indicators to measure such criteria performance. But there appears to be wide consensus that, as quadrennial offerings the two most watched sport events would be the Summer Olympic Games as a multisport event and the FIFA Football World Cup as a single sport event. The 2022 FIFA World Cup in Doha, Qatar, which included 32 national teams, was estimated to be viewed by more than 5 billion people worldwide, with more than 1.5 billion people viewing just the final game between Argentina and France (Beren, 2024). On an annual basis the consensus on the most popular dissipates somewhat and dissension emerges. However, football matches such as the UEFA Cup on an international basis or national football championships such as the English FA Cup are generally considered the most watched sports, followed variously by cricket, hockey and tennis (Wood, 2024). The most expensive sports in terms of equipment, infrastructure and facilities, and participation fees are generally considered to be motor sports, particularly the Formula 1 Grand Prix series, equestrian and horseracing, and arguably golf (Google, 2024).

Amongst the GCC member States, the major sports a generation or two ago were likely to have been camel racing, falconry, hunting with hounds and of course football, and the participants were predominately, if not exclusively, male. However, within the timeframe of that generation or two all States and their nationals participated in all of the sports cited above and many more at differing levels and in various guises—not only as an active and or passive participant, but also as host and organiser, owner, investor, management and governance, media and/or broadcaster. And the most notable and engaged in this regard has been Saudi Arabia. Football (not surprisingly) still appears as the pre-eminent sport, with participation ranging from global elite in famous stadiums to remote village matches on rough-hewn dirt patches. The following are just a few selected examples of recent involvement of the various States in hosting sporting events at the elite international level:

- Bahrain: race on the Formula 1 Grand Prix motor racing calendar since 2004;
- Kuwait: Men's World Open Squash Championships 2009, Asian Judo Championships 2007, and various Asian Championships flagship regional events;
- Oman: primarily Arab regional championships in different sports;
- Qatar: Formula 1 race since 2022, FIFA Football World Cup 2022, 2019 World Athletics Championships, 2014 FINA World Swimming Championships, 2011 Pan Arab Games, 2006 Asian Games;
- Saudi Arabia: Formula 1 race, the MotoGP Grand Prix, Saudi Dakar rally, 2024 World Esports Championship, 2023 World Weightlifting Championships, 2021 ICC Cricket championships 2010 Men's World Open Squash Championships;
- UAE: Abu Dhabi Formula 1 race since 2009, 2024 World Rugby 7s, 2021 FINA World Swimming Championships (short course), 2021 World Karate Championships, 2021 ICC T20 Cricket Championships, the Dubai Rugby 7s (men since 1999 and women since 2011), 2018 Asian Cup (cricket), 2019 AFC Asian Cup (football).

2 GCC Regional Visions on Sports Development and Fitness

All six GCC member States have embraced the concepts of IP rights, AI and emerging frontier technologies, the digital economy and economic growth and development, and their mutual linkages and intersections. They have all crafted national development plans highlighting their 'visions' or ambitions and national priorities over varying timeframes ranging from an objective year of 2030 (Bahrain, Qatar, Saudi Arabia), through 2031 (UAE) and 2035 (Kuwait), to 2040 (Oman). Some of these visions are a continuum of a series of earlier plans, but with an added emphasis on, or change of direction to include, the digital and knowledge-based economies and emerging technologies.

The primary focus in almost all of these plans is one of sustained and broad-based economic development in which broadening economies away from the current reliance on their oil-based resources is given high priority.

All vision statements have a similar theme and structure, although they differ significantly in dimension. However, the character and position of the society and members is not overlooked and features prominently in most plans. While all make general reference to population general health and provision of appropriate services and facilities, some also express concerns for the well-being of the young and their levels of fitness. Hence, the health environments and associated services and industries become key components of the statements. Some also make specific reference to the importance of sport and sporting facilities—not only promoting perspectives and visions beyond national boundaries.

Bahrain, for example, lists amongst its 'Aspirations for Society' the strategy of providing more—and more attractive—public spaces for families and the provision of more modern facilities that promote regular cultural and sports activities (Bahrain *Our Vision*, p. 23). The Vision Statement's 2019–2022 Action Plan expresses support for creativity, excellence, the role of women and youth, and sports in all government programmes and initiatives as key objectives.

Kuwait, in its *Second National Development plan* 2020–2025, advocates improving youth well-being by combating substance use and road injury and promoting sports, and adopting a *Sports for All* strategy as part of the implementation strategy for its vision strategy. It also includes the promotion of new sports clubs and introducing a new law to allow privatisation of sports and recognise athletes in sports clubs and national teams as career professionals (p. 129) and generally enhancing Kuwait's capacity to host international events by partnering with international organisations and providing competitive facilities (Kuwait Second National Development Plan 2020–2025, p. 213).

Oman, in its *2040 Oman Vision*, declares in its 'Well-being and Social Protection Priority' that "focusing on sports activities has direct benefits and developmental gains across the different sectors and various age categories, and enhances Oman's presence on the global sports map" (p. 26). It also includes the objective of creating "An environment and ecosystem conducive for sports to contribute to the economy and compete globally" (p. 26).

Qatar gives sport a rather lower profile than the other States, simply listing "participation in a wide variety of cultural and sports activities" as one of the objectives under the 'Human Development Outcomes' of its *Qatar National Vision 2030* (p. 21). The UAE adopts a similar conservative approach in *We the UAE 2031*, with the only specific sport reference appearing within the Plan's pillar of a 'Forward Society' as part of the objective for an inclusive and empowering society by "enabling individuals to prosper mentally, physically, socially and economically, and strengthens social cohesion through community building activities, cultural events and sports" (p. 23).

3 Development of the Saudi Arabia Sporting Vision and Strategies

Saudi Arabia, on the other hand, makes an unequivocal statement in its national vision statement, *Vision 2030*, on the significance that it places on the position and potential of sport in both economic and societal development. The Vision states that a healthy and balanced lifestyle is an essential mainstay of a high quality of life. It acknowledges that opportunities for the regular practice of sports have often been limited, but this is going to change. Within its pillar of a 'Vibrant Society', it declares that:

> We intend to encourage widespread and regular participation in sports and athletic activities, working in partnership with the private sector to establish additional dedicated facilities and programs. This will enable citizens and residents to engage in a wide variety of sports and leisure pursuits. We aspire to excel in sport and be among the leaders in selected sports regionally and globally. (*Vision 2030*, p. 22)

One of the Vision's stated goals for 2030 is to "increase the ratio of individuals exercising at least once a week from 13% of the population to 40%", a statement which is accompanied by photos of a top-class football stadium to reinforce the message (*Vision 2030*, pp. 25–7).

This focus on sport promotion is taken to another dimension when read in association with the Vision's declaration on the roles and objectives of the state-controlled sovereign wealth fund, the Public Investment Fund (PIF), and its domestic and international investment portfolio. It was established in 1971 to invest Saudi government funds, was restructured and transformed in 2015, and has since been under the chairmanship of Crown Prince and Prime Minister Mohammed Bin Salman Bin Abdulaziz Al Saud. The Vision statement declares that the Fund will become the world's largest sovereign wealth fund (*Vision 2030*, p. 42). The Vision states that it will not compete with the private sector, but instead help unlock strategic sectors requiring intensive capital inputs to contribute towards developing entirely new economic sectors and establishing durable national corporations.

The PIF's website currently (as at October 2024) records that it has so far achieved approximately US$925 billion in assets under management, created 1.1 plus million direct and indirect jobs domestically and globally, and created 95 portfolio companies across 13 strategic sectors (Public Investment Fund, website). Although very difficult to guestimate with any degree of certainty, the dollar value of investment in the sports business appears very significant as a percentage of PIF total assets but is also very significant in terms of spread, dimension and impact.

However, when interviewed by BBC Sport in December 2023, Saudi Arabia Sports Minister Prince Abdulaziz bin Turki Al Faisal stated that the Kingdom's unprecedented investment in sport—estimated at £5 billion over the past three years—was to help inspire a young population to take up physical activity and exercise, open the country up to the international community, boost tourism, create jobs and provide sports federations with growth potential (BBC Sport, 2023).

In August 2023, the PIF reported that it was establishing a new sports investment company, SRJ Sports Investment, to accelerate the growth of the sports sector in the Kingdom and Middle East North Africa (MENA) region. The new company will focus on acquiring and creating new sports events IP, commercial rights of sports competitions, and hosting major global events in Saudi Arabia. The company also plans to target businesses offering "unique fan engagement activities" and "transformative sports technology" across the industry (Dixon, 2023; PIF Press Release, 2023).

Over the duration of virtually one generation, Saudi Arabia has demonstrated its capacity to change the shape of some of the world's most prominent professional and most-watched sports. Through the PIF, which currently reportedly boasts assets exceeding US$950 billion, the Kingdom has acquired significant stakes in major sports organisations and teams. It has lured high-profile athletes to Saudi Arabian football teams, acquired ownership of a leading English Premier League football club, secured the right to host the 2034 FIFA World Cup, effectively forced the world's and the United States' leading golf powerhouse into a global partnership, demonstrated its intention to become a major influence in global motor sports, and established itself as global hub for esports.

3.1 Football

Football is the most popular sport in Saudi Arabia, both in terms of participation and in spectator support, with over 80% of the population playing, attending or following it. As the country's national sport, it is also experiencing unprecedented growth. It is perhaps not surprising, then, that it has attracted considerable attention and support from the Saudi officials and corporate services to bolster the game nationally and to take advantage of the sport's global profile by expanding Saudi influence and investment in the international arena. It has a strong local professional league with five levels for men and three for women, encompassing almost 200 clubs. It has won the AFC Asian Cup on three occasions and been runner-up multiple times. In 2008, Saudi Arabia Telecom Company entered into a sponsorship agreement with Manchester United, while in 2013 Prince Abdullah bin Musaid al Saud, former chairman of Saudi Arabia's Al Hilal football club, acquired a 50% stake in Sheffield United.

Nationally, investment has expanded significantly following the launch of *Vision 2030* and the redevelopment of the PIF. The sport has seen even further and dramatic investment since 2022, generating an influx of some of the world's most iconic football personalities. In early 2023, Crown Prince Mohammed bin Salman announced the launch of the 'Sports Clubs Investments and Privatisation Project', aimed at encouraging and enabling corporations and public sector organisations to invest in sports and then enabling the clubs to be privatised. Under this project, in June 2023 the

PIF took controlling stakes in four Saudi Premier League clubs, namely, Al-Ahli, Al-Ittihad, Al-Hilal and Al-Nassr, and brought in significant financial backing (PIF, 2023, p. 54). Four other clubs transitioned into the hands of state-owned entities, namely, Aramco, the Royal Commission for al-Ula, the Diriyah Gate Development Authority and the NEOM mega-city project.

The inflow of investment funds enabled the Saudi Professional League clubs to make unheard of transfer offers to some of the world's leading footballers. In December 2020, Cristiano Ronaldo agreed to join the Al-Nassr club from Manchester United on a three-year contract for a sum reputed to be in excess of US$200 million per year including salary and endorsement deals. As a result of Ronaldo joining Al-Nassr, the value of the club has reportedly jumped 33%, with the value of its trademarks and other IP rights and broadcasting rights also positively impacted (Fox Sports, 2024). In the same year, Ronaldo was joined by other elite football players, including Karim Benzema, French winner of the 2022 *Ballon d'Or.* In August 2023, Brazilian star Neymar joined Al-Hilal from Paris Saint-Germain for a reputed US$100 million per year. By the end of 2023, the Saudi league had spent a total of US$957 million, with the most notable signings being Neymar, Gabri Veiga (Celta Vigo), Riyad Mahrez (Man City), Sadio Mane (Bayern Munich), Aleksandar Mitrovic (Fulham) and Ruben Neves (Wolves) (ESPN, 2023).

The Saudi Pro League, which boasts players from over 40 different countries and has seen attendance increase by nearly 150% in the last year, aims to be amongst the top 10 leagues in the world. Furthermore, the above Project aspires to raise the League's commercial revenues from SAR 450 million in 2022 to over SAR 1.8 billion annually while generating private-sector investment opportunities and increasing the market value of the Saudi League from SAR 3 billion to more than SAR 8 billion by 2030. According to a recent study by Deloittes, the League clubs had a net expenditure of US$907 million in 2023 for acquiring new players, ranking second only to the English Premier League, which recorded a net expenditure of almost US$1.4 billion (ESPN, 2023).

Internationally, in October 2021, an investment group led by the PIF completed a 100% acquisition of English Premier League football club Newcastle United. For the Fund, the acquisition was in line with its strategy of focusing on key sporting sectors and the opportunity to harness the Club's potential and build upon its long and famous legacy (Newcastle United, 2021). In May 2022, Argentinian legend Lionel Messi, multiple

Ballon D'Or winner and hero of Argentina's 2022 World Cup victory, became an ambassador for Saudi Arabia's 'Visit Saudi' tourism campaign for a rumoured US$25 million three-year contract. The contract was reportedly a contributing factor for his departure from his national club, the Qatari-owned iconic Paris Saint-Germain club (*The New York Times*, 2023).

On 4 October 2023, Saudi Arabia announced its intention to bid for hosting the 2034 FIFA World Cup. Crown Prince Mohammed Bin Salman asserted that the Kingdom's intention reflects the comprehensive development it has achieved across all sectors and levels, as this has positioned it as a leading centre and an international venue for hosting major and significant global events across various fields, and is supported by its economic assets and rich cultural and historical heritage (Saudi Arabian Football Federation, 2023).

On 29 July 2024, the Kingdom officially submitted its bid file while in Paris for the Olympic Games, during a ceremony held by FIFA. The host nation was announced on 11 December 2024, but with no other bids for 2034 submitted (following the withdrawal of Australia's bid) and with endorsement by other national football federations, Saudi Arabia's appointment was a formality (Saudipedia, 2024).

3.2 Golf

In 2021, PIF invested US$1 billion in the establishment of Saudi-based LIV Golf, an international professional golf tour which it states aims to improve professional golf for all stakeholders, including fans, players and owners. LIV Golf offered a restructured series of tournaments with 48-man fields, no mid-tournament cuts and up to $25 million in prize money, and a team component per tournament. The winner's share at each event was $4 million, and the last-place finisher was guaranteed $120,000 (whereas the winner of the 2022 PGA Masters Tournament received $2.7 million, which was increased to $3.24 million in 2023.) The creation of LIV Golf attracted many of the sport's top players away from the US-based PGA Tour and Europe-based DP World Tour (Isidore, 2023).

LIV Golf's organisers hope to position their Tour as a player-focused alternative to the United States' PGA Tour, the global premier golfing competition. But it is essentially a rival league to the US-based PGA Tour and the Europe-based DP World Tour. LIV Golf attempted to sign on the top players in world rankings with bonuses estimated at US$100 million.

It managed to sign 13 former major champions, including Phil Mickelson, a six-time major tournament winner, for a reported fee of US$200 million, and Dustin Johnson, a Masters and US Open Champion, for a reported fee of US$150 million. Both Mickelson and Johnson were suspended by the PGA, as were any other professionals who signed on (PIF Annual Report, p. 85).

The competition for control of world golf generated litigation by both parties in the US courts and a hearing by a US Senate Subcommittee. However, on 6 June 2023 the two sides announced that they were dropping all litigation and setting up a new company to combine their commercial interests. The PGA would hold the majority stake in the new company, while the PIF would invest more than US$1 billion and would initially be the exclusive investor alongside the PGA Tour, with the exclusive right to further invest. LIV Golf has been trying to turn its 12 teams into franchises but it appears that so far there have not been any sponsors committing (Associated Press, 2023).

3.3 *Motor Racing*

Saudi Arabia's connection with Formula 1 motor racing goes back almost 40 years, with Kingdom business initially sponsoring teams in the late 1970s. In 1977, Saudia Airlines became the major sponsor of the legendary Williams F1 Racing team, the first Saudi company to do so. It was later joined by TAG and Albilad Hotels. The influx of sponsorship at a time when Williams was struggling to compete dramatically transformed the team. During the period of Saudia's sponsorship until 1985, Williams won the Constructor's Championship in 1980 with Australian Alan Jones, also taking out the Driver's Championship, and again in 1982 with Finnish driver Keke Rosberg. According to its website, Saudia has continued to participate in many major sporting events, having been a sponsor of the Formula E Diriyah race since 2019. In 2023, Saudia Airlines returned to Formula 1 as the official global airline partner of the Aston Martin team.

In July 2021, the PIF invested some US$518 million for an equity stake in the McLaren F1 racing team, apparently with the intention of endeavouring to relocate it to the Kingdom. It since announced, in December 2023, that it was selling its stake to the Bahraini sovereign wealth fund Mumtalakat, giving that fund virtually full ownership of McLaren Racing. However, the Saudi Fund has recently increased its former minor stake in Aston Martin to just over 20%. Aramco secured a new five-year agreement in December 2023, to become the team's exclusive title sponsor, renaming the team Aston Martin Aramco Racing Team.

Since 2021, Saudi Arabia has hosted a race in the Formula 1 racing, with the new track circuit in Jeddah already enjoying a reputation for being a high-speed challenge for drivers while entertaining the audiences (and thereby the media and their audiences and sponsors). The circuit is utilised for multiple purposes such as Formula 2 and other formulas, GT cars, local racing and even go-karting events. Saudi Arabia is in the process of building another Formula 1 circuit in the city of Qiddiya near Riyadh as part of a mega city for entertainment, tourism and sport. When completed, it will presumably need to compete with the Jeddah circuit for the right to host the Saudi Formula 1 race, since it is unlikely that two races could be held annually in one country considering the strong competition from other countries to become a Formula 1 event host.

US venture capital corporation Liberty Media Corporation acquired Formula 1 as the sport's controlling body for $4.4 billion in 2017. Since then, the valuation of the sport has doubled, largely due to the success of the very popular Netflix original docuseries on the various teams. The docuseries has arguably been the biggest reason why viewership of races expanded by 30% between 2017 and 2021, and has continued to grow since (Hajarnavis, 2024). In 2021, the number of unique users across both Formula 1's website and app grew to 113 million, a 63% increase from 2020, resulting in the league making a profit of $563 million and generating a substantial revenue of $2.5 billion in 2022 (an increase of 17% from 2021) (Hajarnavis, 2024).

3.4 Gaming and Esports

In the last decade, the esports (electronic sports) sector has experienced phenomenal growth with the emergence of new markets, professional players, teams, leagues, funding and prizes. Worldwide revenue generated from esports is expected to reach US$1.86 billion by 2025, nearly doubling the US$996 million revenue generated in 2020. This expected growth is mainly driven by rising investments, live streaming, surging viewership, ticket sales and demand for tournament infrastructure globally (Statista, 2023).

In January 2022, the PIF launched the Savvy Gaming Group (SGG) with the objective of developing it into the leading national and international games and esports company. The launch is in line with the National

Gaming and Esports Strategy, which aims to establish 250 games companies, create 39,000 jobs, and raise the sector's GDP contribution to SAR50 billion by 2030 (PIF Annual Report, 2023). Contributing to that strategy, and with the PIF investment, SGG was able to acquire the American games publisher and developer Scopely for $4.9 billion in July 2023.

The first Esports World Cup was held in Riyadh during July and August 2024, with more than 1500 players from over 100 different teams in 21 different games, and a total of US$62.5 million in prize money. It was organised by the ECW Foundation, a non-profit organisation which is funded by the PIF (ECW, 2024).

Saudi Arabia recognises the immense potential of gaming and esports and aims to position itself as a global leader. In the last two years through major international tournaments, including the inaugural Esports World Cup, Saudi Arabia has hosted more than 1500 elite players from over 80 countries. Further underlining its hosting credentials for esports events, nearly four million esport fans have visited Saudi Arabia for live experiences in the Kingdom, with a further 1.3 billion views globally across a variety of streaming platforms. The Saudi Esports Federation asserts that around 23.5 million Saudis, of whom more than 10 million are female, representing 67% of the Saudi population, consider themselves to be gamers, with an ever-increasing number (currently 100) of pro esports players pursuing full-time careers (Saudi Esports Federation, 2024).

Conservative sports hardliners would no doubt consider that online gaming and esports cannot be considered as a form of sport in any guise at all. Gaming refers to the act of playing video games, with or without an audience, while esports focuses on professional and competitive video gaming, typically with an audience. Esports, a subset of gaming, involves competitive video gaming for spectators and prize money (Saikali, 2022). However, the International Olympic Committee (IOC) itself has given esports formal recognition and endowed upon it the cachet of legitimacy in recognition of its booming growth over the last decade or so in terms of participation and audience numbers, global spread, financial inflow and investment. On 24 July 2024, the IOC created the Olympic Esports Games, with the inaugural Games to be held in Saudi Arabia in 2025.

Prince Abdulaziz bin Turki Al Faisal, Minister of Sport and President of the Saudi Arabian Olympic and Paralympic Committee, commented that esports in Saudi Arabia already had a rich past, an exciting present and a promising future. "And the reason why is the same reason why we are investing across all sports – our young people. Our commitment to esports is simply a reflection of the world our young people live in, and we know all have the chance to write new Olympic history together. The chance to inspire new dreams and new ambitions for literally millions of athletes around the world" (International Olympic Committee, 2024).

3.5 The Olympic Games

Beyond establishing its own sports competitions, Saudi Arabia has expressed a firm interest in hosting the 2036 Olympic Games, and commenced the necessary informal positioning during the Paris Olympics. However, it appears that it will face some strong competition with Chile, India, Indonesia and Turkey having already confirmed bids, and Canada, China, Denmark, Egypt, South Africa South Korea and even Qatar reportedly considering submitting bids (Chadwick, 2024; Wikipedia, 2024). The Host city will likely be named at the 2026 IOC Session. But even if not successful in its 2036 bid, a hosting opportunity for the Kingdom could still arise if one of the earlier hosts falters and withdraws (as occurred in the case of the city of Athens in 1996).

Saudi Arabia has won just two silver and two bronze medals at past Games but has yet to win gold. In general, host countries inevitably enjoy a performance advantage that would not otherwise be present. With the national pride and appropriate investment across the broad spectrum of Olympic sports and across all elements of an individual sport, it is sure to rectify that perceived discrepancy.

4 Intellectual Property, Artificial Intelligence and the Economy Contribution: The Interface

Saudi Arabia's Vision statement also enunciates a clear and obvious interaction between IP rights, AI and economic development. This close and interdependent relationship that appears across the country's national vision was given further emphasis and public attention by Crown Prince and Chairman of the Council of Economic and Development Affairs Mohammed bin Salman Al Saud during the public launch of the Kingdom's new National Intellectual Property Strategy in December 2022. During the launch, Crown Prince Mohammed bin Salman underlined his aspirations to stimulate creativity and innovation in the Kingdom for the next five years through the Strategy:

> We have minds and energies passionate about innovation and creativity, and by enabling them, the Kingdom of Saudi Arabia will become a vibrant environment for a knowledge economy based on an integrated Intellectual Property ecosystem that develops innovative technologies and industries, and contributes to growth of enterprises. (Asharq Al-Awsat, 2022)

However, that interface, notably between IP and AI, will not necessarily be unchecked. The Saudi Government has given notice of a proposed new IP law, which will formally acknowledge the interface between IP and AI, and issued a draft for public consultation during mid-2023 (Al-Balushi, 2023). The new law builds upon the current legislation to update and address contemporary IP issues, as well as the IP/AI interface. While the draft is light on detail in this latter regard, presumably relying on future subordinate regulation to expand, it nonetheless establishes a relationship between the two. Chapter 3, titled "Intellectual Property related to artificial intelligence and emerging technologies, and supporting their catalysis" provides just four illuminating articles, as follows:

> Article 17:
> Intellectual property generated by artificial intelligence is protected whenever a person's natural contribution to it is prominent.
> Article 18:
> The owner of intellectual property rights generated by artificial intelligence is the person who has arranged for access to the intellectual property.
> Article 19:
> IP generated by AI shall be in the public domain in cases where (it does not highlight) the contribution of the natural person to its creation does not emerge, or where the artificial intelligence is created independently of the person.
> Article 20:
> The fields of intellectual property shall be taken into account in innovations related to modern emerging and advanced technologies and artificial intelligence, and the authority may provide a fast track to examine them and stimulate their protection.

The intended meaning of Article 20 could be open to speculation, but the reference to fast-track examination and protection is a reasonable indication that AI-generated IP could still be developed and exploited. It has been suggested that the article can be read as "IP inventions associated with emerging and advanced modern technologies or aided with AI shall be financially sponsored" (Murray et al., 2023).

The Explanatory Memorandum to the draft law provides little clarification to the above articles but does reinforce the existence of that IP/AI complementary relationship by declaring in Section 4(3) that one of the objectives of the new law is to address emerging IP issues at the national and international levels, and provide a systemic framework for its practice, including provisions for the concentration of IP assets, and enabling its exploitation and enforcement, modern technologies and AI in an IP context.

The crucial detail on the practical application of the above proposed legislation if or when it comes to enactment will rest with the accompanying implementing regulations, a step that the Authority will need to take in order to tackle and answer a range of unresolved issues and questions that are already part of the comprehensive debate on IP and AI.

5 Intellectual Property, Artificial Intelligence and the Economy Contribution: The Sports Trifecta

5.1 The Intellectual Property Rights Perspective

In its recent guide to 'Sustaining Sport and its Development through IP', the World Intellectual Property Organization (WIPO) stresses that the sports industry is an industry that relies on the efficient protection of IP rights, since it derives an important part of its revenues from legal control over those rights relating to sports events or sports institutions. The existence of protection frameworks makes it possible to commercialise the rights in a manner fruitful for third parties, such as broadcasters, through granting of exclusive broadcasting rights for sports events, or official sponsors of sports events or sports teams, at all geographic levels (including at the global level). This protection can benefit all stakeholders in the sports industry, including individual athletes, teams and sports federations, which can derive revenues from the commercial exploitation of their IP rights (WIPO, 2022, p. 7).

There is potential for virtually the full spectrum of IP rights as enshrined in the global benchmark of the WTO's TRIPs Agreement to reside in sports events, particularly when those rights can enjoy some value because of the nature of the event. This is particularly apt where the event may be conducted at a competitive or elite level, which involves the use of infrastructure and facilities and even more so where the sport involves investments, which in turn depends on performance and results for its ongoing availability. The main areas of IP in the sports context involve the so-called "big four" of copyright, patents, trademarks and designs.

Trade secrets or confidential information may be understood as any information which is not generally known or available to the public, and which the owner whether a company or organisation keeps secret because of the value of the secret and the advantage over its competitors. A classic exemplar of a trade secret is the Coca-Cola formula. Trade secrets can encompass manufacturing or industrial secrets and commercial secrets, practice, formula, process, pattern, instrument, or compilation of information not generally known or reasonably ascertainable by other. In sports, this includes information such as players' personal records, game plays and strategies, comparative analysis of competitors, games statistics and coaching methods.

And even seemingly distant areas of IP such as breeders' rights could conceivably have application in sports involving animals, such as the thoroughbred industry, where tailored feed stocks to enhance performance may be based on or include specific new plant breeding varieties. Furthermore, outside the bounds of the traditional categories of IP rights are further rights which also play a role in the advancement of sport and which are protected by other legal rights, such as the right of personality, the right of privacy and the right of publicity (WIPO, 2022, p. 6).

However, it must be stressed that, while there are international treaties and complex top-down rules on sports governance and international arbitration bodies (such as the Court of Arbitration for Sport in Switzerland), IP protection and legal relief against infringement is primarily jurisdiction-based and the laws of the host country may prevail in the case of disputation.

5.2 *Trademarks*

Trademarks are perhaps the most critical aspect of IP protection for sports brands. They shape brand identity for teams, events and gear, fostering loyalty and premium pricing. They cover team and association logos and names, slogans, and even distinctive sounds associated with a sports team or athlete. Athletes can also trademark their names or unique signatures, allowing them to control merchandising and endorsement deals. Both Roger Federer and Usain Bolt hold registered name, word and design trademarks, for example. Equally important are event trademarks referring to specific sports events, such as Olympic Games or world championships, and protection though legislation or registration to prevent third parties from ambush marketing, whereby a third party unlawfully attempts to use a trademark that creates an impression of association with or endorsement by an event. Qatar was forced to resort to litigation in Switzerland to prevent PUMA from using the words "World Cup 2022" and "Qatar 2022" as trademarks in respect of a sports bag, sportswear and sporting articles (European Commission, 2022).

5.3 *Copyright and Related Rights*

Copyright protection encompasses original creative works in material form, including team plans, sport and player descriptions content, photographs, performances and music, and broadcasts. This can extend to team anthems, promotional videos and related promotional documentaries. Copyright law ensures that the team retains control over the distribution and reproduction of this content, preventing or obtaining damages for unauthorised copies or adaptations.

But the major area of copyright in sports is broadcasting rights, which are generally enjoyed by international governing bodies with only certain residual rights residing with the team or players. Sports organisations require broadcasters for live event coverage to engage audiences and service fans as well as to attract sponsors. Broadcasting rights underpin the relationship between sport, television and other media. Their commercial value has increased dramatically in recent years, with broadcast organisations willing to pay significant sums for the exclusive right for live coverage initially but also for subsequent replays, spin-off productions and resales. Broadcasting and media rights are now arguably the largest source of revenue for most high profile sports organisations.

5.4 *Patents*

While less common, patents can be crucial for protecting inventions in sports technology. They can encourage technological breakthroughs in sporting equipment. They can include running shoes such as Nike's

HyperAdapt 2.0 smart shoes, featuring advanced self-lacing technology, and swimsuits such as Speedo's Fastskin full body suit, which was later banned by FINA for providing unfair advantage.

Patents might include new equipment operation, training devices or even software used for performance analysis. Patents provide the inventor with exclusive rights to manufacture and sell the invention, fostering innovation and investment in sports technology.

However, patents rarely arise in Formula 1 race cars, primarily because the life cycle of some components can be very short, while patent applications can be an extended process and require the subject of an application to go through a process of public scrutiny. The details of those components are most likely to be protected under trade secrets provisions.

5.5 *Designs*

Design protection is important not only for protecting the appearance of major sports events, but also for developing team loyalty and support. Hence, protection can constitute a highly valuable component of an IP strategy for companies in the sports industry and for attracting sponsorship. Design rights protect the visual appearance of event or team products, which is particularly relevant and crucial for sports merchandising. This includes the design of uniforms, footwear and equipment. Sports merchandise is a significant revenue stream for sports entities. By securing design rights, teams and athletes can ensure that their products remain unique and appealing to fans, while also deterring counterfeiting.

6 The Artificial Intelligence Perspective

AI has become an essential component in the management of virtually any sport which is played at a competitive level, and particularly at elite level, which involves the use of infrastructure and facilities. This is particularly the case where a winning margin may be determined by a fraction of a second or a centimetre, and even more so, where the sport involves investment, which in turn depends on performance and results for its ongoing availability.

One estimate of the global AI penetration in the sports industry has placed the value at US$2.2 billion in 2002, and projected that it would reach US$29.7 billion by 2032, growing at a rate of 30% per year over the decade (Allied Market Research, 2024).

International Consulting corporation PwC suggests that a very simplified construct of AI in sport might initially be divided into event-specific and non-evident categories. For example, in football, the former could encompass:

- Talent identification and selection or player recruitment;
- Pre-game preparation: training and coaching, and personnel in respect of nutrition, physical and mental well-being, injury management, skills and technique development, and team selections;
- In-game activity: real-time performance analysis and feedback, specialist replacement strategy, and umpiring;
- Post-game analysis: analysis and feedback, recovery, and injury management.

The non-event-specific categories could encompass:

- Management and operations: competition management, club and team management, venues, events and ticketing, sponsorship, merchandising, and short-/long-term strategic planning and development;
- Media and fan experience: fan relationship management, news and content, factory sports, esports, sports betting, and media rights (PwC, 2019).

Formula 1 is arguably the most technologically advanced sport in respect of AI applications. During any period of testing at the workshop or the track itself, multiple monitors receive and analyse in real time data from the race car in respect of, for example, tyre performance, braking, acceleration, fuel consumption, main component temperatures and stresses, as well as driver reaction and concentration. During a race, artificial and data modelling can generate simulations as to the potential impact of impending weather conditions, the negative impact of other cars on the track, and to determine best pit-stop scheduling, overtaking timing or track position.

Jad Haddad (2023), writing in the *Arab News*, argues that "Generative AI is about to change the game – and this is happening at a time when the Kingdom is in the unique position of being able to invest heavily in its future". He suggests that since Saudi Arabia is not an IP-intensive economy, it could rapidly leapfrog economies that have spent trillions of dollars building IP-intensive ecosystems. With generative AI opportunities, it could soon reach the same level as countries that have spent decades building up IP-intensive infrastructures. AI will impact large swathes of the global economy, and the shape of many jobs will change profoundly. But in terms of quality of life and potential for citizens in the Kingdom, embracing these shifts could add steam to *Vision 2030* goals (Haddad, 2023).

7 The Contribution to the Economic Development Perspective

Sports have evolved from normal activities to multi-billion-dollar global industries. They contribute to economies worldwide, bridging cultural gaps and promoting peace. They create jobs and entertain. They serve as the catalysts for incentivising innovation, driving advancements in sports equipment, event branding and broadcasting.

Formula 1 races also lead to enormous economic benefits for host countries. For example, it is estimated that Monaco's GDP expands by $110 million during its race week. In addition, the race also leads to a considerable increase in the local population, with the population multiplying by five times in the build-up to the weekend of the race, which in turn benefits local businesses greatly (Hajarnavis, 2024).

The Bahrain Grand Prix has contributed considerably to national economic prosperity, with direct economic benefits from the race estimated to amount to an average of US$100 million annually. The race has also boosted the country's tourism sector, with hotel occupancy rates increasing by 70% to 100% during race weeks. Furthermore, this has also led to greater investment in sports infrastructure, for example the Bahrain Sports City project, which is forecasted to also stimulate enormous economic growth (Hajarnavis, 2024).

Sussan Saikali reported in 2022 that the Saudi gaming and esports market surpassed US$1 billion and projected it would each US$6.8 billion by 2030 (Saikali, 2022). Yet, market growth has significantly exceeded these predictions. PwC's examination of the state of the Saudi gaming and esports market in August 2024 revealed that the market could contribute US$13.3 billion to GDP and generate nearly 39,000 jobs. This phenomenal growth is in large part attributable to technological advancements across the whole value chain, thriving gaming communities, substantial government investment, and hosting of the Esports World Cup. The esports sector is witnessing a rapid transformation with Saudi Arabia becoming the leader in the region and a major player globally.

A primary objective of the PIF was to contribute to the development of a national economy moving towards non-oil sectors. In its latest report, in 2023, the Fund reports that, in terms of expected economic impact by 2025, it will contribute SAR1.5 trillion to non-oil GDP and create 1.8 million direct and indirect jobs. By the end 2023, PIF had delivered an annual average total portfolio return of 8.7% since 2017, primarily driven by investments within Saudi Arabia, as well as international portfolio growth (PIF, 2023).

8 Concluding Remarks

Since 2016 and the public reveal of the Saudi Vision document, overall sports participation levels have more than tripled to almost 50% of the country's population, and the number of sports federations has also increased threefold from 32 to 98 over the same period. Women's sport in particular has witnessed rapid growth, with over 330,000 registered female athletes and nearly 40 women's national teams competing internationally. Sport is part of the school curriculum for all girls, as demonstrated by the 70,000 schoolgirls playing in the school football league each week. In addition, reforms have enabled women to compete internationally in sports, and ensured there is female representation on the boards of all sports federations. And female athletes receive the same level of pay as male athletes when on national duty in their sport (International Olympic Committee, 2024).

In 2020, Saudi Arabia hosted its first professional international tournament for female golfers, the Ladies European Tour, where Saudi women played alongside international female players (Hausheer Ali & Stansbury, 2024).

There is little to suggest that the rate of investment in sports by the PIF and other Saudi bodies is going to abate, at least in the short/medium term. It is more than likely going to continue to increase. The Kingdom is clearly aiming to make its Saudi Pro League one of the world's top domestic football leagues to rival the English Premier League, Ligue 1 (France), Bundesliga (Germany) and La Liga (Spain). It has provided significant funds to the domestic clubs, financed transfers of some of the sport's leading elite players to its league, and positioned itself to host the 2034 World Cup. Its LIV Golf strategy and creating a tour to effectively rival the PGA has succeeded in forcing it into a reluctant partnership with global reach. Rumours continue to abound that Saudi interests have tried, and are still trying, to acquire control of the governing body for Formula 1.

Tennis, cricket, boxing and professional fighting are all receiving attention. In February 2024, the PIF signed a five-year partnership deal with the men's tennis body ATP which includes naming rights and holding major ATP events in the Kingdom; it is also seeking a similar deal with the WTA, the women's tennis body. And it is interested in investing some US$5 billion in Indian Premier League cricket with a view to expanding it into other countries. The PIF has acquired a minority stake in the United States' Professional Fighters League, a rival to the UFC, in a deal to launch a league and super fight division in Saudi Arabia (Hausheer Ali & Stansbury, 2024).

However, it is worth noting that the Saudi experience in international sport investment is not unique, but more a matter of dimension. For example, other GCC member States also own or are influential investors in European football clubs. Bahraini interests own the Paris Football and Cordoba; Kuwaiti interests own Milton Keynes (English League 2); Qatari interests own Paris Saint-Germain, and have invested in Malaga, Barcelona and Bayern Munich; and UAE interests own Manchester City and have invested in Real Madrid, Manchester United, Arsenal and AC Milan (Middle East Political Science, 2024).

Three other GCC member States also host their own event on the Formula 1 calendar, and were doing so well before Saudi Arabia's recent participation. And before LIV Golf emerged, Dubai was arguably the region's biggest golfing attraction. Dubai's DP World has been the lead sponsor for the European Tour now for some years, with the tour now culminating in the DP World Tour Championships.

In esports in the MENA region, Egypt hosts the largest gaming community, while the UAE has the highest revenue per user and Saudi Arabia leads in gaming revenue. The present penetration of esports indicates significant potential for continuing growth due to high mobile Internet penetration, a large young population, and a strong interest in digital technologies across the Gulf States (Statista, 2023).

Put simply, Saudi Arabia's financial riches derived primarily from oil revenues are transforming the domestic and global sporting landscape, with a profound and sometimes controversial shift in influence gathering pace. This drive to transform reflects the Crown Prince's statement in September 2023 that sport had helped increase his country's GDP by 1%

and that he was hoping for a further 1.5% growth from the sector (BBC Sport, 2023). In so doing the Kingdom is successfully utilising sport to move closer towards achieving the objectives of its *Vision 2030.*

References

Abuamer, M. (2024, October). The Rise of Gulf States' Investments in Sports: Neither Soft Power nor Sportswashing?. *Middle East Political Science.* https://pomeps.org/the-rise-of-gulf-states-investments-in-sports-neither-soft-power-nor-sportswashing

Al-Balushi, R. (2023, April 9). Saudi New Draft Intellectual Property Law. *Riyadh Al-Balushi Blog.* https://riyadh.om/2023/saudi-new-draft-intellectual-property-law/

Artificial Intelligence in the Sports Market Size, Share, Competitive Landscape and Trend Analysis. (2024, February). *Allied Market Research.* https://www.alliedmarketresearch.com/artificial-intelligence-in-sports-market-A12905

Artificial Intelligence: Application to the Sports Industry. (2019, February). *PwC.* https://www.google.com/search?client=firefox-b-e&q=Artificial+IntelligenceApplication+to+the+Sports+Industry+PWC

Beren, D. (2024, July 16). Most Watched Sporting Events in the World. *WallSt.* https://247wallst.com/sports/2024/07/16/most-watched-sporting-events-in-the-world-2/

Bids for the 2036 Summer Olympics. (2024, October 11). *Wikipedia.* https://en.wikipedia.org/wiki/Bids_for_the_2036_Summer_Olympics

Chadwick, S. (2024, August 21). Saudi 2036 Olympics Ambitions: Long Race Full of Major Hurdle. *Amwaj Media.* https://amwaj.media/article/saudi-2036-olympics-ambitions-long-race-full-of-major-hurdles

Cristiano Ronaldo Says He's 'Likely' to Finish Playing Career in Saudi Arabia. (2024, August 27). *Fox Sports.* https://www.foxsports.com/stories/soccer/cristiano-ronaldo-says-hes-likely-finish-playing-career-saudi-arabia

de Werra, J. (2022). *Reference Guide to Sustaining Sport and its Development through Intellectual Property Rights.* World Intellectual Property Organisation (WIPO).

Dixon. (Ed.). (2023, August 8). Saudi Arabia's PIF Launches New Sports Investment Company. *SportsPro Media.* https://www.sportspromedia.com/news/saudi-arabia-pif-srj-sports-investments-company/

FIFA World Cup Qatar 2022. (2022, November 30). *European Commission.* https://intellectual-property-helpdesk.ec.europa.eu/news-events/news/fifa-world-cup-qatar-2022-2022-11-30_en

Gough, C. (2023, December 13). Revenue of the Global Esports Market 2020–2025. *Statista.* https://www.statista.com/statistics/490522/global-esports-market-revenue/

Haddad, J. (2023, June 10). Tomorrow Belongs To Those Who Can Harness AI. *Arab News.* https://www.arabnews.com/node/2318966
Hajarnavis, K. (2024, February 4). Fuelling Fortunes: The Economics of Formula One. *Etonomics.* https://etonomics.com/2024/02/04/fueling-fortunes-the-economics-of-formula-one/
Hausheer Ali, S., & Stansbury, J. (2024, January 18). The Real Reason the Saudi Government is Investing in Sports. Hint: It's Not to Impress You. *Atlantic Council.* https://www.atlanticcouncil.org/blogs/menasource/saudi-arabia-sportswashing-investment-sports/
IOC Announces Olympic Esports Games to be Hosted in the Kingdom of Saudi Arabia. (2024, July 12). *International Olympic Committee.* https://olympics.com/ioc/news/ioc-announces-olympic-esports-games-to-be-hosted-in-the-kingdom-of-saudi-arabia
Isidore, C. (2023, June 7). Saudi Arabia's Public Investment Fund just Reshaped Pro Golf. It's Not Stopping There. *CNN Business.* https://edition.cnn.com/2023/06/07/investing/saudi-arabia-pif-golf-liv/index.html
KSA Emerges as a Significant Player in the Global Esports Market. (2024). https://www.pwc.com/m1/en/industries/government-public-services/sports-advisory-hub/centre-of-the-game.html
Kuwait National Development Plan 2020–2025. (2020, September). https://www.media.gov.kw
Mohammed bin Salman: 'I Don't Care' About 'Sportswashing' Accusations. (2023, September 21). *BBC Sport.* https://www.bbc.com/sport/66874723
Murray, M., Gaugeler, R., & Batarfi, S. (2023, July 6). Saudi Arabia Pioneers' Regulation of Artificial Intelligence in the Gulf Region with Proposed New Intellectual Property Law. *Bird & Bird.* https://www.twobirds.com/en/insights/2023/global/saudi-arabia-pioneers-regulation-of-artificial-intelligence
Nuckels, B. (2023, July 11). *Saudi Investment in PGA Tour will Top $1 Billion.* Associated Press. https://apnews.com/article/pga-tour-liv-saudi-arabia-congress-59465133a521143535de84e80fadfdd5
Our Vision: the Economic Vision 2030 for Bahrain", Bahrain, Vision_2030.pdf
PIF Establishes SRJ Sports Investments Company to Elevate Sports Sector in Saudi Arabia and MENA. (2023, August 6). *Public Investment Fund* (Press Release). https://www.pif.gov.sa/en/news-and-insights/press-releases/2023/pif-establishes-srj/
Premier League. PIF, PCP Capital Partners and RB Sports & Media Acquire Newcastle United Football Club. (2021, October). *New Castle United.* https://www.newcastleunited.com/en/news/pif-pcp-capital-partners-and-rb-sports-media-acquire-newcastle-united-football-club
Public Investment Fund. (n.d.). *Kingdom of Saudi Arabia.*
Saikali, S. (2022, March 17). A New Virtual Reality: The Growth of Esports and Gaming in Saudi Arab. *Arab Gulf States Institute in Washington.* https://agsiw.org/a-new-virtual-reality-the-growth-of-esports-and-gaming-in-saudi-arabia/

Saudi Arabian Football Federation Announces Intention to Bid for 2034 FIFA World Cup™. (2023, October). *Saudi Arabian football federation*. https://www.saff.com.sa/en/news.php?id=2560

Saudi Crown Prince Launches National Intellectual Property Strategy. (2022, December 22). *Asharq Al-Awsat*. https://english.aawsat.com/home/article/4057626/saudi-crown-prince-launches-national-intellectual-property-strategy

Saudi Pro League Transfer Roundup: Neymar, Benzema, More. (2023, September 8). *ESPN*. https://www.espn.com.au/football/story/_/id/37884523/saudi-pro-league-transfers-2023-deals-talks

Sports Events in Saudi Arabia. (2024). *Saudipedia*. https://saudipedia.com/en/article/1074/society/sports/sports-events-in-saudi-arabia

Taking Hold of the Controls: The Immense Potential of Esports in Saudi Arabia. (2024). *Saudi Esports Federation*. https://sponsorcontent.cnn.com/int/saudi-esports-federation/the-immense-potential-of-esports/

Ten Most Expensive Sports in the World. (2024, October). *Google*. https://www.google.com/search?q=Top+10+most+expensive+sports+to+organise+in+the+world&client=firefox

Vision 2030. (2016). *Kingdom of Saudi Arabia*. https://www.vision2030.gov.sa/en/

Why is Saudi Arabia Spending So Much on Sport?. (2023, December 14). *BBC Sport*. https://www.bbc.com/sport/67713269

Wood, R. (2024, October). Top-10 List of the World's Most Popular Sports. *Topend Sports*. https://ipv6.topendsports.com/world/lists/popular-sport/fans.htm

Zidan, K., & Panja, T. (2023, June). Lionel Messi, Saudi Arabia and the Deal That Paid Off for Both Sides. *The New York times*. https://www.nytimes.com/2023/06/18/sports/soccer/lionel-messi-saudi-arabia.html

CHAPTER 3

Intellectual Property in the Metaverse and Artificial Intelligence: ChatGPT in the GCC Member States

Dina Widyaputri Kariodimedjo

1 Introduction

Technology and innovation in the digital realm are evolving rapidly, with changes occurring on a daily basis. This development was initially marked by the interest in cryptocurrency and continued with the invention of non-fungible tokens (NFT) in the world of art and technology (Wijayanti et al., 2022, 43). The next growing trend is the meta world, the metaverse, which is starting to be adopted by commercial, government, and educational facilities.

The metaverse is an immensely mounted and interoperable web of simultaneous extracted three-dimensional simulated worlds that can be accessed in a synchronous and persistent way by an effectively unlimited number of users, each of which have an individual sense of presence.

D. W. Kariodimedjo (✉)
Business Law Department, Faculty of Law, Universitas Gadjah Mada (UGM), Yogyakarta, Indonesia
e-mail: dinawk@ugm.ac.id

N. Naim et al. (eds.), *Intellectual Property and Innovation*, The Political Economy of the Middle East,
https://doi.org/10.1007/978-981-96-4020-1_3

Accordingly, it is clear from this definition that in its ultimate manifestation the metaverse will be not only be as big as the real world, but also very bit as diverse. It also supports the full transferability of data and digital assets. The metaverse's growing importance has caused the major US tech companies to invest in it: first Facebook (in 2021), then Google, Microsoft, and Nvidia (Tucci & Needle, 2023). It has been projected that the value of the metaverse economy could reach several trillions of US dollars by 2030 (Petit, 2022). This is going to happen, since the economic sectors of retail, gaming, entertainment, and education are all likely to be transformed by the digital economy of the metaverse. Similarly, these trends are likely to mean that e-commerce will become a dominant instrument. These developments are likely to have particular relevance to, and potential impact upon, the countries of the Gulf Co-operation Council (GCC) given the significant levels of digital connectivity and social media usage among their populations.

Another aspect of the metaverse is the potential it has to transform people's lives as one of the most highly anticipated technology evolutions in recent decades, given its ability to parallel the digital and physical worlds, and to interconnect people's social interactions within the two spheres. This transformation of people's lives might include a range of human activities: the way people communicate, the way they entertain themselves, and the way they learn. People can currently access the metaverse through a range of different portals; these can be downloaded, for example, from the Apple App Store, which provides varieties of metaverse experiences, from pleasures to investments. As a result, an unlimited number of people are able to gain access to synchronous cybernetic environment. This can, in turn, be seamlessly connected to a physical world enormously and in three-dimensional quality.

The metaverse itself is grounded in several different and novel technologies: these include, among others, artificial intelligence (AI), virtual reality, and augmented reality. Through the use of such advanced technologies, people can play games, go shopping, create, or take virtual ownership of property. In order for the metaverse to function, it needs a vision for the future of the internet, which has been termed Web 3.0, the third phase, or the 'smart' internet. Web 3.0 will assist the metaverse's function through the use of sophisticated technologies, such as those mentioned above, but also drawing on newer areas of technology such as natural language processing, decentralized autonomous organization (DAOs), decentralized finance (Defi), machine learning, and blockchain.

According to Article 2(viii) of the *Convention Establishing the World Intellectual Property Organization 1967*, intellectual property (IP) operates a regime which is primarily employed to protect human controls of their intangible aspects rather than the more usual laws on property which might apply in the case of a physical object such as a creative work, a distinctive sign, or a technical innovation. Article 1.2 of the *Agreement on Trade-Related Aspects of Intellectual Property Rights* (TRIPs Agreement), in Part II Sections 1–7 Intellectual Property, grants creators of IP exclusive rights through copyright, trademarks, patents, industrial designs, trade secrets, and lay-out designs and integrated circuits (WIPO, n.d.). From the main objective of IP and the aspect of the metaverse as a parallel connection between the digital and the physical world, it can be concluded that the metaverse user is required to respect the IP rights of the creator, inventor, or owner. Accordingly, such users must seek permission, prior consent, or license from the IP creator or owner.

Accordingly, there are a number of challenges which are faced by the IP creator, inventor, or owner, such as the application of de minimis use, the implied license, and the fair use doctrines in copyright. Further, the challenges in trademark are on classifications and exhaustion of rights applied for virtual goods or branded virtual goods. In addition, there are a number of challenges in patents related to the ownership of patents upon inventions which are invented by an AI, or patents granted for software inventions.

Furthermore, along with blockchain and Web 3.0-based technological innovations, the emergence of AI-based software technology innovations today is considered to be the latest technological transformation point. One AI trend which has attracted considerable attention in recent years is an AI-based piece of software, ChatGPT (generative pre-trained transformer) (Al Ashry, 2023). ChatGPT is widely discussed, for example, within the context of the world of education. Primarily, it makes it easier to write scientific papers that uphold academic honesty. However, it cannot be denied that the world of education is also one of those sectors which has increasing business aspects. The question therefore arises as to how educational actors and the general public should behave regarding the use of AI in various sectors, especially in terms of IP rights.

The world is simultaneously experiencing both the development of the metaverse and the spread of ChatGPT. Countries around the globe, including those belonging to the Gulf Cooperation Council (GCC), are beginning to develop policies and regulations to deal with this trend, as are discussed in this chapter. For example, one GCC country, the United Arab Emirates (UAE), has collaborated with the technology company Metapolis to implement the 'Metaverse as a Service' concept, which was first implemented in the UAE and is intended to be adopted by other GCC countries (Nurfaudzi, 2022).

Based on the background outlined above, this chapter aims to discuss both the regulatory and policy developments, as well as the legal issues concerning the metaverse and the use of ChatGPT within the perspective of IP rights, its challenges, and to propose solutions and recommendations, focusing in particular on the experience of the Gulf countries. The analysis serves as an opening move to formulate a solid legal foundation to deal with the metaverse and ChatGPT trend in these states. The chapter uses the examples of the Gulf countries in order to draw some more general lessons. It has been estimated that the metaverse could generate annual revenues of US$15 billion dollars for the Gulf economy by 2023 (National News, 2022). The chapter also uses the example of the author's country of Indonesia, which has the largest economy in South-East Asia, and which has much to gain from the exploitation of the metaverse given that it ranks fourth in the world in terms of the number of social media users (Antara, 2021). Two principal analytical methods are used in what follows: strengths, weaknesses, opportunities, and threats (SWOT) analysis and qualitative data analysis.

2 Development of the Metaverse and AI ChatGPT in the Perspective of IP in the GCC Countries

2.1 United Arab Emirates (UAE)

2.1.1 Metaverse Development in the UAE

The UAE is one of the countries most committed to realizing technological transformation through projects focused on the metaverse, NFTs, and Web 3.0. In 2018, the UAE announced its 'National Blockchain Strategy' (Emirates Blockchain Strategy, 2022) with the intention of adopting and driving blockchain innovations in various sectors, including finance, health, and education. Some four years later, the UAE collaborated with the Singapore-based technology company Metapolis to build the 'Metaverse as a Service' (MaaS) software, and to launch a microverse product in which users would be able to transact virtual land and NFT parcels (2022) (Nurfaudzi, 2022).

In the government domain, the UAE has established a Ministry of Virtual Economy in the metaverse (Economic Times, 2022). In support of the metaverse industry, several emirates have implemented a series of policies and regulations that encourage the development of the metaverse, including establishing a law on virtual assets and a policy regulatory body to deal with cryptocurrencies (Daily Star, 2022). In addition, a policy has been introduced to ease visa issuance for freelancers, entrepreneurs, and creative workers employed in the metaverse in the UAE.

The UAE consists of seven separate emirates, which offers some advantages in terms of policy coordination. Several of these emirates have already adopted regulations on virtual assets, although at the time of writing these do not specifically address the metaverse or virtual assets at the federal level. Ras Al Khaimah (RAK), for example, has implemented a free trade zone policy for digital and virtual asset companies, known as the RAK Digital Assets Oasis (RAK DAO) (Pandey, 2023). This free trade zone was established to facilitate service providers of digital asset technologies, such as metaverse, blockchain, NFTs, and other Web 3.0 businesses. The provisions regarding this free trade zone are governed by Law No. 2 of 2023 on the Ras Al Khaimah Digital Assets Oasis and Law No. 1 of 2023 on the Establishment of the 'Department of the Future' (Nagraj, 2023). In March 2022, Dubai and the Dubai Virtual Assets Regulatory Authority (VARA) passed a law regarding virtual assets, namely Law No. 4 of 2022 Regulating Virtual Assets in the Emirate of Dubai, which was enacted to provide legal certainty and legal protection for crypto asset investors and to set standards for the digital asset industry. In September 2022, the Financial Services Regulatory Authority (FSRA), the regulator of the Abu Dhabi Global Market (ADGM), issued Guidance: Regulation of Virtual Asset Activities in ADGM (VER04.280922), which is a set of guiding principles and approaches in regulating and supervising new types of assets and their service providers (ADGM, 2022).

Despite some emirates having established authorities and regulations on virtual assets, including those which relate to the treatment of NFTs in the metaverse, there remain a number of weaknesses. The UAE has not yet introduced national legislation on this specific issue at the federal level even though it has a huge potential to become a pilot country for metaverse development among GCC countries. The existence of regulations and authorities on virtual assets in several emirates creates clear standard procedures and market conducts for businesses and creative workers in the field of metaverse technology, which offers the opportunity to increase the UAE's national income and create a variety of jobs in the virtual sector.

The threats or obstacles for the UAE in implementing the metaverse can be seen from both legal and socio-economic perspectives. The first obstacle is in relation to data protection and privacy. The metaverse allows for the interaction and processing of user data. Both data protection and user privacy boundaries may face challenges as there is an evolution in trends and technologies. It is therefore essential to consider whether the practices in the metaverse comply with the applicable principles and laws under UAE federal law and international law. In addition, from a social and economic perspective, the projected relatively rapid development of the metaverse in the UAE in the future also poses a threat. While some emirates have highly developed regulations for virtual assets, others do not have any specific laws on the issue. This creates the potential for legal uncertainty. In addition, there is a challenge to establish a set of regulations to cope with the impact of the future surge in the flow of creative workers from the virtual sector.

2.1.2 AI ChatGPT in the UAE

In November 2022, OpenAI's ChatGPT took the internet by storm when it was first launched; shortly thereafter, it was followed by the launch of similar AI-based software by Microsoft and also Bard, launched by Google (Dhawan & Prasad, 2023). The emergence of ChatGPT poses a number of new legal challenges, especially in the area of IP. This is because the datasets trained by the AI model may include materials belonging to others that are protected by copyright (Dhawan & Prasad, 2023). Another question that arises when ChatGPT generates works such as stories, articles, or song lyrics, is: who has the right to be regarded as the copyright owner of the creation generated by the AI?

In April 2023, Astra Tech, backed by the Abu Dhabi-based AI company G42, announced that it had created the world's first Arabic ChatGPT (Essaid, 2023). Just one week after the announcement, 3000 open letters were signed, highlighting the growing public concern that AI was not being regulated clearly enough (Essaid, 2023). Among the concerns are the ability of AI to create new, unprecedented content in the form of audio, text, or images that may violate local laws. For example, AI may be used to generate an image of the Prophet Muhammad, something which is forbidden in Islam (Essaid, 2023). Another legal concern was that

ChatGPT could put some people out of work, although there are debates as to whether or not the adoption of AI will cause a net gain or loss in overall employment.

The UAE government has committed itself to setting a strong framework for the ethical development of AI within the country. In this case, the UAE government sees more of the positive side of AI in terms of its ability to improve government efficiency. This can be seen as being embodied in the appointment of a UAE Minister of State who has the specific duty of handling AI issues, His Excellency Omar Sultan Al Olama, who is a part of the Ministry of Economy. His remit includes matters relating to ChatGPT. Similarly, the Office of AI, Digital Economy, and Remote Work Applications, under the Ministry of Economy, also launched 'Generative AI,' a comprehensive guide on utilizing applications, including ChatGPT, for cash flow management or technical checks on website development (Dhawan & Prasad, 2023).

At the time of writing, the UAE has no specific laws regarding the governance of either ChatGPT or AI as a whole. Instead, the UAE utilizes a 'patchwork' of regulations to deal with AI in its national laws (Dhawan & Prasad, 2023). These provisions can be found in various separate laws and regulations, including the UAE Federal Law Combating Discrimination and Hatred, the Federal Data Protection Law, the Federal Consumer Protection Law, the Federal Cybercrime Law, and a number of IP laws, namely Federal Decree-Law No. 36 of 2021 on Trademarks, Federal Law No. 38 of 2021 on Copyrights and Neighboring Rights, and Federal Law No. 31 of 2016 promulgated by Law No. 17 of 2022 on Regulation and Protection of Industrial Property of Patents, Industrial Drawings and Designs.

The commitment and enthusiasm of the UAE government regarding the presence of ChatGPT in the country further opens opportunities for the UAE to become a country or place that has a positive atmosphere for the development of AI software, in terms of both law and IP. If it continues to be implemented and developed properly and wisely, ChatGPT can improve the running of the government across all ministries.

In future, the absence of regulations or laws at the UAE federal level regarding ChatGPT or AI more widely might be seen as a threat. It is clear from the public response to the launch of the first Arabic ChatGPT by Astra Tech, which is supported by the Abu Dhabi-based AI company G42, and the threat of ChatGPT that many people are concerned about the possibility of AI creating works that would violate Islamic Sharia and laws, including IP law (Essaid, 2023). Another fear is the possibility of AI taking on an increasing number of roles, meaning that many people will lose employment (Essaid, 2023). The infringement of IP rights, in this case, may occur due to the concept of AI that only summarizes or mixes the works of others, which may be protected by IP laws. The lack of clear regulations that can be used as a reference in the occurrence of public concerns or beyond will make the function of the law suboptimal due to the legal vacuum in certain cases in relation to AI software such as ChatGPT.

2.2 *Saudi Arabia*

2.2.1 *Metaverse Development in Saudi Arabia*

Saudi Arabia is another of the countries with the highest commitment to developing metaverse technology. This was clearly seen at the Leap 2023 Conference in Saudi Arabia with the signing of a memorandum of understanding between the government of Saudi Arabia and the Sandbox company to establish long-term cooperation to develop metaverse projects (Fortis, 2023). The government has also launched the 'Virtual Hacerulesved' metaverse project, which presents the Kaaba in a virtual form, thereby allowing Muslims to simulate the Umrah and Hajj pilgrimages and see relics of Islamic history (Kusuma, 2023).

Although the metaverse has already been implemented in order to simulate religious rituals such as Hajj and Umrah, its use in terms of transactions remains uncertain at present. To date, the use of cryptocurrencies in any transaction undertaken in Saudi Arabia has been forbidden. Any prosecution for doing so will result in the loss of assets. However, there are currently no legal sanctions for those who trade digital assets in the form of cryptos, NFTs, or other forms. Therefore, any NFT transactions that currently take place within the metaverse are considered legal and not something that is prohibited (Hammad and Al Mehdar, 2022).

The metaverse has great economic potential for generating revenue within the Saudi Arabian economy (around $7.3 billion annually by 2030) with tourist destinations and trips in the metaverse contributing $3.2 billion in revenue (Arab News, December 2022). In this case, the metaverse facilitates users to experience and enjoy domestic tourist destinations. It also helps the government to digitize top tourist destinations and historical relics in Saudi Arabia (Arab News, December 2022). New challenges are bound to arise from the metaverse world, of course, For example, the decentralized structure of the metaverse may lead to the elimination of business intermediaries, since banks and brokers are no longer needed to facilitate P2P transactions. As a result, data monetization businesses become ineffective as individuals will have control over their own data. Additionally, regulatory frameworks that apply in the real world cannot be enforced in the metaverse. This raises the question of property rights, the definition of which may extend to copyright, which is conceptually an intangible movable object that can be attached to property rights. One question that may appear is: if a user creates a house with a non-interchangeable token, are other users prohibited from replicating the design? Such questions arise due to the current absence of a legal and policy framework governing the metaverse in Saudi Arabia (Haddad, 2022).

There are a relatively large number of opportunities for metaverse development in Saudi Arabia in various sectors. One such sector is industrial digitalization, which involves the digital simulation of companies or factories, building optimization, and risk mitigation. This is expected to minimize planning errors, which can cost both time and money (Jain, 2023). As has been seen for the discussion above, the biggest challenge to the development of the metaverse in Saudi Arabia is that legal instruments in the real world cannot currently be applied in the metaverse world (Haddad, 2022). Therefore, the government needs to start preparing the legal framework and instruments on the metaverse to clarify the legal basis applicable in the metaverse world of Saudi Arabia.

2.2.2 *AI ChatGPT in Saudi Arabia*

At the time of writing, ChatGPT by OpenAI is not available in Saudi Arabia, although the number of countries in which it operates is being constantly updated (Stella, 2023). At present, some sources state that ChatGPT is not accessible in Arab countries or that Arab countries are not included in the list of supported countries for ChatGPT service (Ankita, 2023). However, the author could not investigate the exact logical ratio of this fact due to the relatively limited sources shedding light on this issue in the context of Saudi Arabia.

2.3 *Qatar*

2.3.1 *Metaverse Development in Qatar*

During the pandemic to post-pandemic period, there was an accelerated adoption of technology in Qatar's education sector. In 2022, Qatar University became the first university in history to enter the metaverse (Ibrahim, 2022). This step was made possible through a memorandum of understanding signed between the university and Metavisionaries, a group of change agents and business professionals who were committed to expanding the economy and to the application of leading-edge technology to address current and future challenges (Ibrahim, 2022). The partnership opens up access for students to space curriculum and the latest technologies, including the ever-evolving Web 3.0.

In addition to the education sector, Qatar's metaverse has ventured into both the accommodation and entertainment sectors. In April 2022, Qatar Airways became the first international airline to introduce a MetaHuman cabin crew named 'Sama', who will take users of its airline website to experience virtual reality (VR) with Qatar Airways. As a result, users are able to conduct a virtual tour of Hamad International Airport, and also to check in through the metaverse. The Qatar Airways Chief Executive, Akbar Al Baker, has said that users could see the interior of the economy to the business class cabins through a script with narration, which guiding users through virtual tour of Qatar Airways (Qatar Airways Group, 2022).

Another exciting innovation related to the metaverse in Qatar surfaced in 2022, when the football World Cup was taking place in the country. Upland, a partner of the Fédération Internationale de Football Association (FIFA), provided a blockchain-based metaverse experience. Supporters who logged into FIFA's metaverse could virtually "fly" to Doha for only about $5 per flight and would experience a representative wait of one-fifth of the expected travel time while "flying" (Huet, 2022). They could also stroll around the digital stadium and purchase souvenirs from shops around the stadium, or from other virtual properties.

The metaverse entry into a variety of Qatar's sectors is believed to strengthen its presence in the country. A survey conducted by the Chalhoub Group, a luxury goods company and the largest retail operator in the Middle East, proves that Qatar and the UAE have the highest awareness of the metaverse, each with 53% of their populations confirming knowledge (Chalhoub Group, 2022). Although the survey is aimed at the luxury consumer community, it aligns with Qatar already having its own National Blockchain Strategy. As outlined above, this finding may not be surprising: Qatar is the first country to have a university, an airline, and a World Cup offering a taste of the metaverse. These facts certainly have a positive impact on the advancement of education, economy, and technology in the country.

The Qatar Central Bank and Qatar Financial Center Regulatory Authority have each issued circulars and press releases prohibiting virtual asset transactions in Qatar (Earley, 2023). Later, the Qatar Communications Regulatory Authority and Qatar Investment Authority expressed interest in using blockchain widely for other purposes (Earley, 2023). Placing a ban on virtual asset transactions could be a drawback from a national revenue standpoint. While Qatar chooses to ban virtual asset transactions domestically, other countries that allow such transactions will benefit from the additional national income derived from such transactions.

With many sectors of the country's development now touched by the metaverse, it is not uncommon for Qatar to be the first in certain fields in the world. The country also has many fresh opportunities in various aspects, such as education, industry, and entertainment, which can extend even further. This is because Qatar is gaining increasing recognition as a fairly advanced country in this early stage of the metaverse.

The advancement of the metaverse in Qatar is characterized by an increase in the size of the metaverse, whose foundations are currently just forming and beginning to grow (Caserta, 2023). The journey of metaverse development needs coordinated and collaborative navigation on the part of the government, industry groups, and market players (Caserta, 2023). Currently, Qatar has a Data Privacy Law that can be used to regulate blockchain without the need for new laws relating to this form of decentralized finance (Earley, 2023). However, the regulation of how any legal regime of IP rights in the metaverse will be protected is one of the key challenges, threatening the legal certainty of ownership of metaverse developers and users in Qatar.

2.3.2 AI ChatGPT in Qatar

As outlined, Qatar is among the countries actively promoting digital innovation and transformation. In 2004, the country established the Qatar Science and Technology Park (QSTP). Then, in 2010, it established the Qatar Computing Research Institute (QCRI) (Moubarak, 2012). Both of these institutes focus on AI research and development. Furthermore,

Qatar is also a member of the International Telecommunication Union (ITU) and engaging in active discussions on developing global AI policies and codes of conduct.

To date, there has been no ban on the use of ChatGPT in Qatar. However, the use of the software has stirred up a debate. Reporting from Doha News, the controversy around ChatGPT usage in education is often associated with plagiarism (Kilani, 2023). From the students' point of view, ChatGPT is considered very beneficial, making it easier for them to complete their assignments.

The chair of the Artificial Intelligence Committee at the Ministry of Communications and Information Technology, Hassan Jassim Al Sayed, has explained that ChatGPT is a chatbot that simulates human conversations in order to provide efficient textual responses or answers (Al Sayed, 2023). Al Sayed explained that ChatGPT is helpful for many applications, such as developing chatbots for customer service or automated responses for customers online. He further remarked that the Ministry has developed a national strategy for AI that includes several matters, among which are: building an enabling environment for research and innovation in the field of AI; investing in education by setting up academic curricula and specializations to develop human resources in the field of AI; and establishing incentives and facilities to encourage entrepreneurship and programs aimed at attracting international companies in the field of AI. In its development, Qatar's national strategy for AI is threefold in nature: to promote its use in the public and private sectors; to develop programs to raise public awareness for the optimal use of AI; and to prepare regulations and guidelines related to the AI ethics to protect the rights of the parties as well as legal adjustments. Based on the description above, it can be seen that Qatar has ambitions to improve the AI sector. Such ambitions are reflected through the establishment of research centers for AI and regulatory adjustments in order to help achieve one of these national strategies.

Al Sayed has also explained that AI could lead to biased decision-making and have an impact on the employment market; hence the Qatari government should take measures to avoid the misuse of AI technology (Al Sayed, 2023). For example, measures could be taken to regulate the use of such technology through laws and policies that restrict the utilization of AI software to specific purposes only or grant licenses to AI development companies. There has not yet been a ban on the use of ChatGPT in Qatar to date. Judging by Qatar's trend to promote AI technology, the use of ChatGPT is likely to increase further (The Peninsula, 2023). Qatar does not yet have regulations that specifically address AI. However, some of the existing legislation may apply to different aspects of AI, such as personal data protection, cybersecurity, IP, and labor law. These laws may provide a legal framework for the growing practice of AI today. The Qatari national laws applicable in the context of ChatGPT are Law No. 13 of 2016 on Personal Data Privacy Protection, Law No. 7 of 2002 on the Protection of Copyright and Related Rights, Law No. 14 of 2014 on Cybercrime Prevention, and other laws and regulations.

Reflecting on Qatar's socio-economic potential, as well as the country's focus on promoting AI, the country may develop a comprehensive and specific legal framework regarding AI. The surge in the use of ChatGPT also presents an opportunity for Qatari society and businesses to improve user experiences, ranging from education to customer service.

The rising trend in the use of AI and ChatGPT has the potential to result in reduced work opportunities for people. In addition, AI is still considered to pose a threat in the form of biased decision-making. Therefore, a specific regulation is required to limit the use of AI, especially ChatGPT (Al Sayed, 2023).

2.4 Oman

2.4.1 Metaverse Development in Oman

A consistent definition of the 'metaverse' is currently difficult to come by as its foundations are still being laid. The underlying technologies are still in their early days, and many areas remain to be developed about the metaverse, including the laws that should govern it (Caserta, 2023). All countries are facing this new trend called the metaverse, and Oman is no exception to this. In this country, there is as yet no separate regulation on the metaverse. However, the country is committed to embracing future digital trends such as the metaverse and virtual assets.

The Capital Market Authority (CMA), which serves as Oman's financial market regulator, is working to create a new regulatory framework for the virtual asset industry (de Ramos, 2023). The CMA has announced that the objective of this new regulation is to establish a market regime for virtual assets with rules to prevent market abuse, including comprehensive supervision and enforcement mechanisms. According to a CMA Press Release published on February 14, 2023, this new regulation will cover the supervision of virtual assets, licensing for virtual asset service providers

(VASPs), and a framework for identifying and mitigating the risks of the new asset class.

Through the CMA, Oman has committed to creating a system of regulation to accommodate activities for the virtual asset industry (de Ramos, 2023). Virtual assets are closely related to the metaverse, NFTs, and crypto. Accordingly, the framework for virtual asset regulation is a strength for the metaverse in Oman; it establishes clarity of market regimes and monitoring and enforcement mechanisms. In October 2022, the Central Bank of Oman (CBO) revealed that the current currency banking law has yet to protect digital currencies and any activities involving their users (de Ramos, 2023). However, according to the report a law or regulation on virtual assets would soon be drafted to rectify the weaknesses or shortcomings of Oman's previous legal system. The virtual asset regulation will be aligned with Oman's Vision 2040, an initiative to digitally transform the country's economy while drawing global players to the area(de Ramos, 2023). The ease and the legal certainty offered by Oman further opens up opportunities for it to become a leading country in virtual asset adoption in the Middle East. At the time of writing, the risk of fraud and issues related to copyright ownership of virtual assets are threats that Omani regulators need to mitigate. The CBO seems to be very cautious with regard to the treatment of cryptocurrencies. The CBO recognizes the threat or risk of using them by repeatedly urging Omani citizens to exercise caution when transacting with cryptocurrencies (de Ramos, 2023).

2.4.2 AI ChatGPT in Oman

The Public Authority for Special Economic Zones and Free Zones (OPAZ) recently announced that it has started to employ AI techniques in its operations. It encourages the utilization of ChatGPT as a tool to speed up data processing for more efficient and accurate work aimed at enhancing service quality and employee performance without reducing employee numbers (Oman Observer, 2023). ChatGPT is often employed to help employees complete their work more efficiently, especially in terms of communication and routine tasks, such as filling out investor applications. While it facilitates work and improves services to local authorities, from a legal perspective, there are a number of other issues, ranging from privacy concerns regarding the processing of personal data without user consent to civil and criminal liability for the veracity of any information generated by ChatGPT (Al-Balushi, 2023).

Furthermore, from the perspective of IP law, there are questions relating to the extent to which ChatGPT is either compatible or in conflict with copyright law and whether the work produced by ChatGPT infringes the copyright protection of the underlying work from which the information is taken. Suppose ChatGPT simply copies an idea from work on the internet. In that case, it does not infringe copyright as Article 4 of Royal Decree No. 65 of 2008 Promulgating the Copyright and Neighbouring Rights Law states that copyright protection does not extend to abstract ideas, although it does protects the expression of those ideas. However, this is not how ChatGPT works. ChatGPT copies, either temporarily or permanently, any type of work (expression of an idea) found on the internet. This aspect of the process violates the exclusive economic right to reproduce as stipulated by Article 6(a) of the Law.

The utilization of ChatGPT in state institutions such as OPAZ, which is to simplify and streamline OPAZ services, is becoming increasingly beneficial for Omani society. ChatGPT, as implemented by OPAZ and specifically tasked with answering investors' questions about OPAZ services, receives a positive response from the state. This is because ChatGPT is trained to answer using replies taken from OPAZ manual procedures so as not to violate the copyright of other people's works. From the perspective of IP law, particularly copyright, the current Omani legal system is perceived as being relatively slow (Al-Balushi, 2023). The current legal system is also considered incapable of serving as a legal basis that can respond decisively to any issues related to ChatGPT.

State authorities utilizing ChatGPT to improve their services to the public without infringing on the copyrights of others is not against Omani copyright law as presently laid out. If updated wisely and responsibly, such use of ChatGPT has the opportunity to make it easier for the public to secure good government services. It has been mentioned earlier in this section that Oman does not currently have a legal system that can respond to copyright issues in the employment of ChatGPT, when it copies the works of others. Therefore, Oman should supplement its copyright law by specifying detailed measures or conditions that may or may not be carried out in virtual training machines.

2.5 *Kuwait*

2.5.1 Metaverse Development in Kuwait

The metaverse development in Kuwait is no less rapid than in other GCC countries. In the field of education, Kuwait College of Science and Technology (KCST) launched VR technology in March 2022 and applied it when conducting classes at Huawei ICT Academy, in which technology allows students to participate in a 5G training system (Oxford Business Group, 2022).

In the banking sector, Warba Bank, an Islamic bank in Kuwait, confirmed its entry into the Decentraland and the Sandbox metaverses (Zimwara, 2022). Warba Bank's presence in these two popular metaverses makes it the latest banking company in the Middle East and North Africa region (MENA) to enter the metaverse. Warba Bank has indicated that it wants to introduce its digital services to young people through cutting-edge technology. In addition to joining the metaverse, Warba Bank is interested in the AI sector to enable easy access to banking services anywhere and anytime.

In 2022, telecommunications services company Virgin Mobile Kuwait launched a metaverse program, collaborating with Kuwaiti content creators on the Sandbox metaverse (Virgin Mobile, n.d.). Virgin Mobile views the metaverse as an excellent opportunity to accelerate digital skill-sets such as computer programming, content creation, gaming, and e-commerce.

In another development, the Central Bank of Kuwait (CBK) has introduced guidelines for digital banks. According to the 'GCC State of the Metaverse,' although the CBK is considered somewhat behind other banks in the GCC countries in regulating virtual assets, Kuwait allows crypto and NFT trading for individual use. In the context of metaverse development, the country has shown itself to be highly developed in applying these technologies. For example, as outlined above, Warba Bank became the first Islamic bank in MENA to present its entity in the metaverse (Christopher, 2022). Additionally, various programs in education and technology have interacted with the metaverse, for example Virgin Mobile Kuwait and KCST.

In contrast to metaverse application in many sectors in Kuwait, Chalhoub Group's survey, in the report 'GCC State of the Metaverse: and Its Potential for Luxury Retail,' shows that the population of Kuwait (along with those of Bahrain and Qatar) has a relatively low level of awareness of NFT and developments in the metaverse, contrasting strongly with the levels observed in other Gulf countries such as the UAE, Saudi Arabia, and Oman (Chalhoub Group, 2022). A clear regulatory framework has yet to accompany the metaverse application in various sectors in Kuwait. One regulation that comes close to this is that with regard to cryptocurrencies, which ensures clarity on the use of cryptocurrencies, and establishes that they are classified as digital assets rather than legal currencies. Accordingly, cryptocurrencies are not considered as legal tender for any kind of legitimate transactions or payments, for instance in the commercial and banking sectors. However, the CBK does not prohibit private transactions of cryptocurrencies as digital assets.

Considering the development of the application of metaverse technology in various fields, Kuwait can still increase public awareness of the said technology. Furthermore, as in other countries, the utilization of the metaverse can drive an increase in people's income, especially creative workers in Kuwait. This offers a great opportunity, bearing in mind that Kuwait is the second-largest country in terms of TikTok user penetration and the fourth-highest in terms of the percentage of Snapchat users (Virgin Mobile, n.d.).

Kuwait presently has no clear regulations and policies with regard to the metaverse, NFTs, or virtual assets. The low level of awareness of the population on the metaverse and similar technologies compared to other GCC countries is one of the factors to consider for Kuwait to implement policies to regulate virtual assets. As seen, some other GCC countries have enacted more established policies or regulations than Kuwait. The country's authorities should acknowledge that it is crucial to have a legal framework governing metaverse technology to deal with future metaverse trends.

2.5.2 AI ChatGPT in Kuwait

Kuwait is one of the countries supported by ChatGPT (Stella, 2023). Kuwait News Agency (KUNA) has queried ChatGPT about tips to develop the competitiveness of news agencies. ChatGPT, which is said to have the ability to review books and movies, create works of art, and try to imitate humans, replied by giving broad generic terms: investing in technology, embracing social media, strengthening digital journalism, focusing on delivering news to portable devices, and so forth (Al-Haitham, 2023). These answers were very much in line with what KUNA expected.

Based on news from Kuwait Government Online, it would appear that the upgraded ChatGPT-4 is 500 times more powerful than the previous ChatGPT-3 version (Kuwait Government Online, 2023). ChatGPT has the ability to recognize images and create text. Major news agencies such as the BBC, Deutsche Press, New York Times, and others have utilized AI software for various purposes. The London-based digital media consultant Ahmad Al-Sheikh told KUNA that the AI media would grow significantly. More recently, Kuwait News has introduced an AI-generated news anchor named 'Fedha.'

The Kuwaiti government has responded well to the introduction of ChatGPT and other AI software, including AI used in news agencies. For example, Kuwaiti news agencies have also utilized ChatGPT and adopted AI in their journalistic activities. The excellent response of Kuwaiti society to ChatGPT offers some optimism that the country should continue to develop the way in which it should develop ChatGPT and AI software. Accordingly, the legal and sociological foundations have been met to form an ideal regulation or law on ChatGPT and AI software in Kuwait.

What news agencies obtain from ChatGPT may be sourced from other people's works or writings on the internet, which Kuwait's copyright laws may protect. However, the impulsive use of ChatGPT and AI software may violate the exclusive rights of the creators of the original works will cause many copyright problems.

The favourable reception of ChatGPT and software in Kuwait, especially within the journalism sector, allows the sector to thrive still further in line with technological advancements. In addition, it can unlock new investments in this field which will positively impact the country's economy. Additionally, by adopting the BBC's approach, KUNA can establish a special division tasked with creating new technological tools to help journalists (Kuwait Government Online, 2023). Education about AI should also be delivered in colleges or universities with press study programs in order to minimize copyright infringement of works used in journalistic activities. El-Bermawy, writing in *Forbes Magazine*, has estimated that up to one billion jobs might be replaced by AI over the course of the next decade (Al-Haitham, 2023). In addition, Ahmad Esmat has told KUNA that ChatGPT could increase the number of so-called 'deepfakes.' This could be a threat if AI software ChatGPT is exploited by malicious forces, leading to societal chaos.

2.6 *Bahrain*

2.6.1 Metaverse Development in Bahrain

The Bahrain Institute of Banking and Finance (BBIF) has launched its campus in the metaverse. BBIF's Director, Ahmed Al Shaikh, remarked that the BBIF Metaverse digital platform reflects the institute's commitment to innovation and excellence in education (BBIF, 2023). The BBIF Metaverse claims to provide a comprehensive and immersive learning experience for students and professionals in the finance and business sector.

BBIF COO Ahmed Naemi has revealed that the launch of the BBIF Metaverse is a significant milestone for the country's business sector (BBIF, 2023). This is because the innovation and the way in which will revolutionize learning methods in universities in the fields of banking and finance, namely utilizing virtual reality instead of solely relying on video conferencing, will undoubtedly increase students' understanding as well as their skills. Naemi has remarked that the BBIF Metaverse offers immersive learning spaces and networking tools for users to connect with peers and industry experts, and that it allows users to attend events, collaborate on projects, and partake in interactive learning activities, inclusive of videos and tutorials in the virtual world.

In other sectors, such as commerce, the use of the metaverse has a number of areas for potential, one of which relates to the retail trade of luxury goods. According to Chalhoub Group's GCC metaverse report, as many as 100 Bahrainis took part in its GCC-wide consumer survey focused on premium/luxury consumers. One of the pieces of the data generated was that Bahrainis are 40% aware of the use of the metaverse in retailing (Chalhoub Group, 2022). The launch of BBIF Metaverse and its warm reception is concrete evidence that, to date, Bahrain has positively welcomed the metaverse within its education sector. Similarly, the use of the metaverse and its favorable reception from the country's luxury goods retail consumer society shows that the metaverse is also widely accepted in the luxury goods retail trade sector. This can be a strength for Bahrain as the metaverse directly impacts the intelligence of its people and provides a reflection that the country's economy is getting stronger due to the metaverse (BIBF, 2023).

With respect to retail trade, and to the Bahraini economy in general, the Central Bank of Bahrain (CBB) has been implementing cryptocurrency regulations since February 2019 (BIBF, 2023). The CBB's crypto-asset directive or regulation relates specifically to the governance of such assets. However, there are no regulations in Bahrain that either govern or provide a general perception of metaverse regulation in a specific law. A metaverse that has made its way into education, such as BBIF, of which the metaverse is entirely designed and developed by Bahraini talents, has the opportunity to draw in more investors. This implies an opportunity for increased income for designers and those involved in developing the metaverse in education and shopping. Future investors will also have a positive influence on the country's economy. Opportunities for the metaverse's creative design and development community also come with risks. Talents from Bahrain or from abroad working in numerous sectors must pay attention to IP laws when creating works in the metaverse, a world where IP laws and regulations applicable in the real world today may have no force.

2.6.2 AI ChatGPT in Bahrain

According to the News of Bahrain, IT experts have asserted that ChatGPT would have a tremendously positive impact on various sectors in Bahrain. According to Salman Zainuddin, CEO of Libra IT Solutions and Marketing at Magneto IT Solutions, Bahrain has future potential for ChatGPT utilization programs in healthcare services and the workforce as virtual assistants (Ayaz, 2023). This is a challenge which is being faced around the world. In Zainuddin's view, with clear regulations from the government to protect user data, ChatGPT will bring significant benefits to both the people and the government of Bahrain.

Sajin Hentry, Managing Director of Syskode Technology, has said that he does not believe that ChatGPT will have an innately negative impact (Ayaz, 2023). Rather, he asserts that whether the use of ChatGPT is good or bad depends on each user's experience. Currently, chatbots can undertake programming and data analysis work. It is therefore crucial to ensure that the benefits of ChatGPT are widely felt and that the negative impacts are minimized. He has also said that in the spirit of making this happen, policymakers, employers, and workers must anticipate and adapt to this worldwide shift. Despite that, at the time of writing, as mentioned by a number of sources, the ChatGPT service remains unavailable in Bahrain (Stella, 2023), as is also the case in Saudi Arabia, China, and Russia. As of May 2023, Bahrain continues to prohibit ChatGPT.

The prohibition of ChatGPT in Bahrain means that the country has not yet faced any instances of the personal data protection-relevant problems which it causes. In terms of IP rights, the software faced dozens of pros and cons regarding copyright law. Bahrain is currently regarded as a country that provides satisfactory protection for copyright owners (Balloch & Fennessy, 2015). Copyright in the country is recognized and protected under Copyright Law No. 22 of 2006 as amended by Copyright Law No. 5 of 2014. As ChatGPT is banned in the country, the direct consequences of copyright infringement from its use do not apply. However, the absence of ChatGPT in Bahrain also means that the rewards from its successful deployment cannot be reaped (Ayaz, 2023). It cannot yet be deployed to streamline healthcare, programming, data analysis, and other strategic sectors.

Technology experts in Bahrain observe that the country does have the potential to use and develop ChatGPT. However, ChatGPT is not yet authorized for use in Bahrain. The stance of not allowing ChatGPT, even for public services, may make the effectiveness of public service delivery in the country inferior to those utilizing ChatGPT for similar purposes. Investors, scientists, and developers may prefer countries that have utilized and developed ChatGPT or even those in the early stages of the race to develop ChatGPT as a place or location for updating ChatGPT technology. This particular activity may increase the country's revenue and enhance the transfer of knowledge and the transfer of technology in association with the development of ChatGPT in Bahrain. If the Bahraini government does not immediately anticipate and adapt to ChatGPT, it could be possible to pose foreseeable threats such as loss of potential revenue, slow pace of government from home and abroad, and lagging technological innovation in certain areas that are the focus of ChatGPT.

3 ChatGPT in Scientific Writing in the Perspective of IP in Indonesia

Given the extensive use of ChatGPT, the comparative examples and analysis in this chapter are focused on ChatGPT in scientific writing in Indonesia from the viewpoint of copyright protection, ethics, and plagiarism. As the *New York Post* observed: "*Welcome to the new age of academic dishonesty*" (Mitchell, 2022). Based on the author's research, academic dishonesty in practice occurs within the framework of the negative utilization of technology, in this case, AI.

As outlined earlier, ChatGPT, the AI software which was developed by OpenAI, is a chatbot platform that has the ability to interact and provide highly accurate human-like responses in accordance with the instructions written by users. It is powered by a large language model (LLM) that can summarize, recognize, predict, and generate text and can be used for all text-related purposes. ChatGPT is capable of answering complex questions since, unlike search engines such as Google, users can vary the desired query or instructions, and the chatbot will provide a complete explanation of the matter, including explanations through easy-to-understand analogies. It is a tool commonly used for assignments and coding.

3.1 Originality vs. Plagiarism

Chat GPT's codes are mostly undetectable by plagiarism detectors, making it difficult for lecturers or universities to identify whether or not a paper was sourced or written by an AI. With the lecturer's experience, and through paying attention to a person's writing style, suspicion of a paper that does not meet the element of originality can arise and be identified from several characteristics—for example, the use of sentences/language which might be deemed too complex for a student's age or language level. To prove or avoid AI in the production of assignments, lecturers can request or prompt students to deliver examples and analysis using their own sentences to show evidence of their own knowledge, ability, and analysis of a theme or topic in writing or orally. Chat GPT outputs can be regarded as a form of plagiarism if they quote the work of others, without citing the source.

Aside from the possibility of Chat GPT resulting in plagiarism, this application is widely banned by schools or universities due to its negative impact on the learning process of students and concerns about the security or misinformation of the responses, as well as the accuracy of the content of the resulting papers. Some sources have asserted that other AIs, such as originality.ai, constentscale.ai, and writer.com, can easily detect Chat GPT-3.5, including the free version of Chat GPT, which has certain writing patterns that help enable detection by lecturers; one of the tools to perform such is OpenAI GPT2 Output Detector (Montti, 2022). Turnitin stated the same in February 2023 (Turnitin, 2023).

The Oxford English Dictionary defines 'plagiarize' (verb) as to: "Take and use as one's own" (the thoughts, writings, inventions, etc., of another person); copy (literary work, ideas, etc.) improperly or without acknowledgment; pass off the thoughts, work, etc. of (another person) as one's own. It defines 'plagiarism' (noun) as: "the action or practice of taking someone else's work, idea, etc., and passing it off as one's own; literary theft" (Oxford English Dictionary, 2024). Therefore, the elements of plagiarism include taking or using, etc. thoughts, writings, inventions, ideas, etc. belonging to others; inappropriately or without mentioning the source (not giving proper acknowledgment); and pretending/assuming them as one's own.

Plagiarism is not the same as copyright infringement, however, although there are similarities in terms of their essential elements. On the one hand, the scope of plagiarism contains works, thoughts, inventions, ideas, or the like, as well as violations of ethical norms in general, which evolve into law violations under certain conditions. Plagiarism is known in academic circles as the undertaking of a dishonorable act worthy of public exposure and social sanction, which damages the integrity and reputation of the perpetrator. Copyright, on the other hand, is a regime that protects already tangible works of intellectual output—there must already be an expression as a form or output of the results of thought or idea, with a term of protection of the lifetime of the creator plus an additional 50 or 70 years (lifetime plus 50 or 70 years). Furthermore, copyright infringement is a violation of IP law, particularly the copyright regime.

Article 1.1 of Indonesian Law No. 28 of 2014 on Copyright states that "copyright is the exclusive right of the creator that arises automatically based on the declarative principle after creation is realized in a tangible form without reducing the restrictions in accordance with statutory provisions". Embodiment or expression in a particular form must have an original nature/contain originality. Article 1.2 of the Law also states that a creator is a person (or several persons) who, individually or jointly, produce a distinctive and personal creation. Original, or containing originality, means that it has a unique and personal nature and is not a copy. Thus, plagiarism is not the same as copyright infringement, although there are some similarities.

The Indonesian government passed the Minister of National Education Regulation No. 17 of 2010 concerning Prevention and Countermeasures of Plagiarism in Universities. Article 1(1) of this regulation provides that "plagiarism is the act of intentionally or unintentionally obtaining or attempting to obtain credit or value for scientific work by quoting part or all of the work and/or scientific work of another party recognized as their scientific work without properly and adequately stating the source". Most universities and educational institutions, including in Indonesia, have similar policies regarding plagiarism. Plagiarism policies translate universal ethical norms into offences (not necessarily in a criminal sense) in accordance with the rules prescribed by the university's code of conduct. Sanctions for plagiarism generally range from grade reduction, declaration of course failure, academic suspension, or probation to expulsion from the study program.

As an example, Universitas Gadjah Mada (UGM), the author's university, has Rector Regulation No. 771/P/SK/HT/2013 concerning the UGM Student Code of Conduct (UGM, 2013). There is also an Anti-Plagiarism Guide prepared by the UGM Library, which determines the scope of plagiarism, namely: (a) quoting words or sentences of other people without using quotation marks and without mentioning the identity of the source, (b) using ideas, views, or theories of other people without mentioning the identity of the source, (c) using facts (data, information) of other people without mentioning the identity of the source, (d) recognizing writings of other people as one's own, and (e) paraphrasing (changing other people's sentences into one's own sentence structure without changing the idea) without mentioning the identity of the source (UGM Library, 2023).

3.2 Regulation and Policy on AI ChatGPT

It is unfortunate that Indonesia does not yet have regulations governing AI software ChatGPT, so there is no definition, scope, legal certainty, and legal protection for relevant offenses occurring in the country. The IP rights regime recognizes property specific to human creations, not the output of any AI, be it ChatGPT or any other AI, for example, related to inventions, software, or music, thus solely protecting human legal subjects. There is a statement of originality of works in the copyright protection and IP rights registration process. Thus, if the registered works are not original, they are in violation of their own declaration. In the event that there is no technology capable of detecting ChatGPT, the central element to be tested is whether or not the threshold of originality is met. Suppose a work results from someone plagiarizing or falls into the category of a computer-generated fake work without the person identifying the source. In that case, the work is essentially not the original work of the person. Although the work has uniqueness, the author believes that it still does not fulfil the personal nature of the creator that corresponds to the meaning contained in the original element of a work subject to copyright protection.

Many authors presently have included ChatGPT as an author—for example, in Scopus. In the future, it remains unclear whether reputable journals will accept this practice further, as it will be interesting if the works produced by ChatGPT are unique. Moreover, the fact is that there are so many words in this world, and whatever ChatGPT is ordered to do, it will execute the prompt well. This phenomenon will be a challenge in law, including IP rights for the author or researcher, and the government to regulate ChatGPT. An example of a guide model was published in April 2023 by the United Nations Educational, Scientific and Cultural Organization (UNESCO) and UNESCO International Institute for Higher Education in Latin America and the Caribbean (IESALC) (Sabzalieva & Valentini, 2023). This provides an overview of how ChatGPT works, and the way in which it might be used in higher education. The guide mainly focuses on some of ChatGPT's main encounters and its ethical consequences.

If AI works are to be recognised and allowed, several things need to be anticipated because of the simultaneous technological developments, and these conditions require humans to adapt to produce quality work. The first issue is to validate the work. For example, somebody has an idea and asks AI to program it, after which the person will incorporate innovations into it. Another occurs when an individual wants to design a bottle. They give the details of shape, size, and color, but it is AI that will proceed with the design. In some respects, AI is actually similar to computers, but it is a more sophisticated type of technology; thus, banning AI is tantamount to banning the use of computers. In the past, one could draw a design with Photoshop; today, however, the designer can simply talk to the AI, and it will create an image with alternatives.

The principles in IP rights, especially copyright, do not protect ideas alone. In the concept of IP rights, the idea will be worked on together by an individual or several people in a team of creators (and the participating AI must also be assigned a role). If that person or team works for a company, the company will usually be declared the copyright holder, while the person or team is regarded as the creator. This is what lies behind the current concept of IP law. The author agrees that AI should not be entirely banned. However, in the case of material submitted for the purpose of assessment for an academic assignment or degree, the work must be original. If AI is doing the research, it should be clearly specified which parts are the original work of the person and which the work of AI. In essence, the technology should be working for humans, rather than humans working for technology.

The author observes that the use of AI has yet to show clear legal consequences, let alone legal sanctions. As can be seen in the case of Indonesia, and in common with the other nations considered in this chapter, both the phenomenon, and the issues associated with it, are relatively new. The author argues that the concept of originality should be the approach adopted with regard to IP rights when it comes to the treatment of AI, as explained earlier. What is more, it is still difficult to determine legal sanctions because if this AI issue is linked to plagiarism, then anything resulting from copying can be categorized as copyright infringement. In fact, the concept of plagiarism stands on its own, without any notion of copyright infringement. Plagiarism includes the use of ideas and thoughts with no clear mention of the source, and with those ideas and thoughts being treated as if they belong to the perpetrator. The key aspect of copyright is the element of originality, and this concept is different from patents that prioritize the element of novelty, in which the earliest applicant to register is the one who obtains the patent. In addition, that should not be a problem if the same idea or thought inspires a work. However, the embodiment or expression of the idea must be original, such that the work can still be copyrighted.

4 Conclusion

As demonstrated, the GCC countries have adopted a range of approaches to the development of the metaverse and AI software. Most countries have made relatively substantial efforts and improvements to utilize the metaverse and AI in areas which accommodate public needs, especially in economic and socio-cultural sectors. Besides having advantages and opportunities, countries also deal with several disadvantages and obstacles in developing the metaverse and AI in their region. The absence of metaverse- and AI-specific law and regulation becomes the key element in this process. It is quite a challenge to make laws and policies that will be able to anticipate practices in the metaverse and AI, while people are still attempting to understand and study it. In addressing the metaverse and AI, it is necessary to be informed by people who understand the legal and technical sides, the metaverse, AI systems, and the concept of technology as a new invention, along with diverse challenges related to law and technology in general, and to AI in particular.

Regarding ChatGPT, it is emphasized that humans must have ethics, and not cheat or steal ideas. Academic honesty is required to clarify the origin and source of what they express in the context of scientific writing or scientific work. Humans with emotions, intelligence, and creativity can capture the context of what is found in computers to craft intellectual work that simplifies and improves lives, product development, production, and new ideas, with the assistance of AI. The keywords are ethics, morals, and honesty. The other matters become homework and challenges. Anything related to AI and its regulation can be further improved. The rule of law on the issue of AI software ChatGPT should consider a balance in which education emphasizes not only cognitive and psychomotor abilities but also affective abilities or attitudes.

Regarding copyright protection, ethics, and plagiarism in the use of ChatGPT in scientific writing, the author proposes several recommendations. First, universities should prohibit the employment of Al chatbots for writing papers, especially for works used to obtain assessments for certain degrees. Furthermore, universities and all stakeholders should increase awareness and uphold ethics, especially in avoiding plagiarism that uses AI. Moreover, universities should also set and assess indicators of plagiarism for which AI is used.

Bibliography

Al Ashry, A. (2023, March 22). *ChatGPT and Its Legal Impact on Society as a New Form of AI.* https://alshamsilegal.com/legal-article/chat-gpt-legal-impact?utm_source=mondaq&utm_medium=syndication&utm_term=Intellectual-Property&utm_content=articleoriginal&utm_campaign=article

Al Sayed, H. J. (2023, January 17). ChatGPT technology is an Addition to the Technological Development and Its Related Concerns are Overrated. *Qatar Ministry of Communications and Information Technology.* https://www.mcit.gov.qa/en/media-center/news/chairman-artificial-intelligence-committee-chatgpt-technology-addition

Al-Balushi, R. (2023, April 26). *Is ChatGPT Legal Under Omani Copyright Law?* https://blog.decree.om/2023/chat-gpt-oman-copyright/

Al-Haitham, S. (2023, January 19). AI Revolution … Fears and Hopes—'ChatGPT is Scary Good'. *Arab Times Online.* https://www.arabtimesonline.com/news/ai-revolution-fears-and-hopes-chatgpt-is-scary-good/

Ankita. (2023, April 15). How to Use ChatGPT in Saudi Arabia. *MLYearning.* https://www.mlyearning.org/chatgpt-in-saudi-arabia/#:~:text=Share%20this%3A-,Is%20ChatGPT%20available%20in%20Saudi%20Arabia%3F,not%20available%20in%20your%20country%E2%80%9D

Artificial Intelligence Sees Exponential Growth in Qatar. (2023, April 4). *The Peninsula Newspaper*. https://www.zawya.com/en/business/technology-and-telecom/artificial-intelligence-sees-exponential-growth-in-qatar-d78apgsn

Ayaz, Z. (2023, February 9). Does ChatGPT Hold Bahrain's Future? *News of Bahrain*. https://www.newsofbahrain.com/bahrain/88005.html

Bahrain Institute of Banking and Finance (BBIF). (2023, March 8). *Shaping the Future of Learning: BIBF Bahrain's First-Ever Educational Institute on the Metaverse*. https://www.bibf.com/bibf-bahrain-first-ever-educational-institute-on-the-metaverse/

Balloch, H., & Fennessy, C. (2015, September 23). Bahrain: Perlindungan Hak Cipta di Bahrain. *Mondaq*. https://www.mondaq.com/copyright/429164/copyright-protection-in-bahrain#

Caserta, R. (2023, January). The Metaverse: Why Governments Should Care. *KPMG*. https://kpmg.com/xx/en/blogs/home/posts/2023/01/the-metaverse-why-governments-should-care.html

Chalhoub Group. (2022, January 1). *GCC State of the Metaverse and Its Potential for Luxury Retail*. https://www.chalhoubgroup.com/en/media/194/gcc-state-of-the-metaverse-and-its-potential-for-luxury-retail

Christopher, J. (2022, July 4). Warba Bank—The First Islamic Bank that Enters Metaverse. *Today NFT News*. https://www.todaynftnews.com/warba-bank-the-first-islamic-bank-that-enters-metaverse/

De Ramos, H. (2023, February 17). Oman to Establish Regulatory Framework for Virtual Assets. *Cointelegraph*. https://cointelegraph.com/news/oman-to-establish-regulatory-framework-for-virtual-assets

Dhawan, A., & Prasad, V. (2023, May 10). United Arab Emirates: Legal and Regulatory Concerns with ChatGPT. *Mondaq*. https://www.mondaq.com/new-technology/1313414/legal-and-regulatory-concerns-with-chatgpt

Earley, M. (2023, January 26). Qatar: Blockchain Technology in Qatar. *Mondaq*. https://www.mondaq.com/fin-tech/1275284/blockchain-technology-in-qatar#

Essaid, S. (2023, April). Middle East Unlikely to Slow Down on AI, ChatGPT Rollout. *Al-Monitor*. https://www.al-monitor.com/originals/2023/04/middle-east-unlikely-slow-down-ai-chatgpt-rollout

Fortis, S. (2023, February 8). Saudi Arabia Partners with the Sandbox for Future Metaverse Plans. *Cointelegraph*. https://cointelegraph.com/news/saudi-arabia-partners-with-the-sandbox-for-future-metaverse-plans

Guidance—Regulation of Virtual Asset Activities in ADGM (VER04.280922). (2022).

Haddad, J. (2022. July 2). Is Saudi Arabia Ready for the Metaverse and Its Related Challenges and Opportunities? *Arab News*. https://www.arabnews.com/node/2115146

Hammad and Al Mehdar. (2022, April 4). The Regulation of Digital Assets in Saudi Arabia. *Lexology*. https://www.lexology.com/library/detail.aspx?g=2bca5d91-7961-4b6d-9de9-93cd47e1fe0b

Huet, E. (2022, November 16). Metaverse Fans Can 'Fly' to Qatar to 'Experience' World Cup. *Business Live*. https://www.businesslive.co.za/bd/life/arts-and-entertainment/2022-11-16-metaverse-fans-can-fly-to-qatar-to-experience-world-cup/

Ibrahim, M. (2022, August 14). Qatar University Makes Historic First Step into the Metaverse. *Doha News*. https://dohanews.co/qatar-university-makes-historic-first-step-into-the-metaverse/

Indonesia's Digital Economy Largest in Value in SE Asia: Indrawati. (2021, December 11). *Antara—Indonesia News Agency*. https://en.antaranews.com/news/204037/indonesias-digital-economy-largest-in-value-in-se-asia-indrawati

Jain, A. (2023, January 19). Saudi Arabia Bolsters Talent Pool to Strengthen Its Industrial Metaverse. *Crypto News*. https://crypto.news/saudi-arabia-bolsters-talent-pool-to-strengthen-its-industrial-metaverse/

Kilani, H. (2023, January 14). 'Opportunity, Not a Threat': How Do Students and Tech Experts Feel about ChatGPT in Qatar? *Doha News*. https://dohanews.co/opportunity-not-a-threat-how-do-students-and-tech-experts-feel-about-chatgpt-in-qatar/

Kusuma, D. (2023, March 2). Arab Saudi Bikin Proyek Kabah di Metaverse. *IDX Channel*. https://www.idxchannel.com/news/arab-saudi-bikin-proyek-kabah-di-metaverse

Kuwait Government Online. (2023, April 9). *American Company Produces High-Powered Chatting Robot*. https://www.e.gov.kw/sites/kgoenglish/Pages/ApplicationPages/NewsDetail.aspx?nid=8088843

Metaverse Expected to Add 15 Billion Annually to GCC Economies by 2030. (2022, November 2). *The National News*. https://www.thenationalnews.com/business/technology/2022/12/07/metaverse-expected-to-add-15-billion-annually-to-gcc-economies-by-2030/

Metaverse to Contribute $7.6bn to Saudi Economy by 2030: Report. (2022, December 7). *Arab News*. https://www.arabnews.com/node/2212141/business-economy

Mitchell, A. (2022, December 26). Professor Catches Student Cheating with ChatGPT: 'I Feel Abject Terror'. *New York Post*. https://nypost.com/2022/12/26/students-using-chatgpt-to-cheat-professor-warns/

Montti, R. (2022, December 16). What is ChatGPT and How You Use It. *Search Engine Journal*. https://www.searchenginejournal.com/what-is-chatgpt/473664/

Moubarak, M. (2012, June 7). Qatar Science & Technology Park Overview. *Al Misnad Law*. http://almisnad-law.com/qatar-science-technology-park-overview

Nagraj, A. (2023, March 20). Ras Al Khaimah Issues Law to Set Up Free Zone for Digital and Virtual Asset Companies *The National News*. https://www.thenationalnews.com/business/cryptocurrencies/2023/03/20/ras-al-khaimah-issues-law-to-set-up-free-zone-for-digital-and-virtual-asset-companies/

Nurfaudzi, B. (2022, November 2). *Uni Emirat Arab Menjadi Negara dengan Bisnis Metaverse as a Service Pertama di Dunia!* https://www.smarteye.id/blog/metaverse-as-a-service/

OPAZ Introduces ChatGPT to Develop Services. (2023, April 24). *Oman Observer*. https://www.omanobserver.om/article/1136099/oman/community/opaz-introduces-chat-gpt-to-develop-services

Oxford Business Group. (2022). *How Institutions of Higher Learning are Embracing the Metaverse*. https://oxfordbusinessgroup.com/reports/kuwait/2022-report/education-health/the-metaverse-in-education-building-a-digital-landscape-in-institutions-of-higher-learning/

Oxford English Dictionary. (2024, June). https://doi.org/10.1093/OED/3549092311

Pandey, S. (2023, March 3). *UAE Announces World's First Free Zone for Digital and Virtual Asset Companies*. https://beincrypto.com/uae-emirate-rak-announces-digital-assets-free-zone/

Petit, M. (2022, June). Value Creation in the Metaverse. *McKinsey and Company*. https://www.mckinsey.com/capabilities/growth-marketing-and-sales/our-insights/value-creation-in-the-metaverse

Qatar Airways Group. (2022, April 2). *Qatar Airways Steps into the Metaverse with 'QVerse' Virtual Reality and World's First MetaHuman Cabin Crew*. https://www.qatarairways.com/press-releases/en-WW/215125-qatar-airways-steps-into-the-metaverse-with-qverse-virtual-reality-and-world-s-first-metahuman-cabin-crew

Sabzalieva, E., & Valentini, A. (2023). *ChatGPT and Artificial Intelligence in Higher Education: Quick Start Guide*. (Document code: ED/HE/IESALC/IP/2023/12). United Nations Educational, Scientific and Cultural Organization and the UNESCO International Institute for Higher Education in Latin America and the Caribbean (IESALC). https://www.iesalc.unesco.org/wp-content/uploads/2023/04/ChatGPT-and-Artificial-Intelligence-in-higher-education-Quick-Start-guide_EN_FINAL.pdf

Stella. (2023, May 31). *Supported Countries, Regions, and Territories for ChatGPT*. https://www.minitool.com/news/chatgpt-supported-countries-and-territories.html

Tucci, L., & Needle, D. (2023, May 23). What is the Metaverse? An Explanation and In-Depth Guide. *TechTarget*. https://www.techtarget.com/whatis/feature/The-metaverse-explained-Everything-you-need-to-know

Turnitin. (2023). *Turnitin Announces AI Writing Detector and AI Writing Resource Center for Educators.* https://www.turnitin.com/press/turnitin-announces-ai-writing-detector-and-ai-writing-resource-center-for-educators

UAE Digital Government. (2022, November 24). *Emirates Blockchain Strategy 2021.* https://u.ae/en/about-the-uae/strategies-initiatives-and-awards/strategies-plans-and-visions/strategies-plans-and-visions-untill-2021/emirates-blockchain-strategy-2021#:~:text=In%20April%20 2018%2C%20the%20UAE,the%20blockchain%20platform%20by%202021

UAE to Launch Economic Ministry in the Metaverse. (2022, October 3). *The Daily Start.* https://www.thedailystar.net/tech-startup/news/uae-launch-economy-ministry-the-metaverse-3134016

UAE's Latest Bet on Tech: A Ministry in the Metaverse. (2022, October 3). *The Economic Times India Times.* https://economictimes.indiatimes.com/news/international/uae/uaes-latest-bet-on-tech-a-ministry-in-the-metaverse/articleshow/94610487.cms

Universitas Gadjah Mada. (2013). https://hukor.ugm.ac.id/download/peraturan-rektor-uam-nomor-711-0-sk-ht-2013/

Universitas Gadjah Mada Library (UGM Library). (2023). *Panduan Anti Plagiarisme.* https://lib.ugm.ac.id/wp-content/uploads/sites/1681/2023/01/panduan_anti_plagiarisme.pdf

Virgin Mobile Kuwait Announces Metaverse Programme. (n.d.). *Unlock Communications.* https://www.unlock23.com/virgin-mobile-kuwait-announces-metaverse-programme/

Wijayanti, M., et al. (2022, December). Hak Kebendaan dan Keabsahan Perjanjian Kebendaan Virtual Land di dalam Metaverse Ditinjau Berdasarkan KUHPerdata. *Majalah Hukum Nasional, 52*(2). https://doi.org/10.33331/mhn.v52i2.176

World Intellectual Property Organization (WIPO). (n.d.). *What Is Intellectual Property?* https://www.wipo.int/about-ip/en/

Zimwara, T. (2022, July 3). Kuwait-Based Islamic Bank Enters the Metaverse. *Bitcoin.* https://news.bitcoin.com/kuwait-based-islamic-bank-enters-the-metaverse/

CHAPTER 4

Development of New Technologies and Intellectual Property Regulations in the Sultanate of Oman

Muhanna Hamed Al Zuheimi

1 Introduction

The Sultanate of Oman is an emerging player in global trade, utilizing its strategic geographic location and rich natural resources. Acknowledging the pivotal role of new technologies in facilitating trade and enhancing its competitive advantage, Oman has invested in research and development (R&D) activities to diversify its economy, reduce oil dependency, and facilitate sustainable economic growth. Through the advent of Internet connectivity, e-commerce platforms, and cloud computing, productivity and efficiency gains have been achieved, revolutionizing the way that its international trade is conducted (United Nations, 2014).

One key area where technology has made substantial contributions is trade facilitation. Automation and digitization of customs processes have streamlined trade clearance procedures, reduced paperwork, and enhanced

M. H. Al Zuheimi (✉)
Legal Department, Ministry of Higher Education, Research and Innovation, Al Seeb, Muscat Governate, Sultanate of Oman

N. Naim et al. (eds.), *Intellectual Property and Innovation*, The Political Economy of the Middle East,
https://doi.org/10.1007/978-981-96-4020-1_4

transparency. This has resulted in shorter processing times, lower costs, and improved reliability, making Oman a more attractive destination for foreign investors and trading partners. Innovative technologies such as artificial intelligence (AI) and big data analytics drive efficient market research, enabling businesses to identify emerging trade opportunities and gain a competitive edge (Al-Bulushi, n.d.). Oman recognizes that effective utilization of new technologies is essential to diversify its trade portfolio and reduce reliance on oil exports. By embracing digitalization, Oman has expanded its export base and increased its competitiveness in non-oil sectors such as manufacturing, information technology, and tourism. This has allowed it to tap into new markets, attracting foreign investments and fostering economic growth (Ministry of Higher Education, Research, & Innovation, 2017). Investments in technological innovation have played a crucial role in diversifying its trade portfolio, reducing trade barriers, and enhancing its global competitiveness. As Oman continues to prioritize the development of new technologies, it is well poised to seize new opportunities in the international trade arena, foster sustainable economic growth, and secure a prosperous future (International Telecommunication Union, 2023).

2 Development of New Technologies in Oman

Oman's strategy encompasses critical elements such as human capital development, infrastructure creation, adoption of e-government practices, trust establishment, and the formulation of relevant frameworks and legislation. The success of this strategy heavily depends on the commitment and expertise of professionals. Additionally, Oman has made significant strides in adopting and successfully implementing various technologies, leading to notable transformations in infrastructure, communications, healthcare, and renewable energy sectors. This has elevated Oman as a significant player in the global technological landscape (Ministry of Transport, Communications, & Information Technology, 2024). A specific example is the government's digital transformation program for 2021–2025, which aims to cultivate a sustainable knowledge society and enhance public sector productivity and efficiency. This initiative promises bolstered national capacity, improved infrastructure, a flourishing IT industry, and more efficient government services and delivery methods. It also ensures streamlined service processes for citizens, businesses, and government institutions (Ministry of Transport, Communications, & Information Technology, 2024).

Innovation and entrepreneurship are the engines of digital development, driving the creation of new technologies and growth of new industries that improve lives and connect society to new opportunities. Oman understands the importance of these two concepts in building a sustainable, progressive, and digitally connected society. It has made tremendous strides with various information and communication technologies (ICTs) investments and its Digital Economy program and continues to address opportunities toward the Oman Vision 2040 (Zavazava, 2023 cited in, International Telecommunication Union, 2023).

2.1 *Infrastructure Development*

Infrastructure development utilizes advanced technologies to improve connectivity and transportation systems. There are numerous infrastructure projects, including constructing modern airports, highways, railways, and cultural landmarks (Oxford Business Group, 2023a, 2023b). The Batinah Expressway, for example, is recognized as one of the most sophisticated highways in the region and has transformed the transportation industry by reducing travel time and enhancing road safety. Substantial investments have been directed toward transportation, particularly in roads, maritime ports, and airports. Ongoing efforts aim at establishing a national railway network that will benefit Oman and align with a broader GCC-wide network, creating a more extensive and interconnected system. The recent improvements to the Sultanate's public–private partnerships law are anticipated to incentivize increased private investment in future projects, further strengthening this network (Oxford Business Group, 2023a, 2023b).

2.2 *ICT and Communications*

There has been significant investment in expanding high-speed fiber-optic networks, ensuring Internet access even in remote regions. This connectivity push has facilitated communication for individuals and paved the way for the advancement of e-commerce, e-learning, telemedicine, and other digital services. Furthermore, Oman's National Broadband Strategy has opened doors for a digital economy, creating fresh employment prospects and promoting innovation (Oxford Business Group, 2023a, 2023b). ICT policies and regulations encompass many areas, from cloud governance to social media. The ITU ICT Regulatory Tracker has granted Oman an impressive score of 85.33 out of 100, attesting to the solid domestic regulatory authority and competitive frameworks for ICT and telecommunications. This paves the way for significant innovation in the sector. However, the urgency and importance of adjustments are necessary to fully capitalize on this potential to tackle the challenges presented by advanced technologies such as drones and cloud services and clarify ambiguous areas pertaining to access and utilization (Oxford Business Group, 2023a, 2023b). A critical issue is the slow pace of policy revisions, largely due to security concerns, which has deterred innovators from venturing into certain areas. To create an environment that promotes innovation and technological progress, it is crucial for authorities to address these concerns. This will provide clearer guidelines for emerging technologies usage, ensuring the security and protection of all stakeholders and encouraging their participation (International Telecommunication Union, 2023).

2.3 *Healthcare Advancements*

The Oman Health Vision 2050 aims to establish a stronger healthcare system. Oman is dedicated to enhancing healthcare accessibility, quality, and outcomes for its people through strategic policy interventions and substantial investment in healthcare infrastructure and services (AlKaabi, 2023).

In recent years, Oman's healthcare sector has undergone rapid and transformative progress, with significant advancements and innovations. This progress is a testament to the dedication and hard work of all stakeholders, including policymakers, healthcare professionals, and citizens. The comprehensive healthcare reform program, establishment of a national health system providing accessible and affordable nationwide healthcare services, healthcare infrastructure investment, and healthcare professional training are all achievements in which stakeholders can take pride. Additionally, there has been a strong emphasis on preventive healthcare measures, with initiatives such as vaccination programs, health education campaigns, and screening services for conditions such as diabetes and hypertension significantly impacting Oman's healthcare landscape.

Health is a top priority under Oman Vision 2040, and the industry has made remarkable progress with further development on the horizon (Al Khabouri, 2021). However, these advancements have not been without their challenges, as the shortage of skilled healthcare professionals, especially in specialized fields, has impacted the quality of care provided and led to longer waiting times for patients and non-communicable diseases such as diabetes, cardiovascular diseases, and obesity. Leveraging cutting-edge technology, Oman's healthcare sector has achieved significant milestones, elevating patient care and strengthening the country's medical infrastructure. The government's proactive approach has led to pioneering initiatives such as electronic healthcare records, telemedicine services, and remote monitoring systems. These digital innovations have revolutionized information sharing among healthcare providers, significantly improving the efficiency and effectiveness of care delivery and ultimately alleviating the burden on healthcare facilities (Oxford Business Group, n.d.).

2.4 Renewable Energy and Sustainability

Oman has made remarkable progress in its sustainable development journey, particularly in renewable energy. The country's focus on solar and wind energy projects, as part of its Renewable Energy Initiative, is notable for utilization of abundant solar and wind resources. This forward-thinking approach reduces dependence on non-renewable energy sources and contributes significantly to the global fight against climate change. Embracing sustainability promotes economic diversification and creates job opportunities in the renewable energy sector, paving the way for a brighter and more sustainable future.

In alignment with global initiatives to reduce carbon emissions, the Ministry of Energy and Minerals collaborated with OQ and Hydrogen Oman (Hydrom) to expedite the regulations for the hydrogen industry. This collaboration has been instrumental in implementing the necessary legal frameworks to expand the industry. The Ministry has also focused on allocating viable production sites to attract investment, localizing this technology, and compiling essential studies. The broad range of uses of hydrogen, contributing to diversifying energy sources, reducing carbon emissions, and fostering economic growth, has led to the launch of investment incentives in the sector. More than 50,000 square kilometers have been allocated for staged green hydrogen projects. Ambitious plans aim to generate over a million tons of green hydrogen by 2030 and almost 8 million tons by 2050 using 30% of the already permitted space.

The Ministry is pivotal in promoting local added value policies, localizing hydrogen-related industries, enabling strategic studies, research, and development, building national capacities, raising public awareness of clean energy, and other related policies. This comprehensive approach underscores Oman's commitment to sustainability and its strategic objectives. Oman's energy security is a top priority, guided by integrated planning for traditional and renewable energy resources. This strategic approach supports transition to a more energy-efficient economy, fostering regional and global economic diversification while enhancing Oman's status as a significant and competitive player in the world energy market (Ministry of Energy & Minerals of Oman, 2022).

3 Oman's Short-, Medium-, and Long-Term Economic Plans

Oman Vision 2040 embodies Oman's long-term development strategy. The government has executed executive programs, action plans, key milestones, and targets to realize this vision. The primary focus is on bolstering economic growth in essential short- to mid-term sectors to achieve long-term goals. The government has recently formulated comprehensive and strategic economic plans to achieve immediate, intermediate, and long-term financial objectives. These plans involve identifying crucial strategies and initiatives to facilitate economic expansion, diversification, and sustainability (Ministry of Higher Education, Research, & Innovation, 2017).

The national innovation system is implemented in three integrated stages. The short-term stage focuses on initiatives with immediate and high impact on national sustainability, including developing digital and Internet services, removing regulatory obstacles, and promoting the development of policies for small and medium-size enterprises (Ministry of Higher Education, Research, & Innovation, 2017). Oman is undergoing a significant transformation to achieve sustainable growth and development in the medium term. Its focus is on economic diversification, infrastructure development, and promoting knowledge-based industries (Ministry of Higher Education, Research, & Innovation, 2017).

3.1 Short-Term Economic Plan

There is an ambitious short-term financial strategy to address ongoing economic challenges and reinforce economic stability and resilience. At the core of this approach is the diversification of the economy away from reliance on oil, with a strategic focus on fostering growth in such sectors as tourism, logistics, manufacturing, and fisheries, which offer significant potential for expansion. The government is making substantial investments in infrastructure, introducing incentives for both domestic and international investors, and cultivating a business-friendly environment to accomplish this goal (International Telecommunication Union, 2023). Human capital development is a crucial priority in Oman's economic agenda, emphasizing vocational training programs, educational reforms, and investments in R&D. The government is deeply committed to providing the workforce with the necessary skills and knowledge to succeed in a rapidly evolving job market, with a strong focus on education and skill development. With 50% of the population under 25, Oman boasts a high-value ratio of human capital. Young innovators are enthusiastic, creative, and hard-working, particularly in digital innovation. However, they require essential business building and operational skills, including sales and marketing, critical thinking, project management, financial management, human resources management, and client management. While some skills can be acquired through on-the-job experience, there is a genuine need for more training, mentorship, and exposure to foster innovation (International Telecommunication Union, 2023).

3.2 Medium-Term Economic Plan

Oman's medium-term economic plan aims to reduce its heavy dependence on oil and gas revenues by expanding and developing sectors such as tourism, manufacturing, logistics, and renewable energy. This strategic shift aims to create a more resilient and balanced economy that is less susceptible to oil price fluctuations while fostering innovation and creating new employment opportunities (Ministry of Higher Education, Research, & Innovation, 2017). The economic plan emphasizes the development of robust infrastructure to support economic diversification and enhance Oman's global competitiveness. Critical investments in transportation, telecommunications, energy, and other infrastructure projects are pivotal to unlocking the country's growth potential and improving its citizens' overall quality of life (Ministry of Higher Education, Research, & Innovation, 2017).

In line with global trends in the digital economy and the Fourth Industrial Revolution, Oman is intensely focused on advancing knowledge-based industries through investments in education, research, and innovation. This approach aims to build a skilled workforce capable of driving technological advancement and creating high-value products and services. Key strategies include promoting entrepreneurship, technology transfer, and protecting IP rights (Ministry of Higher Education, Research, &

Innovation, 2017). Environmental sustainability is being addressed through integrating green initiatives and sustainable practices, such as reducing carbon emissions, promoting renewable energy sources, and preserving natural resources for future generations, demonstrating a firm commitment to environmental protection and sustainable economic growth (Ministry of Higher Education, Research, & Innovation, 2017).

The medium-term economic plan emphasizes achieving sustainable growth and promoting knowledge-based industries through economic diversification, infrastructure development, and sustainability initiatives. It also prioritizes innovation, education, and environmental stewardship, to thrive in the competitive global economy (Ministry of Higher Education, Research, & Innovation, 2017). Economic diversification involves reducing reliance on traditional industries like oil and gas and expanding the economic base through investments in non-oil sectors. This strategy facilitates sustainable economic growth and boosts resilience against external shocks. Focus areas include enhancing non-oil sectors, developing tourism infrastructure, improving regional connectivity, and attracting foreign investments in renewable energy, technology, and medical services. Key to the plan is expanding tourism infrastructure to stimulate economic activity. Investments in this sector can create job opportunities and revenue streams while attracting visitors globally (Ministry of Higher Education, Research, & Innovation, 2017).

Attracting foreign investment in renewable energy, technology, and medical services is crucial for economic diversification. Renewable energy sources reduce carbon emissions and decrease dependency on fossil fuels, stimulating energy security and sustainability. Similarly, investments in technology and medical services drive innovation, enhance healthcare delivery, and create high-value job opportunities, promoting economic diversification and knowledge exchange (Ministry of Higher Education, Research, & Innovation, 2017). Improving regional connectivity through efficient transportation networks further supports economic growth, trade volumes, and cooperation with neighboring countries, opening new markets and opportunities. Investing in transportation infrastructure, including roads, ports, and airports is essential for improving connectivity within Oman and neighboring countries. This expedites the movement of goods and people, benefiting local businesses and attracting foreign direct investment. Enhanced infrastructure also boosts tourism by showcasing the country's natural beauty and cultural heritage to a broader audience (Ministry of Higher Education, Research, & Innovation, 2017).

3.3 *Long-Term Economic Plan*

Oman's current economic strategy to shift from reliance on oil to building a knowledge-based economy outlines three main objectives. Firstly, Oman aims to position itself as a hub for innovation, research, and development. This involves boosting productivity through innovation, fostering collaboration between academia and industry, and supporting start-ups and knowledge-intensive industries. Secondly, it is committed to investing in education and skills development to cultivate a workforce with advanced technological and digital skills, thereby enhancing its competitiveness in the global economy. Thirdly, it is enacting measures to ensure economic and financial stability. These measures include diversifying revenue sources, reducing dependence on oil revenues, and attracting investment in tourism, manufacturing, logistics, and renewable energy sectors. Additionally, initiatives are in place to improve budget planning and execution, strengthen public financial management, and enhance debt management practices (International Telecommunication Union, 2023). Measures to enhance governance and increase the disclosure of financial information are designed to build trust with investors, improve the efficiency of public spending, and mitigate the risk of corruption. This commitment inspires confidence among stakeholders (International Telecommunication Union, 2023).

Overall, Oman's comprehensive strategy aims to diversify the economy, reduce reliance on oil, and promote sustainable growth. Supported by the country's commitment to achieving its economic objectives, these efforts promise a prosperous future and enhance its attractiveness as an investment and business destination (International Telecommunication Union, 2023).

4 Role of Industry in Supporting Economic Growth

The close relationship between manufacturing, technology, and innovation contributes to economic development. Oman's focus on innovation as a vital factor for future progress necessitates a thoughtful consideration of the interaction between innovation and manufacturing (Ministry of Commerce & Industry & the United Nations Industrial Development Organization, 2019). Over the past few years, Oman has significantly emphasized the diversification of its economy, pivoting toward industrialization to stimulate growth and advancement. This strategic initiative necessitates thoughtful deliberation on establishing new industries and the requisite government initiatives and strategies to accomplish this objective. The government's role in prioritizing five essential elements—creating employment opportunities, fostering economic diversification, facilitating R&D expenditure, ensuring government effectiveness, and investing in infrastructure—is crucial for the success of this industrialization drive (Ministry of Commerce & Industry of Oman, & the United Nations Industrial Development Organization, 2019).

Firstly, creating employment opportunities is a crucial factor. Industries play a pivotal role in generating employment. Oman has made noteworthy strides in developing sectors such as manufacturing, petrochemicals, and logistics, creating many job prospects for both skilled and unskilled workers. This has effectively contributed to reducing unemployment rates and enhancing the nation's economic landscape. Secondly, the focus on economic diversification has been a significant strategic development driver. The emergence of industries has effectively mitigated the nation's reliance on oil-based revenues. The government has actively promoted and implemented policies such as tax incentives, streamlined regulatory processes, and investment in education and training to encourage investment in non-oil sectors. Critical industries such as manufacturing, renewable energy, and tourism have driven diversification, attracted foreign direct investment, and nurtured local entrepreneurship (Ministry of Commerce & Industry & the United Nations Industrial Development Organization, 2019).

Moreover, Oman's flourishing industries have facilitated the transfer of technology and innovation, drawing multinational corporations and foreign investors who bring cutting-edge technologies, knowledge, and expertise to the region. This influx has led to the adoption of best practices and increased productivity for local industries, rendering them more competitive on a global scale. Their establishment has also fostered a vibrant environment for research and development, ultimately driving innovation and the emergence of new products and services. The rise of industries has served as a vital catalyst for economic growth in Oman, contributing to job creation, economic diversification, technological innovation, and increased value of natural resources. The government's efforts to attract investments and create a favorable business atmosphere have yielded positive results, significantly bolstering the nation's overall economic development. Through the strategic establishment of industries, Oman is on track to achieve sustainable economic growth and reduce its reliance on oil revenues. Notably, an important point to stress about innovation is that country size does not affect innovation capacity. While large countries may be able to develop a broader range of innovation capabilities and may be involved in multiple economic activities by focusing on selected areas of excellence, smaller countries can also compete and thrive in the world economy (Ministry of Commerce & Industry & the United Nations Industrial Development Organization, 2019).

5 Role of Local Communities in Technology Development

Technological progress can be enhanced by harmonizing the academia, government, and industry sectors to cultivate applied technology. The potential for technology development via collaboration between the academic, government, and industry sectors is immense. With the pooling of knowledge, resources, and expertise from these sectors, innovation can be fostered, technology transfer facilitated, and economic growth stimulated for the direct benefit of Oman. Academic institutions are instrumental in driving the progress of applied technology. Their faculty members and researchers possess extensive expertise and actively engage in R&D initiatives. They accelerate technological advancements through their fundamental research and partnerships with government agencies and industry. By consistently staying abreast of scientific advancements, academic institutions foster the growth of highly skilled professionals and cultivate innovative research outcomes (Ministry of Commerce & Industry & the United Nations Industrial Development Organization, 2019).

The academia, government, and industry-integrated approach to applied technology development through local, regional, and international R&D project networks set the stage for numerous positive outcomes. For example, the Helmholtz Association and Oman signed an agreement reiterating their plans to build a technology center in Oman. Research at the new institute will focus on improved oil and gas extraction, water resources technology, and renewable energies. Four Helmholtz centers are involved in this cooperation so far: the GEOMAR Centre for Ocean Research Kiel, Potsdam Centre, the German Research Centre for Geosciences, the Centre for Environmental Research and the German Aerospace Centre. Oman can leverage this approach to foster a culture of research and innovation, drive economic diversification, attract foreign investments, and nurture a skilled workforce capable of tackling global challenges. Moreover, the knowledge, discoveries, and technologies generated through these networks can have widespread societal impacts, improving Oman's standard of living, healthcare, and sustainability (Ministry of Commerce & Industry & the United Nations Industrial Development Organization, 2019).

6 Bridging the Gap: Technology Advancements in Product Manufacturing

Oman has been making significant strides in economic development, particularly within the manufacturing sector. To sustain this momentum, Omani enterprises should prioritize investing in innovative technologies to enhance product quality. This can be achieved through the acquisition of off-the-shelf technology solutions and the development of customized ones to meet specific requirements. By embracing innovative technologies, manufacturers can streamline their operations, reduce production costs, improve efficiency, and elevate product quality. Additionally, integrating advanced equipment can enhance a company's manufacturing capabilities, enabling them to offer a more diverse range of products to meet both local and global market demands. Furthermore, prioritizing and investing in local R&D fosters innovation and creativity within the manufacturing sector, ultimately leading to increased competitiveness and long-term sustainability (Ministry of Commerce & Industry & the United Nations Industrial Development Organization, 2019).

Government initiatives promoting R&D and collaboration between academia and industry are crucial for creating an innovation-driven culture within the manufacturing sector. By combining technology acquisitions and locally developed innovations, Oman can establish an adaptable, efficient, and globally competitive manufacturing sector capable of meeting the demands of today's markets (Ministry of Commerce & Industry & the United Nations Industrial Development Organization, 2019).

7 Governmental IP Rights Legislation and Assistance for Oman's Trade Positioning

Safeguarding IP in Oman is a top priority and is upheld by solid government legislation. The country acknowledges the substantial economic advantages of protecting IP rights, which not only enhance its position in global trade but also stimulate economic development, promote innovation, and attract foreign investment. This positive outlook on growth and innovation in Oman directly results from implementing robust IP regulations (Ministry of Justice & Legal Affairs, 2008).

To protect IP, Oman has enacted several crucial legislations. Royal Decree 65/2008, the Law on Protection of Copyrights and Related Rights, safeguards literary, artistic, and scientific works and neighboring rights for performers, producers, and broadcasters. Royal Decree 67/2008, the Law of Industrial Property Protection, encompasses patents for inventions, trademarks for distinctive signs, industrial designs, geographic indications, and trade secrets. Oman has also enacted Royal Decree 49/2009, the Law on Protection of New Plant Varieties, to protect new plant varieties and regulate breeders' rights. Moreover, Oman's involvement in international agreements, such as the World Intellectual Property Organization (WIPO)'s Berne Convention for the Protection of Literary and Artistic Works and Paris Convention for the Protection of Industrial Property, and the WTO's Agreement on Trade-Related Aspects of Intellectual Property Rights, further bolsters Oman's comprehensive framework for safeguarding IP rights. This comprehensive IP framework provides a secure operational environment for businesses and individuals (Ministry of Justice & Legal Affairs, 2008).

7.1 Importance of Intellectual Property Regulations

Intellectual property encompasses the legal rights that safeguard products of the mind, such as inventions, literary works, artistic designs, and symbols. These rights enable creators and innovators to manage and benefit from their creations. Vigorous enforcement of IP regulations can yield numerous positive effects on nations involved in global trade (WIPO, 2008). Robust IP protection protects domestic industries from unauthorized use and exploitation. This safeguard ensures that creators and innovators receive just compensation for their intellectual pursuits, motivating them to continue producing innovative works. In contrast, lax IP regulations can lead to widespread piracy and counterfeiting, impeding innovation and economic progress. Hence, local talent is encouraged to push the boundaries of technology and creativity, knowing that their efforts will be adequately protected (WIPO, 2008).

Stringent IP regulations also attract foreign direct investment (FDI) by establishing a secure environment for companies to develop and commercialize their innovations. A clearly defined IP framework boosts investor confidence. It enables businesses to safeguard their assets and thrive in fair competition, fostering a sense of security and confidence in the global trade landscape. Implementing effective IP regulations contributes to nurturing international collaborations and partnerships, laying the groundwork for a more interconnected and innovative world. When countries have reliable and equitable IP laws, businesses are more likely to engage in joint ventures, research initiatives, and technology transfers. This facilitates the exchange of knowledge and expertise across borders, leading to mutually beneficial progress in various industries (WIPO, 2008).

7.2 *Benefits for Oman's Global Trade Positioning*

The enhancement of Oman's IP regulations can significantly improve its global trade status and pave the way for substantial economic growth and diversification. Strengthening IP laws and enforcement mechanisms can create an environment conducive to innovation and entrepreneurship, attract foreign direct investment, and facilitate the transfer of advanced technologies, knowledge, and resources. This, in turn, can spur economic growth and diversify Oman's economy. Furthermore, robust IP regulations play a crucial role in enriching Oman's innovation ecosystem. By providing a secure framework for local innovators to develop, safeguard, and commercialize their IP, Oman empowers them to create high-value products and services, promote technological advancements, and nurture a culture of innovation and creativity. This is essential for a knowledge-based economy and underscores the value of local talent. Harmonizing IP laws with international standards can significantly enhance Oman's global market position by streamlining trade agreements and partnerships. This could potentially lead to expanded market access, increased export opportunities, and the establishment of mutually beneficial economic alliances with other nations, which could significantly boost Oman's competitiveness on the international stage (U.S. Embassy Oman, 2009).

7.3 *Role of Governmental Legislation and Assistance*

Oman's government is instrumental in safeguarding the well-being of its citizens and driving economic, social, and cultural progress. Implementing robust IP laws is crucial to fostering innovation, safeguarding investments, and facilitating knowledge transfer. Therefore, the government's IP system must be aligned with these objectives. The multifaceted nature of the government's involvement underscores the complexity of this matter, necessitating a comprehensive approach that addresses all pertinent elements. The gravity and significance of this task, which cannot be overstated, highlights the need for a thorough and all-encompassing strategy (WIPO, 2005).

Domestic implementation is a primary consideration. The government's commitment to ensuring that IP laws offer sufficient protection to creators while also balancing public and private interests is crucial. This balance is key to fostering a fair and equitable environment for all stakeholders. Comprehensive IP regulations are essential and pivotal to maintain a competitive position in the global trade arena. Recognizing this, the government plays a proactive role in instituting and upholding these regulations. This is achieved through the enactment of extensive laws that safeguard various forms of IP, including patents, trademarks, copyrights, and trade secrets. The laws also encompass enforcement mechanisms, dispute resolution, and penalties for infringement, demonstrating the government's unwavering commitment to protecting IP (WIPO, 2005).

Moreover, the government's provision of financial assistance and incentives is crucial in bolstering IP creation and protection. This may involve funding research programs, establishing specialized training centres, and offering tax benefits or grants to encourage innovation, IP registration, and support local industries. The government's support in this area is a significant boost to IP development and protection. Capacity building and educational initiatives are also crucial to enhancing local understanding and IP awareness. Organizing training programs, workshops, and awareness campaigns for businesses, entrepreneurs, and the public can effectively disseminate knowledge about IP protection. By enacting robust IP laws, Oman can attract foreign investment, foster innovation, and fortify its position in international trade. Legislative measures, financial assistance, and education initiatives can establish an environment conducive to creativity, innovation, and the protection of IP rights, ultimately contributing to the nation's overall growth and prosperity. This promising future is within reach with the implementation of robust IP laws (WIPO, 2005).

8 Innovation and Growth: Government Agencies as IP Commercialization Custodians

The digital era, powered by transformative technologies, has significantly reshaped the landscape of IP generation, distribution, and utilization on a global scale. This shift has elevated the role of IP assets such as patents, trademarks, copyrights, designs, and trade secrets to a pivotal position in fostering innovation, driving economic growth, and safeguarding national interests. In this context, it is crucial for government agencies to proactively engage in the acquisition, importation, and protection of IP to promote commercialization and innovation. In economic growth and development, innovation serves as the primary driver, enabling the introduction of new products, services, and production processes into the market. It becomes imperative to establish a well-balanced, cost-effective, and dependable system of IP rights. Such a system not only shields the substantial investments of innovative companies from potential imitators but also provides essential incentives for undertaking these investments in the first place. However, not all entities, including academic institutions and innovative businesses, possess the requisite financial and technical capabilities to bring their inventions or creations to the market independently. This underscores the critical need for global partnerships, particularly in markets such as biotechnology, where international presence is not only beneficial, but also crucial for success (United Nations Economic Commission for Europe, 2011).

In the commercialization of biotechnology innovations, it is essential to acknowledge the extended lead times between initiating commercialization activities and realizing substantial revenues. Consequently, alternative funding sources are critical to bridge this gap, particularly when the risk of commercial failure is perceived to be high. To realize commercial returns from IP, certain conditions must be fulfilled, including the existence of customers or the ability to create them, as well as an entity controlling the manufacture and sale of the resulting products. Furthermore, a shift from closed to open innovation models is evident, indicating a fundamental change in how organizations innovate and bring new ideas to the market. In IP valuation, it is crucial to identify valuable IP within a portfolio for complete protection. Equally important is the recognition of underutilized IP, as it presents an opportunity to create diverse revenue streams and foster innovation. Achieving cost efficiencies in IP development, protection, and utilization is also a key consideration in this process (United Nations Economic Commission for Europe, 2011).

8.1 Protecting and Enforcing IP

The Ministry of Commerce, Industry, and Investment Promotion has established a national Intellectual Property Office to oversee IP rights and a department dedicated to inspections and enforcement to address IP infringements. Nevertheless, challenges still need to be addressed in dealing with IP violators and deficiencies in the IP rights enforcement system. Effectively managing IP rights in Oman hinges on several critical principles. One of the most important is developing a comprehensive protection strategy. It is essential to understand that Oman's IP protection and enforcement procedures may differ from those in other countries. Additionally, it is crucial to recognize that most IP rights must be registered and enforced in Oman by local laws. For example, trademarks registered in the United States and patents hold no legal standing in Oman. Copyright protection is not universal, and safeguarding work in a country is subject to its domestic laws. However, Oman grants copyright protection to foreign works through international agreements (International Trade Administration, 2024).

8.2 Enhancing Economic Development

Preserving and capitalizing on critical intellectual properties is imperative for advancing national interests and economic prosperity. As stewards, government agencies can establish conducive environments for businesses and entrepreneurs to maximize their capabilities, leading to the development of new industries, employment opportunities, and enhanced competitiveness in both domestic and global arenas. By fostering economic progress, government agencies contribute to the national collective well-being. The significance of IP has seen a remarkable upsurge, with intangible assets now constituting much of a company's worth. To fully exploit the economic potential of IP assets, businesses, financiers, and investors play a pivotal role in devising market mechanisms and risk-return strategies tailored to intangibles. This evolution, including financial markets, professional entities, governmental policies, and international trading norms, relies on expertise and dedication (Ogier, 2016).

The IP system captures economic value in today's knowledge-based economies, converting intangibles into tradeable economic assets. Nonetheless, the intangibles market must progress to prevent capital from being locked in low- or negative-yielding assets. Promoting this transformation entails various measures, including company IP audits, professionally accredited standards for IP valuation and risk management, common platforms to facilitate IP asset assessment, and a deeper understanding of IP licensing (Ogier, 2016).

8.3 Encouraging Innovation

Governmental entities actively encourage innovation by offering incentives for R&D. These incentives include research grants, tax advantages, and strategic partnerships, motivating businesses, academic institutions, and start-ups to partake in innovative endeavors. By facilitating cooperation between governmental entities and various stakeholders, Oman aims to drive significant advancements across diverse fields, bolstering the country's competitiveness on the global stage. As part of this overarching objective, the Ministry of Commerce, Industry, and Investment Promotion is committed to upholding and strengthening IP rights. The Ministry has implemented various procedures and initiatives to bolster innovation and investment in new ideas (Ministry of Higher Education, Research, & Innovation, 2024a, 2024c).

Furthermore, the Undersecretariat of Research and Innovation of the Ministry of Higher Education, Research, and Innovation has introduced various research funding support programs in different fields. These programs target students, researchers, and government officials, promoting research and innovation and potentially culminating in identifying and developing IP rights. As such, the scientific research and innovation sector is committed to enhancing research capabilities, boosting productivity and efficiency, and offering prompt solutions to researchers' challenges. It also encourages collaboration and aims to finance research proposals that align with national requirements. The sector aims to fortify national capabilities in crucial areas by cultivating skilled personnel and building infrastructure to support research, development, and innovation. Ultimately, its goal is to attain leadership in R&D in areas where the Sultanate holds a competitive edge (Ministry of Higher Education, Research, & Innovation, 2024a, 2024c). Overall, Oman's dedication to fostering innovation, safeguarding

IP, and supporting R&D underscores its commitment to driving economic growth and competitiveness through continual and strategic initiatives.

8.4 Protecting National Interests

When government agencies take custody of IP, they are responsible for safeguarding it, especially in matters related to national security or strategic priorities. By acquiring IP, government entities can systematically examine and assess potential risks associated with foreign technologies or sensitive advancements. This proactive approach ensures that no unintended disclosures of classified information or improper use of proprietary knowledge could compromise national security or put strategic interests at risk (Oman Vision 2040, Implementation Follow-up Unit, n.d.).

> We will protect our national interests, as they are the most important constants of the next phase, the directions and targets of which were set by 'Oman Vision 2040', with the prime aim of transforming all aspects of life. It is a true embodiment of collective national willpower. The success of this vision is the responsibility of us all, dear citizens, without exception, each one acting from his position and within the scope of his abilities and responsibilities. (Haitham bin Tarik, Sultan of Oman (Oman Vision 2040, Implementation Follow-up Unit, n.d.))

8.5 Collaborating with Industry

As key players in the acquisition and importation of IP, government agencies wield significant influence over economic development, innovation, and national security. Their active engagement with industry stakeholders is crucial to fully exploit IP's potential. This engagement can manifest in various forms, such as licensing agreements, joint ventures, grants, or other mechanisms that facilitate access and utilization of the acquired IP assets. Collaboration with industry stakeholders presents government entities with the opportunity to champion the adoption of new technologies, break down barriers to market entry, and bolster the competitiveness of domestic industries. This can pave the way for the emergence of new industries and a boost in national competitiveness. Therefore, it is crucial for government agencies to meticulously plan and leverage their role as custodians of IP to ensure that the economy, society, and overall national interests reap the rewards while mitigating potential risks (Ministry of Higher Education, Research, & Innovation, 2024b).

The collaboration & communication hub for research and innovation program (EJAAD) is a successful example of collaboration between government and industry. This program aims to bridge the gap between the industrial and academic sectors, creating a collaborative environment to enhance R&D. EJAAD is a membership-based platform encouraging meaningful interaction and cooperation among stakeholders from academia, industry, and related fields. The program's strong alignment with 69% and 34% of Oman Vision 2040 Priorities and National Goals underscores its strategic direction and potential to contribute to a knowledge-based economy. Specifically, EJAAD aims to facilitate integrating academic research with industry needs and cultivating a culture of collaboration between them. Emphasizing collaboration is fundamental to EJAAD's success and catalyses stakeholder involvement. Moreover, the program strives to maximize in-country value by directing business R&D requirements to local academic institutions and facilitating the deployment, commercialization, and transfer of technology resulting from research efforts (Ministry of Higher Education, Research, & Innovation, 2024b).

9 IP Enrichment Through Secondary Innovation

Oman boasts a rich historical and cultural heritage, complemented by its significant advances in innovation, technology, and scientific discovery. Leveraging these advances is crucial for enhancing IP through secondary innovations such as commercial licensing and avenues for commercialization. This approach will help convert Omani innovations into profitable ventures, benefiting the country's economy. A well-established IP rights framework can promote innovation and facilitate technology transfer. It should empower inventors and creators, allowing them to focus on their expertise without shouldering the burdens of entrepreneurship. Entrepreneurs will also benefit from reduced uncertainties when bringing innovations to market. However, implementing an IP rights framework requires dedicated support from policymakers, going beyond mere attention. This support is vital to incentivize and facilitate innovation effectively and is crucial to the framework's success (United Nations, 2014).

As Oman's economy and industries expand, IP rights play a pivotal role in the innovation system. Building the capacity to use IP instruments and recognizing the strategic importance of proprietary and public domains are essential at this stage of Oman's technological development. Policymakers should also consider open access as part of the IP rights policy to ensure that publicly funded research outcomes can be readily accessible. Recognizing IP rights as a critical policy component is fundamental to Oman's transformation into a knowledge-based economy with a functional national innovation system (United Nations, 2014).

9.1 Harnessing Intellectual Property Assets

The significance of IP assets in driving economic growth, supporting innovation, and gaining a competitive advantage is paramount. To fully capitalize on these assets, it is crucial to promote secondary innovations, which starts from technology introduction and imitation and focuses on technology catching up. These are new products, services, and processes developed by reimagining and repositioning existing discoveries and technologies to align with evolving market needs. This approach can lead to the development of new products, services, and processes, enhancing Omani inventions' commercial potential. While Oman's current IP laws generally adhere to WIPO and WTO conventions and their obligations, there is room for further optimization. It is essential to build greater awareness of the utility patents system, a type of patent that is granted for a new and useful process, machine, manufacture, or composition of matter, or a new and useful improvement thereof, to encourage incremental innovation (United Nations, 2014).

Oman is strategically developing various research and innovation areas, such as the Animal and Plant Genetic Resource Centre under the Innovation Center of the Ministry of Higher Education, Research and Innovation, where IP will play a pivotal role. Leveraging genetic material in advanced agriculture, industry, and pharmaceutical development necessitates a fully functional IP framework. However, this also presents a challenge as potential commercial outcomes often arise from combining traditional knowledge and research-driven efforts. This requires a policy that balances openness with protection against unwarranted appropriation. Patents are critical IP tools for fostering innovation and industrial development. Policymakers, particularly the Ministry of Commerce, Industry, and Promotion Investment, which houses Oman's IP Office, must address the need for more capacity to evaluate patent applications. Additionally, the costs associated with applying for and maintaining patents, especially for small and medium enterprises seeking international protection, pose a significant barrier. Potential solutions include joint filings with other stakeholders, financial support, and the broader use of national-only utility models. The benefits of IP must accrue to both the IP owners and society. Therefore, an IP rights policy should emphasize creating linkages between invention, innovation, economic growth, and diversification. Since IP has become integral to the globalized economy, a strategic and objective-oriented approach to IP, in collaboration with top-level policymaking for national development, is imperative (United Nations, 2014).

9.2 Promoting Commercial Licensing

It is common for inventors, innovators, and researchers to work with established companies to bring their ideas to market through commercial licensing agreements, which let individuals and organizations transfer their IP rights to companies. In turn, these companies can use their resources and expertise to make the most of these ideas in the market. The importance of IP rights to technology and innovation-led development is closely tied to microeconomic factors. This includes the technology use and capabilities of different sectors and companies and the competitiveness of local and international markets. Advanced firms and sectors and less developed and competitive sectors can both benefit from technology licensing. By acquiring and implementing new technologies, these sectors can enhance their competitiveness and contribute to the country's overall economic diversification. In these cases, technology owners, such as multinational firms, often prefer to trade within their company or make foreign direct investments. However, these circumstances can be influenced by policy (Lee, 1997).

According to Lee (1997), bolstering Oman's IP capabilities to advance its industrialization involves various significant factors. Firstly, Omani policymakers must be able to identify all pertinent international sources of technology transfer and establish necessary IP rights capacities for their utilization. For instance, technology licensing can stimulate innovation and economic diversification, depending heavily on a functioning IP rights regime. Other strategies, such as those based on FDI or domestic innovation, may necessitate distinct policies, institutions, and capacity-building efforts. These approaches may also require substantial enhancements in enforcing and resolving conflicts related to trade and industrial secrets, non-disclosure, or developing local capacity to facilitate domestic innovation patenting and commercialization. However, having a legal foundation in the form of IP laws is a fundamental yet insufficient prerequisite; it is also crucial to reinforce human and institutional capacity to design an IP rights regime that aligns with the strategic goals outlined in the national development policy, particularly the goal of innovation-driven diversification.

Secondly, domestic R&D and innovation commercialization demand that research institutions and firms develop IP strategies. They should transition from purely "work for hire" policies to enabling shared or joint IP registration and filing to provide more substantial incentives for creativity and innovation among staff while facilitating the commercialization of research outputs. This is especially crucial for smaller countries like Oman, which may increasingly seek worldwide IP protection for their research and knowledge institutions, entrepreneurs, and innovators (Lee, 1997).

Thirdly, policymakers must comprehensively understand the entire scope of IP policy, recognizing that creative endeavors and scientific research thrive on and require access to an ever-expanding global network of scientific and technological knowledge. Critical public policy concerns should encompass making publicly funded research openly accessible and, when appropriate, distributing it under public and open copyright licenses. Conversely, patents resulting from publicly funded research should be considered for licensing under non-exclusive terms and conditions (Lee, 1997).

Deeper collaboration with academic institutions is essential for research and innovation. For example, Oman Refineries and Petro Chemicals (ORPIC) has established ties with academic institutions such as Caledonian University (UK) and Oman's Sultan Qaboos University, focusing on reverse osmosis water treatment. However, the main obstacles to deeper collaboration include the limited capacity for advanced research and the need to align R&D activities with potential commercially viable products. It should be noted that ORPIC relies on licensing technologies rather than conducting in-house R&D. Oman needs a robust legal framework for IP protection to facilitate this process effectively. This framework should be transparent, efficient, and accessible to all parties involved, providing clear guidelines for acquiring, safeguarding, and enforcing IP rights. Additionally, developing an effective Intellectual Property Office and offering guidance and support to researchers and innovators navigating licensing negotiations is crucial. By fostering an environment that supports innovation and entrepreneurship, Oman can encourage local enterprises to pursue licensing agreements with innovators. This will lead to mutual growth and the advancement of the country's technological and scientific progress (Middle East College, 2024).

9.3 *Enabling the Commercialization of Innovations and Technologies*

Implementing technology transfer programs and facilitating collaborative R&D endeavors with foreign companies, local businesses, and academic institutions can promote international and regional integration. Strengthening connections with global research networks is essential due to the relatively limited pool of researchers in various fields within the individual economies of the Gulf Cooperation Council. The National Oil Companies Technology Managers Group in the oil and gas sector illustrates these efforts, and other industries should consider similar collaborative opportunities (Middle East College, 2024).

To support the commercialization process, Oman should establish technology transfer offices (TTOs) in universities, research institutions, and industry clusters. These TTOs will act as intermediaries between inventors and potential investors or commercial partners, assisting with patenting, licensing, funding, and marketing to make Omani innovations more accessible. For example, the Technology Transfer Office at Middle East College was established in collaboration with the Ministry of Higher Education, Research, and Innovation with the primary goal of connecting with the National Technology Transfer Office in the Ministry of Commerce, Industry and Investment Promotion. A TTO focuses on safeguarding IP rights and enhancing academic institution and industry sector connections. Its core mission and vision are to facilitate research, innovation, and discovery by administering IP laws, safeguarding individual rights related to creations and inventions, and granting licenses to third parties. Furthermore, collaborative networks and platforms that bring together inventors, investors, entrepreneurs, and industry experts can create synergistic relationships and facilitate knowledge and expertise exchange. Such initiatives can promote the development of innovative ecosystems that accelerate invention commercialization. For example, the Oman Investment Authority manages two funds: the Future Generations Fund for international assets and investments and the National Development Fund for domestic economic diversification and growth in specific sectors.

The Authority is committed to promoting economic sustainability and development in Oman (Oman Investment Authority, 2024).

As Oman continues to advance in innovation, technology, and scientific discovery, realizing the full potential of these homegrown advancements is essential. Through IP enrichment, commercial licensing, and commercialization, Oman can strategically leverage these valuable assets. By implementing robust IP protection mechanisms, promoting collaborations, and establishing effective support structures, Oman can unleash the transformative power of its IP for the benefit of its economy and society (Al-Jabri et al., 2021).

10 Scientist Participation in Strategic Top-Down Government-Funded Projects

Effective governance demands a robust focus on scientific expertise and technological progress. As significant shapers of progress and change, governments should actively promote the leadership and involvement of scientists and technologists in strategic, top-down initiatives receiving government funding. By leveraging their expertise, fostering innovation, and promoting evidence-based decision-making, governments can pave the way toward a more prosperous and sustainable future (Al-Jabri et al., 2021).

10.1 Harnessing Scientific Expertise

To address the pressing global challenges, leveraging the knowledge and skills of scientists and technologists is crucial. Governments can engage them as leaders and partners in government-funded initiatives to access their invaluable expertise. In climate change, scientists can offer scientific assessments and pioneering methodologies to mitigate its effects. In healthcare, medical scientists can provide invaluable insights to improve public health policies and broaden top-quality healthcare services access. By tapping into scientific expertise governments can promote interdisciplinary collaboration and foster a comprehensive approach to problem-solving (Al-Jabri et al., 2021).

10.2 *Fostering Innovation*

The partnership between scientists, technologists, and governmental organizations catalyzes revolutionary innovation. Scientists and technologists consistently push the limits of advanced research and development, utilizing their expertise to introduce pioneering ideas and technologies. When government-funded initiatives incorporate these fresh perspectives, research findings, and solutions for complex societal issues, they can tap into this synergy. Moreover, this collaboration has potential to generate high-quality employment opportunities and attract exceptional talent, ultimately fostering significant economic growth and prosperity (The Intergovernmental Panel on Climate Change, 2024).

10.3 *Enhancing Public–Private Partnerships*

Collaboration between government agencies, academic institutions, and industry leaders can foster valuable knowledge exchange, leading to innovation and technological advancements. The involvement of scientists in public–private partnerships can guide private-sector initiatives toward the public interest, enabling both sectors to work together toward common goals. This collaboration is crucial for addressing contemporary challenges such as climate change, sustainable energy, and technological transformation. Governments must invite scientists and technologists to lead and become associates in strategic top-down government-funded projects to achieve effective governance. By leveraging their expertise, governments can tackle complex challenges, foster innovation, promote evidence-based decision-making, and enhance public–private partnerships. This approach can result in sustainable solutions, economic growth, and improved societal well-being.

11 Conclusion

To enhance economic growth and trade competitiveness through advanced technology, Oman should consider a range of strategies. First, it should encourage R&D investment to foster innovation by providing government funding, partnering with universities and research institutions, and offering tax incentives to encourage private-sector investment. Oman should promote entrepreneurship and start-ups by establishing an ecosystem that nurtures entrepreneurship and supports start-ups. This can include mentorship and training programs, funding and venture capital access, and simplified business establishment procedures. Fostering collaboration between academia and industry is essential. This can be achieved through partnerships between universities/research institutions and businesses to enable knowledge transfer and commercialization of research, joint research projects, industry internships, and technology transfer offices. Oman should support digital transformation by encouraging businesses to adopt digital technologies and processes to improve efficiency and competitiveness. This may involve providing incentives for digital transformation projects, promoting e-commerce platforms, and establishing digital infrastructure such as high-speed Internet connectivity.

Developing industry-specific technology hubs can help drive innovation in targeted industries. Identifying critical industries with growth potential and establishing technology hubs or innovation clusters is recommended to promote collaboration and idea exchange within those sectors. This can bring together companies, start-ups, researchers, and investors. Enhancing trade infrastructure is crucial for improving trade capabilities. Modernizing logistics and transportation infrastructure, developing ports, airports, and trade corridors, implementing efficient customs procedures, and promoting trade facilitation agreements can all play a critical role.

Strengthening the IP framework is essential to protect innovations and incentivize R&D activities. Robust IP laws and enforcement mechanisms give domestic and foreign investors confidence in Oman's technology sector. International partnerships can provide access to advanced technologies and markets, including collaborations and partnerships with other countries and international organizations. This may involve trade agreements, joint research programs, and international technology conference and exhibition participation. Finally, workforce continuous skill development and training programs can help in adaption to technological advancements, including upskilling programs, vocational training, and retraining initiatives for individuals affected by industry transformation. By implementing these strategies, Oman can leverage technology to drive economic growth, enhance its global trade competitiveness, and remain a key player in the global market.

References

Al Khabouri, M. (2021). Health—A national priority. *Muscat Daily*. https://www.muscatdaily.com/2021/11/17/the-healthcare-sector-in-a-national-priority-under-oman-vision-2040/

Al-Bulushi, A. (n.d.). *Oman's Tech Ecosystem: Why is the Sultanate becoming a technology destination of choice?* https://www.britishomani.org//uploads/downloads/oman_tech_ecosystem_ahmed_al_bulushi.pdf

Al-Jabri, F., Kvist, T., Sund, R., & Turunen, H. (2021). Quality of care and patient safety at healthcare institutions in Oman: Quantitative study of the perspectives of patients and healthcare professionals. *BMC Health Services Research, 21*, 1–8. https://doi.org/10.1186/s12913-021-07152-2

AlKaabi, A. (2023). *Advancing healthcare in line with Oman Vision 2040*. https://www.omanobserver.om/article/1143741/magazine/advancing-healthcare-in-line-with-oman-vision-2040

International Telecommunication Union. (2023). *Digital innovation profile: Oman*. Retrieved September 11, 2024, from https://www.itu.int/dms_pub/itu-d/opb/inno/D-INNO-PROFILE.OMAN-2023-PDF-E.pdf

International Trade Administration. (2024). *Country commercial guide: Oman—Protecting intellectual property*. https://www.trade.gov/country-commercial-guides/oman-protecting-intellectual-property

Lee, Y. S. (Ed.). (1997). *Technology transfer and public policy*. Quorum.

Middle East College. (2024). *The Technology Transfer Office (TTO) at Middle East College*. https://mec.edu.om/en/technology-transfer-office/#:~:text=The%20Technology%20Transfer%20Office%20(TTO)&text=The%20foremost%20initiative%20is%20to,academic%20institutions%20and%20industry%20sectors

Ministry of Commerce and Industry and United Nations Industrial Development Organization. (2019). *'Manufacturing for wellbeing': The Sultanate of Oman's manufacturing strategy 2040* (1st ed.). https://downloads.unido.org/ot/15/44/15446402/Oman%20Manufacturing%20Strategy-%20En%20-%20for%20web.pdf

Ministry of Energy and Minerals. (2022). Sultanate of Oman The future of green energy. *WEALTH Newsletter*. https://mem.gov.om/Portals/0/WEALTH%20Newsletter%20Eng.pdf

Ministry of Higher Education, Research & Innovation. (2017). *Oman's national innovation strategy*. Muscat, Sultanate of Oman.

Ministry of Higher Education, Research & Innovation. (2024a). *Undersecretariat of Research and Innovation of the Ministry of Higher Education, Research, and Innovation*.https://www.moheri.gov.om/InnerPage.aspx?id=6126de59-44b0-4eb5-94c8-24500b33ae06

Ministry of Higher Education, Research & Innovation. (2024b). *EJAAD Platform*. https://orp.trc.gov.om/ejaad/

Ministry of Higher Education, Research & Innovation. (2024c). *Oman Research Portal*. https://orp.trc.gov.om

Ministry of Justice and Legal Affairs. (2008). *Royal Decree 67/2008 Promulgating the Industrial Property Rights Law*. https://qanoon.om/p/2008/rd2008065/; https://qanoon.om/p/2008/rd2008067/

Ministry of Transport, Communications and Information Technology. (2024). *Government Digital Transformation Programme*. https://www.mtcit.gov.om/ITAPortal/Pages/Page.aspx?NID=292734&PID=200797#:~:text=The%20government%20digital%20transformation%20program,of%20government%20services%20and%20its

Ogier, J. P. (2016). Intellectual property, finance and economic development. *WIPO Magazine*. https://www.wipo.int/wipo_magazine/en/2016/01/article_0002.html

Oman Investment Authority. (2024). *Oman investment authority launches future fund Oman*. https://www.oia.gov.om/Index.php?r=en%2Fsite%2Fnewsview&nid=oman-investment-authority-launches-future-fund-oman

Oman Vision 2040, Implementation Follow-up Unit. (n.d.). *Oman Vision 2040*. https://www.oman2040.om/?lang=en

Oxford Business Group. (2023a). *How Oman upgrades transport infrastructure to support diversification*. https://oxfordbusinessgroup.com/reports/oman/2023-report/

Oxford Business Group. (2023b). *The report: Oman 2023*. https://oxfordbusinessgroup.com/reports/oman/2023-report/

Oxford Business Group. (n.d.). *Oman's health care system increasingly ready to meet the population's needs*. https://oxfordbusinessgroup.com/reports/oman/2017-report/economy/on-the-rise-a-growing-population-finds-a-health-care-system-ready-to-meet-its-needs

The Intergovernmental Panel on Climate Change. (2024). https://www.ipcc.ch/

U.S. Embassy Oman. (2009). U.S.-Oman Free Trade Agreement. Muscat, Oman.

United Nations. (2014). *Conference on trade and development: Science, technology and innovation policy review*. https://unctad.org/system/files/official-document/dtlstict2014d1_en.pdf

United Nations Economic Commission for Europe. (2011). *Intellectual property commercialization, policy options and practical instruments*. United Nations Publications.

World Intellectual Property Organization (WIPO). (2005). *National seminar on copyright, related rights, and collective management: The role of government in establishing a modern copyright system*. WIPO Publications. Retrieved September 11, 2024 from wipo_cr_krt_05_2.doc (live.com)

World Intellectual Property Organization (WIPO). (2008). *Intellectual property handbook* (p. 489). ISBN 978-92-805-1291-5.

CHAPTER 5

A Framework Proposal for Islamic Finance-Based Intellectual Property Rights Audit Valuation

Nadia Naim

1 Introduction

This chapter will evaluate the role AI systems can play in IP financing whilst considering Islamic law for the Gulf Cooperation Council (GCC) states, the broader legal landscape pertaining to creating common data spaces in the IP industry, from which to generate more accurate IP comparable data and support IP financing and lending (Williams, 2022). For AI, there is potential to overcome its challenges around ethics and trustworthiness and create AI-assisted and/or AI-generated valuation methods. The UK Intellectual Property Office (IPO) offers an IP finance toolkit which acts as a guide for businesses and supports their IP audit before applying for an IP-backed loan or financing. To further support IP management and commercialisation strategies, as well as raise awareness of

N. Naim (✉)
Associate Dean International, Law and Social Sciences, Aston University, Birmingham, UK
e-mail: n.naim@aston.ac.uk

N. Naim et al. (eds.), *Intellectual Property and Innovation*, The Political Economy of the Middle East,
https://doi.org/10.1007/978-981-96-4020-1_5

finance options available, toolkits can be more useful where AI systems are utilised to address the limitations with current valuation processes.

IP audits can be very insightful and relevant to a company's financial forecast and value. The audit will establish whether the appropriate IP policies and procedures are in place and what IP rights a company has. The more detailed and accurate, the more reliable the audit is, in terms of validity and status. The audit aims to identify the most valuable rights as core assets. IP due diligence is critical for identifying and verifying IP assets and liabilities, in relation to an IP transaction (Calboli, 2021).

The IP audit and due diligence of all relevant IP assets, including registered assets such as patents and trademarks and also unregistered assets that include copyright, trade secrets and know-how, contribute to the valuation of a company. To fully exploit the IP a business owns, the three different valuation methods, namely cost, market and income based, can monetise IP and generate revenue. However, valuation priorities are different for each approach and depend on the purpose of the IP audit such as securitisation, collateral, licensing, franchising or equity financing (Brassell, 2022).

The chapter analyses the potential role AI can play in the development of audit and valuation methods to expand the current market limitations on ascertaining the most accurate value of IP assets and creating more opportunities for IP financing and technology whilst considering issues around AI trustworthiness and ethics. This is relevant to the Gulf Cooperation Council (GCC) states as they are embarking on significant transformation and there is an opportunity for the region to lead on ground-breaking AI-led IP financing valuation processes.

2 Commercialisation and IP Strategy

Of the top 1% companies, many of them are able to utilise their IP value as part of their exit strategy. For example, Cadbury sold their business for $11.5 billion in 2010 (Mullen, 2024). Forty-one per cent of Cadbury's enterprise value was attributed to its trademark portfolio when the US company Kraft successfully took over the historic British chocolatiers company (Milliemn, 2014). The extent to which Cadbury secured all of its various IP assets, especially its trademarks, highlights the value IP can add to the balance sheet and, more importantly, how it is monetised to add significant value to the company. However, when you are not a top 1% company, it is much more difficult to secure your IP value on your financial audit. Successful mergers and acquisitions are underpinned by strong IP rights, for the GCC, it is tapping into their IP potential for value and economic growth. Despite there being legal recognition of IP as collateral, there is less actual recognition from banks and financial institutions. In the GCC, Saudi Arabia is the most complaint with Islamic banking principles, with all other GCC states having Islamic banks and Sharia-compliant products. There is therefore a need to establish IP valuation standards and the IP valuator certification processes that can harmonise IP laws with Islamic law for economic growth. The GCC states can promote and support IP financing and securitisation by regulating IP finance with Islamic law. This can be achieved by establishing infrastructure for IP financing through auditing and due diligence frameworks, building capacity to improve the confidence and the experience in IP financing as IP fuels the creative economy. Knowledge-based assets underpin the revenue generated by IP-rich companies and could be a vital competitive edge for start-ups and businesses who are unable to use their IP assets as collateral. For the GCC, ASEAN and MENA regions, Islamic finance can play a crucial strategic role in business productivity. IP is rarely sufficient, in and of itself, to create businesses or, indeed, to create significant economic value. It needs to be incorporated into a commercialisation plan. IP audit and valuation mechanisms can enhance a business portfolio by creating an IP business strategy for maintaining and exploiting its IP rights.

3 Overview of the UK IP Audit System

An IP audit is a subsidiary of the traditional tangible asset audit that a business or company carries out to assess the current financial value of the organisation by an independent auditor. The financial audit includes a balance sheet, an income statement, a statement of changes in equity, a cash flow statement, and notes comprising a summary of significant accounting policies and other explanatory notes. The purpose of the audit is to reflect the financial position of the organisation based on the financial report presented in the audit for all of the assets owned by the business or company (Price Water House Coopers, 2017). An IP audit assesses the value of the IP assets, identifies current IP, requires systems in place to manage risks, identifies priorities for the business and has both core and non-core assets, and formulates protection strategies on how to manage the IP assets. The UK Intellectual Property Office (UK IPO) have developed extensive IP toolkits and diagnostics to support IP auditing in the UK and measure the value of IP assets (Innovate UK, 2018).

The purpose of the IP audit is to build and preserve the value of IP assets in the business to give it monopolies, which in turn strengthens the business case to investors as the IP assets can act as the unique selling point. Other purposes of the IP audit include access to licensing and selling assets to generate revue or use as collateral. Relevant to the sustainability of the business, the IP audit facilitates the implementation of processes and policies and the upskilling of internal staff. The IP audit process can be broken down into key stages, comprising the business plan, discovery, investigation, review, report and action. For the business context, the audit will normally start with the IP assets a business has in relation to core assets, the territory and markets. The next step is to identify who has been involved in creating the IP assets and the documents that are in place for them. For IP assets, the main legislation in the UK is the Copyright, Design and Patent Act 1988, Trademark Act 1994 and Intellectual Property Act 2014. The registered IP rights are for patents, trademarks and registered design rights. For unregistered rights, the main IP rights are copyright, unregistered designs rights and trade secrets.

The investigation stage is concerned with carrying out relevant searches as the onus is on the applicant to ensure they are not infringing on existing IP assets of registered owners. This is an essential step as for a patent application to be successful and also to avoid potential litigation in the future, the applicant must have taken extensive steps to ensure the patent doesn't infringe existing patented inventions. The review stage is the most technical, as it requires a strategic assessment of the search results, to enhance the IP audit and valuation; it is important to identify gaps and how to approach these. It could be that collaborations are the most appropriate way forward and/or commercialisation, as well as using external third parties. There may also be a need to involve developers and manufacturers. The reporting stage involves an internal report that identifies the key action and the main priorities for the business. The final stage is what action a business needs to take. If there are patents, patent attorneys would need to be instructed as professionals with expertise in making patent applications, and likewise for trademarks, a trademark attorney would be required. For other issues such as rebranding, marketing experts are essential. Copyright issues include ownership, assignment, licensing, software development and royalty collection (Koglin & Guriqbal, 2023).

Non-disclosure agreements and confidentiality agreements are important actions from an IP audit.

The UK has a breadth of knowledge and expertise in IP audits and due diligence with robust and efficient systems and models. The UK IPO has invested heavily in supporting the IP economy and providing significantly subsidised IP auditing professional support in partnership with Innovate UK Edge (Innovate UK, 2018). The UK can be an ideal exemplar for an IP auditing system in the GCC as the UK has demonstrated how innovation is a major driver for its economic growth. The success of the UK IP auditing scheme has harnessed IP for the benefit of businesses and the UK's vision for a more prosperous Britain through its Industrial Strategy and making the UK the most innovative country in the world (Moss, 2018). Larger companies are more likely to easily secure mainstream finance as they often have a critical mass of tangible assets. This means for small and medium-sized enterprises (SME), there is a funding gap. In response to this, NatWest bank has launched the first ever IP-backed lending scheme in the UK (NatWest Group, 2024). The global SME finance gap now stands at $5.7 trillion (International Finance Corporation, 2024). The UK can act as an exemplar to address the growing SME funding gap especially in developing countries like the GCC where the states have developed national visions and strategies to be knowledge-based economies. An Islamic law-compliant IP auditing and due diligence model that embeds AI and emerging technologies could help address the SME finance gap in the GCC and globally. In order to propose and recommend a framework that is viable and fit for purpose, how Islamic law can be utilised to support a novel framework, within the context of the GCC, will be considered next.

4 Islamic Law in the GCC States

Islamic law, according to the Shariah scholars, refers to the comprehensive system of laws and principles derived from the primary sources, defined from the Quran and the Sunnah. Accepted translations of the Quran are available at www.quran.com. For the Sunnah, Sahih Al Bukhari wrote the collection that is often described as the most accurate companion to the Quran, demonstrating in practical terms the meaning behind the Quranic verses. The Sunnah has the status of a primary source as it is very important as a source of Islamic law as the acts, practices and statements attributable to Prophet Muhammed (PBUH), which were recorded and fixed in tangible form for the Muslim world to follow (Hallaq, 1997). Therefore, many argue that the Quran and Sunnah in themselves are a form of intellectual property from which new inferences should not be made (Khan, 2000). The primary sources encompass the complete guidance on various aspects of life, including law, morality, ethics, social justice, economics and governance. They serve as a divine and ethical framework that Muslims are encouraged to follow in their personal lives and in the community (Arif, 2023). The Sunnah provides examples and explanations of core themes covered by the Quran. For example, in reference to Islamic business law, the Quran emphasises the importance of fair dealings in contract law (Surah Al Mai'dah, Quran). The Sunnah then provides examples of how to conduct fair dealings in business contracts and transactions (Bukhari, Book 34, n.d.).

The GCC states are historically Islamic states and they have all incorporated Sharia law into their written constitutions, which makes the GCC a unique regional union when compared to the European Union or the African Union. The influence of Sharia law principles is not universal among all six of the GCC states as each state has its own sovereignty and autonomy over how it governs and develops national laws in line with its religious beliefs. However, there are commonalities in certain areas among all the GCC states, most notably all the GCC states have the main primary source of Sharia law as the Quran (Naim, 2022). The differentiation between the states can be seen by what weight Sharia law has in influencing the law-making process as legislative developments differs from state to state. Saudi Arabia has Sharia as the source of law (Saudi Arabia Basic Law of Government Article 1), for Oman it is the basis of legislation (Omani Constitution Article 2), and for Qatar, the UAE and Kuwait it is a main source of law (Constitution of Qatar, Part One, UAE Constitution, Part One, Article 7 and Kuwait at Kuwaiti Constitution, Part 1, Article 2). This leaves Bahrain with Sharia as a principle source of law at a constitutional level (Constitution of the Kingdom of Bahrain, Part One, Article 2).

Islamic jurisprudence (Fiqh) refers to the understanding and application of Islamic law. It involves the systematic study, interpretation and derivation of legal rulings from the primary sources of Islam, namely the Quran and the Sunnah. Islamic jurisprudence covers a wide range of legal, ethical and social issues, providing guidelines for personal conduct, family matters, business transactions, criminal justice and legal maxims (Alam, 2011). Relevant to Islamic finance, the jurisprudence sets out the permissible parameters in which Islamic finance can operate and an understanding of Islamic jurisprudence is needed to underpin a Sharia-compliant IP auditing and due diligence model. Islamic jurisprudence contributes to a dynamic and diverse legal landscape within Muslim-majority societies, enriching the legal tradition and accommodating the varied needs and circumstances of the community.

The foundational principles of Islamic jurisprudence across the Hanafi, Maliki, Shafi'i and Hanbali schools are understood as variations in interpretation rather than as conflicting principles. These schools are all considered valid and respected within the broader Islamic tradition, and each school's approach is seen as a legitimate way of understanding and applying Islamic law. All schools of Islamic jurisprudence recognise the concept of Ijtihad, which allows scholars to interpret Islamic law in light of changing circumstances. This enables the adaptation of Islamic principles to new issues and challenges such as IP and emerging technologies as well as AI. The analysis of Islamic jurisprudence is focused on Islamic finance law as this will create a novel framework for IP auditing and due diligence that is compliant with Islamic finance law for the benefit of the local communities in the GCC.

5 Islamic Jurisprudence and Financial Law

The Islamic ontological framework is essential to understanding Islamic financial law and integrating emerging technologies and AI into the IP auditing and valuation systems. Islamic ontology focuses on worldview and differs from conventional views as it goes beyond the realities and observations from realists, positivists and postmodernists. Its methodology integrates the seen and unseen, embracing spiritual reality. In conventional epistemology, the knowledge is acquired and confined within the free thinking of human cognition (Steup & Neta, 2024). However, in Islam, knowledge is obtained by insight from the Quran and Sunnah. The Islamic worldview affirms a monotheistic ontology, emphasising the existence of a single, transcendent God as the ultimate reality, with the universe as the creation of God (Allah). Material existence is seen as contingent upon the will and design of God, with humans as stewards of the Earth (Hashi, 2013). Islamic financial law ranks highly in the Quran and Sunnah with the Prophet Muhammed (peace be upon him) stating the prohibition of interest as a strong tenet of observing the Islamic faith. The Quran has clear statements regarding honouring agreements and the need for certainty whilst forbidding interest (riba) and usury (gharar). There are several references in the Quran which further cement the strength of the Islamic rule against interest. The strongest and clearest references can be found in the Quran in Surah Al Baqarah in Verse 275:

> Those who consume interest cannot stand [on the Day of Resurrection] except as one stands who is being beaten by Satan into insanity. That is because they say, 'Trade is [just] like interest.' But Allah has permitted trade and has forbidden interest. So whoever has received an admonition from his Lord and desists may have what is past, and his affair rests with Allah. But whoever returns to [dealing in interest or usury] - those are the companions of the Fire; they will abide eternally therein. (The Quran)

Through Islamic business law, and the development of the Islamic finance sector, different models of contractual arrangements have emerged which are Sharia-compliant. The Islamic finance sector has been built on the Sharia principles that allow a fair and regulated way for business transactions and investments to take place, and for permissible (halal) return on the capital that has been invested to be earned without breaching the ban on interest. It is the distinction between return on investment and interest that has been the cornerstone of the Islamic finance industry (Naim, 2022). The GCC states have been instrumental in growing the Islamic finance industry. The origins and historical overview of modern Islamic banking and finance can be traced back to the Dubai Islamic Bank, which launched in 1975 as the first fully fledged Islamic world commercial bank. The fundamentals of Islamic finance are that it is interest-free, ethical, asset-backed and asset-based. There are significant international bodies established to study, promote, develop and set standards for the Islamic finance sector, most notably, the International Islamic Financial Market, the Islamic Financial Services Board and the Accounting and Auditing Organization for Islamic Financial Institutions. For the development of IP auditing and valuation schemes, the existing organisations can be expanded to create new rules and regulations for IP valuation utilising Islamic finance for the GCC states and wider region. Islamic financial institutions play a facilitative role in Islamic society and they ensure economic development through supporting liquidity needs of major agents in the economy (Khalid et al., 2023). This includes finance companies, Islamic housing cooperatives, Islamic microfinance institutions, Islamic endowment (waqf) management institutions, private equity/venture capital firms, pilgrimage (hajj) and mandatory charity (zakat) management bodies (Hussain et al., 2015).

Islamic banking was initially based on ideas of equity partnership and partnership modalities, as from the early Islamic finance scholars the emphasis was on developing Sharia-based financing rather than Sharia-compliant financial products. Early jurists employed legal reasoning (ijtihad) in developing Sharia-based products for Islamic finance. In the current era of emerging technologies and digital economies, there is a strong emphasis on innovation in Islamic finance to meet the current needs of the Muslim population in the GCC and globally (Boukhatem & Moussa, 2018). A novel Islamic finance-based IP auditing and due diligence model for the GCC and the wider region that can embed AI and emerging technologies in a legal framework will be a global first for the GCC.

6 The Era of Emerging Technologies and Artificial Intelligence

The EU has legislated on the first AI Act. There is no equivalent Act in the GCC, and how the region marries emerging technologies and AI to Islamic law is imperative to developing a successful IP auditing model in the GCC and wider region. IP commercialisation requires valuation methods for IP rights effectively supporting the unmet need of SMEs and entrepreneurs. Auditing tools for IP identification and valuation for IP rights-holders are crucial for the IP ecosystem and supporting IP growth. Data and AI-based assets are critical emerging asset classes. Understanding the role emerging technologies and AI can play in developing a compliant IP-based financing system has the potential to drive the future of the IP economy, especially in the creative and tech industries where conventional financing is failing SMEs. Lessons can be learnt from the EU AI Act and adapted to suit the GCC states for their own laws in the area of emerging technologies and AI.

The EU has been a global leader in AI legislation. The European Parliament passed a resolution on 16 February 2017 with recommendations to the Commission on Civil Law Rules on Robotics (2015/2103(INL)). The European Parliament followed up with a further resolution of 20 October 2020 on intellectual property rights for the development of artificial intelligence technologies. Members of the European Parliament approved proposals to address long-term opportunities and legal challenges posed by AI in the areas of ethics, civil liability and intellectual property. In December 2023, the EU Commission approved the first ever legal framework on AI, the EU AI Act, which addresses the risks of AI and positions Europe to play a leading role globally (EU Commission, 2023).

The EU AI Act deals with digital risk and utilises strategies and legal risk management to create a tiered-level approach to mitigating risks from AI, set out transparency requirements and support innovation. The AI Act is the first ever comprehensive legal framework on AI worldwide, which makes it a significant piece of legislation as AI becomes more and more dominant in business and society. The EU AI Act aims to foster trustworthiness and risk management with the use of AI in Europe and will have wider-reaching impact. Core principles of the EU AI Act are to have systems in place that respect fundamental human rights, safety and ethical principles, and to address risks of very powerful and impactful AI models (EU Commission, 2023). The EU AI Act sets new rules for risk mitigation and risk management based on low-, medium- and high-risk levels. The new rules address risks specifically created by AI applications, prohibit AI practices that pose unacceptable risks, determine a list of high-risk applications, set clear requirements for AI systems for high-risk applications, and define specific obligations deployers and providers of high-risk AI applications must adhere to. Further, they require a conformity assessment before a given AI system is put into service or placed on the market, and put enforcement mechanisms in place after a given AI system is allowed into the market by establishing a governance structure at both a regional and national level (EU Commission, 2023).

For the GCC, the lesson learnt from the EU AI Act is to create a framework for creativity and innovation by encouraging the use of AI technologies with the interests of human creators as a core ethical principle in line with Islamic law and finance. It is essential to distinguish between AI-assisted human creations and AI-generated creations for the purposes of IP auditing and due diligence. In the GCC, AI has not been endowed with full legal personality, as this could have negative effects on the IP ecosystem for human creators. For a GCC-led IP auditing system, the IP rights should only be granted to natural or legal persons who have created the work legally and only if the IP owner has given permission for the use of the content. The recommendations require AI and emerging technologies to be used for procedural enhancements in the auditing systems and support the granting of IP rights and for the determination of liability for infringements. A clear line needs to be drawn on the limitations of AI and emerging technologies as these should not replace the human review that is carried out on a case-by-case basis, in order to ensure the quality and fairness of decisions. AI and emerging technologies can assist the human review to save time and increase efficiency and accuracy (Naim, 2024).

7 The Development of a GCC-Focused IP Auditing System

A successful GCC-focused IP auditing system that incorporates IP law, Islamic finance and AI will require careful analysis, system development and industry buy-in to address the current unmet funding gap for SMEs in developing economies. A successful system will need a systematic review of all IP assets (registered and unregistered) created, owned, used and/or licensed by a business. As IP assets vary, registered and unregistered intellectual assets that are owned or used by the business require adequate protocols and measures. The starting point will be identifying what IP a business currently has, when it was created or acquired and by whom, where, and from whom. For Islamic law, certainty and clarity are necessary and therefore the more detailed and informed the IP audit guidelines are, the more likely it is that they will comply with Islamic law. Detail includes how the IP assets are protected, how are they maintained and how are they used, as well as how they are enforced.

The robustness of the IP audit system must comply with Islamic law standards and avoid unjust enrichment and speculation (Anwar, 2021). In order to achieve this, the proposed audit system must allow the business to know what assets it has, what are core assets, the controls in place over the IP assets, and the clear actions to strengthen and monetise the IP portfolio. The confidentiality, non-disclosure and IP ownership agreements are accurate and up to date. As Islamic law does not support ambiguous transactions and uncertainty, the IP audit system must clearly define who is responsible for the IP assets and as such have the required policies in place to further the IP strategy in line with the business plan. This dictates the decision-making process as to what assets should be protected and to ensure that all IP rights are logged and maintained to demonstrate that policies are properly followed.

8 IP Audit Performance

Standards need to be set for the IP audit performance. The UK has systems in place that can be applicable in the GCC for consulting patent, design and trademark databases. Internal inventors, research managers, marketing directors and appointed bodies create or work with the registered rights to assess the IP performance and review internal documents. These include business plans, contracts, agreements, licenses, websites, product portfolio summaries and brands.

Dealing first with registered IP rights, a successful IP audit must include a list of all registered and pending assets with the countries in which they are or will be registered. This needs to be supplemented by a record of all maintenance fees and dates of renewal. The next detail is the record of inventors and designers with filing dates and numbers, status and expiry date. For copyright, a copyright policy can separate works into different categories such as advertisements, training materials, webpages and software. The policy can state what is core according to the business needs. The copyright policy is very important as it would address the Islamic finance sector concerns on IP assets as the policy would give the copyright works transparency and operational parameters to satisfy Islamic finance procedural requirements. For example, the copyright policy must include the date the work was created and where, as this determines length of protection and, crucially, provides evidence if there is a dispute over copyright infringement. The author is named in the copyright policy with information as to their status, such as whether they are an employee or commissioned. If the author is commissioned, the policy will need to show if it was an assignment or licence of the copyright, as well asa description of the agreement and the requisite terms, and provide a copy of the agreement for the IP audit. For trade secrets, confidential information and know-how, one named person should be in control of all such information. The identity of this person should be recorded. They should be tasked with identifying, grading, tagging and giving sensitive information an appropriate level of protection. Confidential information should be classified according to its importance to the business and each classification should have corresponding polices dealing with access and on how to then share the confidential information, in line with the policies (Bainbridge & Howell, 2014).

As discussed earlier, for a successful Islamic law-complaint system of IP auditing and due diligence, the IP audit system must comply with Islamic law jurisprudence and legal reasoning. An IP checklist would give the checks and balances needed for strong accountability for the IP audit and satisfy Islamic law. The checklist would need to include a series of detailed information such as name, type, classification, owner, date created, access and level of access, the access control, protection mechanisms, review dates, legal advisor, value and, if applicable, expiration dates. The IP audit is the backbone to developing an action plan in line with overall IP strategy and commercialisation. With the interconnectivity of AI and emerging technology and the creation of IP content, to further enhance the IP auditing and due diligence system in the GCC, an added dimension to the proposal is to not only create IP systems that are complaint with Islamic law but also utilise emerging technology and AI that is ethical and trustworthy. There are several economic benefits to this in the GCC. It would enable earlier lending to attractive growth companies, and the IP audit assessment process enhances knowledge, and reduces risk. The management of risk is a key component of Islamic finance and the assessment process can mitigate risk for lending purposes. The monitoring of IP assets is essential to the auditing and due diligence processes as it looks for opportunities and threats such as new assets to secure or weak management of existing assets. Security is a requirement of Islamic finance, and for the IP assets the audit can align security issues with the purpose of the funds and drivers of cash flows. It can create quantifiable recovery prospects by providing a credible route to IP value recovery. This in turn improves capital efficiency and reduces cost. The reason it is so relevant and timely to the GCC to have an Islamic law-based IP auditing and due diligence system is down to three pertinent areas. Firstly, IP has a strong potential for loan collateral as it is scarce, but highly scalable. Secondly, the risks are firm-specific and not correlated to the wider market, and IP can be closely linked to cash flows and to use of funds raised. Thirdly, IP is the last thing a firm will default on, and stakeholders are well motivated to intervene if a problem arises. Currently, IP is very unlikely to be already encumbered (Brassell, 2022).

9 Conclusion

This chapter has evaluated the role AI systems can play in IP financing whilst considering Islamic law for the GCC states, the broader legal landscape in the IP auditing industry, from which to generate more accurate IP-comparable data and support IP financing and lending. The focus has been on lessons that can be learnt from the UK given its strength in IP as evidenced by the Global Innovation Index, the UK's leading contribution to the World Intellectual Property Organization IP finance landscape and, most importantly, the UK's position as the leading European country for Islamic finance. The chapter has given attention to IP audits and the value these hold for businesses and for economic growth, and has proposed a tailored approach for the GCC that can take into account IP audit processes and practices for successful IP valuation whilst actively creating an Islamic-law compliant model. With the continued interplay between IP and AI, there is potential to seize the opportunity that AI presents for the IP ecosystem and economic growth. The GCC is in a period of transformation and has an opportunity to overcome the challenges around ethics and trustworthiness and create AI-assisted and/or -generated valuation methods that support their national visions and economic viability. The main lessons that can be learnt from the UK IPO are from the UK's IP finance toolkit which acts as a guide for businesses and supports IP audit before applying for an IP-backed loan or financing. To further support IP management and commercialisation strategies, as well as raise awareness of finance options available, toolkits can be more useful where AI systems are utilised to address the limitations with current valuation processes. This is where the real opportunity is for the GCC states to be leaders in the implementation of AI-assisted and potentially AI-generated IP audit systems and processes.

The chapter has highlighted that IP audits can be very insightful and relevant to a company's financial forecast and value. The audit establishes whether the appropriate IP policies and procedures are in place and what IP rights a company or business has. The more detailed and accurate, the more reliable the audit is, in terms of validity and status. The audit can then allow the business to identify the most valuable rights as core assets. IP due diligence is critical for identifying and verifying IP assets and liabilities, in relation to an IP transaction, and can then give vital collateral for income generation and consequential business growth. For the GCC to be successful as trailblazers in IP auditing systems with AI assistance, and develop robust and informed systems, there is a great deal of knowledge that can be assimilated and applied from the EU AI Act. The GCC can develop a regulatory framework that defines and mitigates for the different levels of risk for AI systems that are in compliance with Islamic law to develop a first of its kind set of AI-related laws and regulations for IP. The EU AI Act deals with AI risk but not IP laws. The GCC are in a unique position where they have strengths in IP, Islamic law and AI to enact the first ever piece of legislation that encompasses all three distinct areas.

References

Alam, M. (2011). *Choudhury Islamic Economics and Finance An Epistemological Inquiry*. Emerald Group Publishing Limited.

Anwar, M. (2021). *Islamic Jurisprudence: The Law of Contracts and Natural Justice*. Foot Ansey. https://www.footanstey.com/our-insights/articles-news/islamic-jurisprudence-the-law-of-contracts-and-natural-justice/#:~:text=Contracts%20in%20Islam%20are%20underwritten,)%20and%20Maysir%20(speculation)

Arif, S. (2023). Searching for Islamic Economics: A Philosophical Inquiry. *Journal of Critical Realism in Socio-Economics (JOCRISE)*.

Boukhatem, J., & Moussa, F. B. (2018). The Effect of Islamic Banks on GDP Growth: Some Evidence from Selected MENA Countries. *Borsa Istanbul Review, 18*(3). https://doi.org/10.1016/j.bir.2017.11.004

Brassell, M. (2022). *Challenges in harnessing IP for finance*. Inngot Limited.

Bainbridge, D., & Howell, C. (2014). *Intellectual Property Asset Management: How to Identify, Protect, Manage and Exploit Intellectual Property Within the Business Environment*. Routledge.

Bukhari, Sunan Ibn Majah 2274, Book 12, Hadith 138, Vol. 3, Book 12, Hadith 227. (n.d.).

Calboli, I., & Montagnani, M. (2021). *Handbook of Intellectual Property Research: Lenses, Methods, and Perspectives*. Oxford University Press.

EU Commission. (2023). *Shaping Europe's digital future*. https://digital-strategy.ec.europa.eu/en/policies/regulatory-framework-ai

Hallaq, W. B. (1997). *A History of Islamic Legal Theories, An Introduction to the Sunnī Usúl al-Fiqh*. Cambridge University Press.

Hashi, A. A. (2013). Between Monotheism and Tawhid: A Comparative Analysis. *Revelation and Science, 3*(2). (1435H/2013).

Hussain, M., Shahmoradi, A., & Turk, R. (2015). *An Overview of Islamic Finance*. International Monetary Fund.

Innovate UK. (2018). *Take an IP Audit—Get a better idea of what you own*. https://iuk.ktn-uk.org/perspectives/take-ip-audit-get-better-idea-what-you-own/

International Finance Corporation. (2024). IFC Financial Institutions Group (FIG) MSMEs. https://www.ifc.org/content/dam/ifc/doc/2024/msme-s-factsheet-ifc-financial-institutions-group.pdf

Kadiri, S. (2017). *What is an audit? Price Water House Cooper*, PwC Middle East.

Khalid, H., Abida, M., Haridana, M. D., & Buana, G. K. (2023). *Case Studies on Innovation in Islamic Finance*. UNDP, Islamic Development Bank. https://www.undp.org/sites/g/files/zskgke326/files/2023-09/ins-islamic_finance_june_2023.pdf

Khan, L. (2000). Ali. Islam as Intellectual Property 'My Lord! Increase Me in Knowledge.'. *Cumberland Law Review, 31*(361), 2000–2001, Available at SSRN: https://ssrn.com/abstract=936291

Koglin, L. V., & Guriqbal, S. J. (2023). *Creative Expression, An Introduction to Copyright and Related Rights for Small and Medium Sized Enterprises*. World Intellectual Property Office.

Milliemn, R. (2014). *The Use of Competitive Intelligence in IP Monetisation*. Intellectual Asset Management.

Moss, T. (2018). *Using IP to Access Growth Funding*. British Business Bank. https://www.british-business-bank.co.uk/sites/g/files/sovrnj166/files/2022-11/502-IP-Report_singles.pdf

Mullen, D. (2024). *Cadbury's 200 Years of Takeovers, Triumphs and Transformations*. The Grocer. https://www.thegrocer.co.uk/suppliers/cadburys-200-years-of-takeovers-triumphs-and-transformations/688914.article

Naim, N. (2022). *Islamic Legal Principles and Intellectual Property Rights in the GCC*. Gerlach Press.

Naim, N. (2024). *Developments in Intellectual Property Strategy: The Impact of Artificial Intelligence, Robotics and New Technologies*. Palgrave Macmillan.

NatWest Group. (2024). *NatWest launches Intellectual Property-based lending to fuel high growth businesses*. https://www.natwestgroup.com/news-and-insights/news-room/press-releases/enterprise/2024/jan/natwest-launches-intellectual-property-based-lending-to-fuel-hig.html

Steup, M., & Neta, R. (2024). Epistemology. In *The Stanford Encyclopedia of Philosophy* (Spring 2024 Edition). https://plato.stanford.edu/archives/spr2024/entries/epistemology/

Williams, L. (2022). Anonos Secures $50 Million in IP-Backed Financing to Deliver Data Privacy Technology with 100% Accuracy and Utility to Data-Driven Enterprises, Business Wire.

CHAPTER 6

Intellectual Property Financing for Innovation: Structuring Intellectual Property Securitization for Issuance of Islamic Financial Instrument "*Sukuk*"

Mas Rahmah

1 Introduction

Intellectual Property (IP) owners can monetise their IP assets by assigning, licensing, or using them for financing such as for collateral or for securitization. Securitization is a financial model for rapid finance acquisition by transferring property or assets into tradeable financial instruments. IP becomes a property of achieving future cash flow streams, royalties, or capital by transferring IP assets into securities under IP securitization. IP securitization is one of the IP financing techniques to turn IP such as copyright, trademarks, or patents into marketable securities.

This chapter examines the efficacy of IP securitization as one of the possible IP financing models which is dedicated to accelerating new

M. Rahmah (✉)
Faculty of Law, Universitas Airlangga, Indonesia, Surabaya, Indonesia
e-mail: rahmah@fh.unair.ac.id

N. Naim et al. (eds.), *Intellectual Property and Innovation*, The Political Economy of the Middle East,
https://doi.org/10.1007/978-981-96-4020-1_6

alternative financial support to enhance the development of creativity and productivity in the innovation world. The chapter firstly analyses the prospect of IP securitization as a financial technique to turn the IP asset (including royalties or receivables) into marketable securities such as bonds, or Sukuk (a plural Arabic term for financial asset instruments). As Sukuk are one of several Islamic financial instruments, their issuance under IP securitization may create some problems at the tenet, regulatory, and technical levels. At the tenet level, the main problem is the fundamental issues in respect of Shariah compliance in structuring IP securitization for Sukuk. At the regulatory level, the inadequacy or non-existence of rules may affect the validity of IP securitization. At the practical level, the absence of appropriate systems and infrastructure leads to clumsy and non-confident practices of IP securitization since it involves complex procedures, interdisciplinary laws and professionals, complicated IP asset valuation, and so forth. In addition, the intrinsic risks of IP assets because of the inherent uncertainty of the future delivery of revenues or royalties, the small bespoke market, and IP transferability problems expose the IP securitization challenge.

The chapter concludes with a consideration of how it might be possible to structure Sukuk issuance under IP securitization while at the same time ensuring compliance with Shariah requirements. It suggests that IP securitization is an attractive financing option to support creative and innovation development as Sukuk have a widespread appeal and marketability in Islamic states and other non-Islamic jurisdictions.

Securitization of assets is not novel, but securitization on IP assets became a new technique in capitalising IP when there was an issuance of "the Bowie Bond" transforming song copyright of a singer, David Bowie, into financial debt bonds. The success of the Bowie Bond reveals the evidence that IP assets can be monetised by transforming them into financial securities and provide the opportunity to the IP owners to have cash capital from the securitization.

Under securitization, IP assets are transformed into the tradeable financial instruments called securities, either in the form of conventional securities such as bonds or Islamic securities such as Sukuk. As Islamic financial instruments, Sukuk issuance under IP securitization might introduce problems. The key issue related to Shariah compliance in structuring IP securitization for Sukuk is the fundamental doctrinal challenge. Inadequacy of regulation on IP securitization becomes the main regulatory challenge which may affect the validity of IP securitization transactions. The absence of system and infrastructure of IP securitization which govern complex procedures, interdisciplinary professionals and regulations, complicated IP asset valuation, and so forth are the technical challenges which leads to untrusted practices of IP securitization. In addition, the IP transferability problem and the small IP market because of uncertainty of IP revenues or royalties becomes the critical challenge of IP securitization. To address the doctrinal challenge, the chapter suggests the compatibility and full compliance of Shariah principles in transaction of IP securitization.

To address technical and regulatory problems, this chapter recommends government and stakeholder participation in encouraging IP securitization practises by setting financial and regulatory frameworks, and establishing systems and infrastructures for IP securitization for Sukuk issuance. It suggests that IP securitization for Sukuk issuance can be structured, if such securitization complies with Shariah requirements which necessitate that the transactions are based on asset purchase, interest free, and loss and profit sharing. Such securitization seems to be a new technique for IP owners or innovation industries in searching for a finance method for their operation and further innovation development since Sukuk have widespread appeal and marketability, not only in Muslim jurisdictions in Asia such as Indonesia, Brunei Darussalam, and Malaysia, and in the Gulf States such as Bahrain, Kuwait, Oman, Qatar, Saudi Arabia, and the United Arab Emirates, but also non-Muslim and Western countries. Once IP securitization financing can be successfully structured to support innovation development, further innovative and productive activities can be created for the sake of economic development and community wealth.

2 IP Securitisation

IP securitization is a relatively new asset class of securitization that followed the monumental Bowie Bond securitization. The securitization itself has been defined with several different meanings, although all definitions essentially refer to the process of creating financial instruments by transforming certain property into securities (Fairfax, 1999). The property is monetised, not by securing traditional loans or factoring, but by issuing asset-backed securities (Sylva, 1999). Thomas Fitch and John Gabala have both defined securitization as an asset transformation into tradeable financial instruments in the form of securities to raise capital (Fitch, 2006, 25; Gabala, 2004, 307). In similar fashion, the Indonesian

Financial Service Authority (OJK) extended the definition by including the Shariah-based assets as the underlying assets and Islamic securities as the products of securitization (OJK Regulation No. 11 of 2019, Art. 1.2).

The history of securitization commenced in early 1970 when the United States Government National Mortgage Association (otherwise known as Ginnie Mae) issued securities backed by mortgage (Culver, 1994, 36). In Indonesia, asset securitization was first recognised in 1997 and subsequently formally regulated in 2003 under the Indonesian Financial and Capital Market Supervisory Board Regulation No. IX.K.1 on Guidance of KIK on Asset Backed Securities, which was amended in 2008 (Rahmah, 2015). Currently, securitization has been regulated by the OJK under a series of recent regulatory provisions, namely, POJK.No.11/POJK.03/2019 on Principle of Prudential on Securitization Activities For Banking, POJK No.65/POJK.04/2017 on Issuing and Reporting Asset Backed Securities in the Form of KIK, and POJK No.20/POJK.04/2015 on Issuance and Requirements of Sharia Asset Backed Securities.

Traditionally, securitization is supported by conventional property, such as receivables of credit card, pawn, land mortgage, car loan, franchise (Glasner, 2008, 27), tangible assets, financial obligations (Nikolic, 2009, 324), or the future payment (Garner, 2009, 1479). These assets are naturally similar in representing future payment or other payment obligations (Glasner, 2008, 29).

Currently, an IP asset can be securitised as a form of valuable asset and can generate a payment obligation, such as a trademark or copyright royalty, or proceeds or revenue stream transferred into tradeable financial instruments. Copyrighted subject matter, trademarks, and patents are the IP assets best suited and therefore most utilised for IP securitization. Copyright protects original artistic and literary works. A trademark protects the usage of mark for goods and services designation (Nimmer, 2001, 469). A patent protects the non-obvious, novel, and useful inventions for a limited time (Chu, 1998, 469).

IP securitization is a concept to overcome the choice of monetising property by enabling retention of IP ownership. Randhikla Pandey has described IP securitization as transformation of royalties into capital market securities by which the IP holders get proceeds from the transaction (Pandey, 2006). IP securitization becomes a financial scheme to secure fresh funding or capital by converting the future payment of royalties, receivables, or revenue streams into marketable securities.

IP securitization was first structured in February 1997 with the introduction of a novel scheme to convert the future royalties from rock icon David Bowie's copyrighted music portfolio into securities. The new securities—launched as "Bowie Bonds"—were supported by the IP in the copyright and the forthcoming royalties stream from a 25-album catalogue comprising some 300 songs (Robert, 1997). The value of the bonds offered totalled US$55 million with a 15-year maturity and 7.9% interest rate (Fairfax, 1999; Sylva, 1999). Bowie received cash from the sale of the Bond-based music copyrights. The "Bowie Bonds" were the first product of IP securitization which brought music to bond, and the first new financial product that could merge finance and art.

IP securitization becomes a new trend and innovative financing with IP that can be used not only by copyright holders such as film makers, musicians, and software developers, but also patent holders and trademark owners. The success of the Bowie Bond has been followed by several other musicians to structure music securitization (Morris, 2009).

Film revenues have also become underlying bases for asset securitization, such as future revenues owned by Steven Spielberg from films sold to DreamWorks (Euromoney, 1998). The future cash flow owned by Cecchi Gori has also covered a securitization structured by Merrill Lynch (Serwer, 1998). Vivendi Universal Films and New Line Cinema securitized their film royalties in 1998 and 2003 respectively. Future payment also became the underlying asset of US$650 million bonds issued by PolyGram, a Dutch entertainment company (Davies, 1998).

Although IP securitization was mostly backed by copyrights, there has been some securitization from trademarks, such as the securitization of Dunkin Donuts, Guess, and Billboard. The securitization of royalties from pharmaceutical products such as BioPharma Royalty Trust and Royalty Pharma Finance Trust are examples of patent securitization.

3 Benefits of IP Securitisation

Funding is highly needed by companies to cover their development, production, and promotion requirements. Similar to other businesses, innovation companies need funds for the operation, development, and expansion of respective markets, or financial profile and investment performance. They face challenges in generating instant financial returns on their products and outputs. IP securitization becomes the novel method for financing their creativity and innovation development by tapping their innovation products and inputs protected by IP for capital need. IP securitization provides financial support for innovation companies by transforming their IP property into on-call finance (Scott, 2003).

IP securitization can resolve the problems of accessing significant amounts of funding while still retaining IP ownership. Prior to securitization as a funding-generation option, innovation companies had two options for capital raising, namely, access to bank loans and the sale of assets (Janger, 2002). With securitization, companies are able to secure capital but still retain their ownership of IP assets, as finance providers purchase mostly royalties or future revenue, rather than IP assets themselves.

IP securitization also delivers benefit to society as it offers the chance for public access to wealth allocation and alternative investment. As the products of IP securitization are mostly bonds, the public will get wealth allocation by achieving certain interest from the bonds. IP securitization may also provide alternative public investment by offering tradeable securities which may attract investors to purchase the securities in anticipation of an expected return. IP securitization also enables investors to choose the strategy to invest based on the pool of assets secured against the bank loan (McLean, 2008). IP securitization encourages public participation to support innovative activity by investing in securities. IP securitization also offers new opportunities to open the wealth in IP (Chu, 1998). The more IP securitization succeeds in financing innovative industries, the more innovative and useful products can be utilised for societal wealth.

4 The Nature of Sukuk

Sukuk as an Islamic financial asset instrument are defined by the Accounting and Auditing Organization for Islamic Financial Institutions (AAOIFI) as:

> securities of equal denomination representing individual ownership interests in a portfolio of eligible existing or future assets, or 'certificates' of equal value representing undivided shares in the ownership of tangible assets, usufructs and services or (in the ownership of) the assets of particular projects or special investment activity.

Sukuk are Islamic asset-backed securities which provide remuneration of investment and grant ownership to the holders. Sukuk issuance is a process to obtain funds in order to conduct large-scale projects with various purposes for business productivity, including for infrastructure and economic development projects, or to finance government expenditures.

Similar to bonds, Sukuk have maturity dates and are commonly used for raising funds with various purposes for generation of business productivity in accordance with Shariah principles. However, Sukuk and bonds differ on the nature of asset ownership and the underlying assets. Sukuk have underlying assets owned by the holders, who will participate in profits sharing from the assets (Alam et al., 2013). In complying with financial requirements, Sukuk need to comply with Shariah law, while a bond needs to comply with conventional financial law. However, a conventional bond in a Western finance context is an instrument of indebtedness, and such indebtedness is discouraged in Islam as it is covered by interest. The presence of underlying assets in Sukuk is mandatory since the essence of Islamic economics requires real assets in transaction. Sukuk require underlying assets to back the issuance because Sukuk are in essence the proof of asset ownership. With this structure, the Sukuk holders have interest on the asset profit value, including any risks which may be embedded. This structure corresponds to the Shariah principles of *alghorm bi alghonm* which has the meaning of "risk return trade-off" and *alkharaj bi aldhaman* which has the meaning of 'liability determines profit'. Accordingly, as a financial Islamic product, Sukuk have some major characteristics of:

- serving as evidence of asset ownership;
- requiring underlying assets;
- generating return in profit or margins;
- issuance complying with the fundamentals of Islamic rules.

5 IP as an Underlying Asset for Sukuk Issuance

In the Shariah perspective, IP is recognised by the Organization of Islamic Cooperation Fiqh Academy as property rights that can be bought and sold, even though they have intangible characteristics. With the characteristic of an abstract right, IP can be considered as property which is based on an analogy to property on abstract rights such as licence rights and concession rights as property. Several factors can include IP as an abstract intangible property, namely:

- natural properties with special characteristics;
- consists of ownership value;

- freedom by the owner to benefit from the wealth and to prohibit others from using it without permission or getting involved with the wealth;
- availability and transferability; and
- the wealth is not prohibited according to Sharia (Securities Commission Malaysia, 2009).

According to Islamic rules, IP is acknowledged as *al mal* (property) in the form of *al haq* which has the meaning of rights, or *al manfaah* which has the meaning of benefit (Arif, 2017). IP rights are also recognised under Fatwa No.1/Munas/VII/MUI/15/2005 on IP protection, which rules that:

- IP rights are property from the intellectual effort in creating a useful product or process which is acknowledged and protected by a state;
- IP is acknowledged as Huquq Maliyyah (rights of property) which are protected by law (*mashu*), as well as mal (*wealth*);
- Any form of infringement of IP rights by way of making, using, selling, importing, exporting, distributing, delivering, falsifying, reproducing, plagiarizing, or announcing is unlawful and an injustice; and
- IP rights comply with Islamic law, and therefore these rights can be used as objects for any transactions, both commercial and non-commercial, including for *waqf* and heritage.

The existence of underlying assets or asset participation is essential for Sukuk issuance. The underlying assets to back Sukuk are mostly physical, or intangibles that can be used for transactions relating to leasing (*ijarah*), gaining profits, selling (*bay*), or backing for a loan (*rahn*).

As an intangible asset, there is an important question about the acceptance of IP as an underlying asset for Sukuk in the Shariah perspective. In nature, Sukuk are documents or certificates that represent the value of assets (McLean, 2008). According to the AAOIFI, Sukuk are representative of ownership of tangible assets, services, usufruct, assets in certain projects, or special investment activities. This means that the AAOIFI does not include financial assets, especially debt receivables, which have intangible character as the underlying assets of Sukuk.

According to Muhammad Al-Bashir and Muhammad Al-Amine, one of the main requirements for the issuance of Sukuk is that the assets of the Sukuk must comprise real estate and even currently tangible assets. Real estate and other tangible assets are the most popular asset class for Sukuk (Al Bashir & Al Amin, 2009). However, Natalie Schoon has argued that, although the underlying assets of Sukuk are generally tangibles, the intangible assets, including receivable claims, can also be used as underlying assets for Sukuk (Schoon, 2008). Saiful Azhar Rosly and Mahmood Sanusi also argue that receivables (*al dayn*) can be used as underlying assets for Sukuk, such as receivables in the form of money such as *murabahah* prices (cost-plus sales price) and goods receivables such as receivables for goods in *salam* transactions (Rosly & Sanusi, 1999).

Assets that can be presented by Sukuk include financial assets such as receivables/debts and non-financial assets such as tangible assets, usufruct, and services. The Malaysian Securities Commission, in more detail, includes several types of assets that can be the underlying assets for Sukuk, namely:

- claims to originate from the payment;
- the goods from the order of purchase (*salam* contract);
- ownership of real assets in a lease contract (*ijarah*);
- the right to enjoy rental benefits arising from the lease agreement;
- the right to a *mudharabah* (cost-plus sales contract), or *musyarakah* (cooperation) project; and
- a portfolio of assets that is a combination of receivables from sales contracts, and undivided ownership of tangible assets under a lease contract.

This shows that Malaysia also includes intangible assets as an underlying asset for Sukuk.

In Indonesia, the Sovereign Sukuk Law rules that assets that back Sovereign Sukuk shall be in the form of tangible goods such as land and/or buildings, but they may also include intangible goods that have economic value (Indonesian Sovereign Sukuk Law Article 1(3)). It can be concluded that, when referring to the AAOIFI arrangement, IP rights that are assets as intangible objects, especially in the form of claims/royalties, cannot be used as underlying assets for Sukuk. However, the practice in Indonesia, as well as in Malaysia and several other Sukuk issuances, reveals that intangible assets are allowed to be the underlying assets for Sukuk. Therefore, as one of the permitted tangible assets, IP can be used as underlying assets for Sukuk. It also means that it is possible for IP securitization for Sukuk issuance to be structured.

6 The Process of IP Securitization for Sukuk

IP securitization involves some basic steps. Firstly, the originator who has ownership of the IP asset secures the rights on IP (POJK No. 11 of 03/2019) (Deacon, 2004). Secondly, the originator makes the valuation and pools the asset (Bennett, 2006). Thirdly, the originator assigns the IP assets to a special purpose vehicle, which is specifically established for securitization purposes only (Klee & Butler, 2002). Fourthly, the special purpose vehicle proceeds with the issuance and sells the IP-backed securities to investors in the form of debt or equity. Equity-based securities will give the investors the proportional payment based on cash flow and their share. Debt-based securities give an investment return to holders by providing fixed payments, both principal and interest, which are secured by the receivables based on anticipated cash flow. Fifthly, the revenue from the sale of the securities will be used to pay the originator. Finally, the investment return for the investors will be taken from the payment of receivables (Shaw, 1990).

7 The Prospect and Challenges of IP Securitization for Sukuk

The asset of securitization for Sukuk is mostly tangible assets, although intangible assets can become an alternative option. An effort to include intangible assets in the securitization for Sukuk can be traced to the issuance of the East Cameron Gas Sukuk in 2016, which had the underlying asset of royalties from oil concessions in the Gulf of Mexico offshore. The offering in the United States was the first Sukuk in a non-Islamic jurisdiction. However, although this securitization was governed by United States law, Shariah principles were still accommodated to protect the holder of the Sukuk in a non-Muslim State (Ahmed, 2015).

Another endeavour to back a Sukuk with intangible assets was the Sukuk offered by a German financial company. The intangible assets of the Sukuk were proprietary software and associated IP rights. This Sukuk offering is interesting because it included an asset choice that had not been previously considered. The offering raised about US$55 million under an *Ijarah*-based contract in the form of a sale and lease-back contract with the IP as the underlying asset.

These Sukuk offerings show the growth of a revolutionary asset of so-called intangible assets for Sukuk. What such transactions also demonstrate is the flexibility of Shariah that enables the utilisation of adaptations to the complicated system of intangibles as assets for Sukuk. The Sukuk issuance with IP underlying assets becomes a successful and groundbreaking transaction and demonstrates Shariah flexibility in accepting and adapting IP as underlying assets for Sukuk.

In the various Sukuk restructurings, the crucial part is transferring the ownership of underlying assets. The creation of IP as an alternative for underlying assets has promise to succeed because IP may be possibly assigned under the purchase agreement in accordance with business transaction. The ownership transfer of IP is easier than tangible asset (particularly land) transfer, which requires a rather more complicated process such as the registration of the transfer of the land title in a national land titles agency, while the IP transfer just needs to be recorded in a national IP office as a relatively simple process.

IP as a new asset to back Sukuk is promising since IP is recognised as a very important asset for many large global companies. Leading corporations such as Microsoft, Google, Unilever, McDonald's, KFC, and Toyota use IP as a key foundation for their market dominance and continuing profitability. Their IP portfolios such as trademarks, patents, and trade secrets can have higher value than their tangible assets. In mergers and acquisitions, IP becomes a key objective to achieve in order to enhance market dominance and profitability. In the digital world, new categories of IP rights enable creators to draw economic reward in greater opportunities from various models of streaming, file sharing, digital content, etc.

The prospect of IP as a new asset to back Sukuk is very promising, along with the assumption that the higher the percentage of Muslims in a country, the demand for Shariah-compliant securities will be higher. For Indonesia, the potential for Sukuk growth is tremendous because Indonesia has the biggest Muslim population in the world.

However, the success of creating IP as a new class of asset to back Sukuk issuance will face some challenges. First, IP securitization for Sukuk issuance needs to comply with Shariah, which may create incompatibility and interpretative problems. Second, there is the risk that the IP as underlying asset may achieve low acceptance from Islamic investors. Therefore, it is necessary to design polished Shariah-compliant funding instruments using IP assets that can be accepted by all parties.

In addition, IP can be a risky asset because of the potential for counterfeiting, piracy, and infringements of IP rights, particularly in the digital world context. Electronic platforms, illegal uploading and downloading and streaming, and utilization of IP without permission have led to major problems in achieving greater economic benefit and enforcement of IP rights. As the IP system was designed and established within and for the non-digital age, it has therefore become quite difficult in the digital context. Digital infringements appear to have become uncontrolled in some scenarios. Digital copies can be limitless and measureless and have potential for significantly detrimental impact on non-digital businesses such as the print media and publishing. Electronic copying can also be boundless and can be easily distributed in a borderless manner.

Moreover, appropriate legal and practical frameworks to ensure the IP licence and royalty management can be collected and distributed in a systematic and transparent way are inadequate. Royalties are the most important revenues that can be used as the underlying asset for IP securitization. The problems in royalties' management (collection and distribution) appear at both the regulatory and implementation levels. Inefficient royalties management leads to the loss of income, profits, and future cash flow, which thus leads to the failure of IP securitization in ensuring future economic revenue as the investment return for investors.

Furthermore, IP has some unique attributes, including being given exclusive right to exclude others to use the rights, which are protected and workable against all-comers. However, limited time protection and limitations on IP such as "fair use" that broadly allows copying of IP without permission is also a problem for ownership on IP assets.

Another constraint is related to the notion of possession. As intangibles, IP assets may be employed and used in limitless number synchronously (Tosato, 2010). IP can be copied in limitless number that will affect to less gain of economic benefit because of abundant IP products in market, and thus is very relevant to the premise of the scarcity doctrine that 'the less product available, the more profit will be gained'. There is also risk in IP ownership as the ownership can be subjected to legal suits for ownership cancellation.

The valuation of IP assets is also challenging. The intangible character of IP leads to uncertainty and difficulty in measuring economic value on IP assets. In addition, as intangible asset, IP still entails the problem of bankable and the small market because the banking and current market still relies on safety in tangible assets rather than intangible ones. The valuation of IP is very important and commonly used for the purposes of reporting, taxation, investment or loan financing. However, the current valuation regime fits with copyright, trademarks and patents only, but not for the rest of other IP assets.

Although the valuation is very important in IP securitization, unfortunately, there are no standards for valuation methodologies that are established and enforced over all IP assets in some countries, including in Indonesia and some Gulf countries. A recent effort to establish general valuation includes the Equity Index based on the corporate IP value developed by the American Stock Exchange. There are also plans from the World Intellectual Property Organization (WIPO) for an IP exchange which allows investors to participate in IP-related financial products such as IP-related futures, indexes and options, IP-based securities, initial public offerings of patent corporations, and IP-based exchange products. In 2007, the German Institute for Standardization endeavoured to establish the general principle of valuation for patents. The International Organization for Standardization (ISO) has also endeavoured to create an ISO Standard for the valuation of patents.

The challenges confronting the IP securitization for Sukuk demonstrate that the securitization still has a long way to travel to achieve global and Shariah acceptance and acknowledgment. From a legal perspective, most countries do not have proper legal frameworks for IP securitization, and it seems that there is no strong political will and pressure to initiate significant legal change in regulating IP securitization.

8 Conclusion

IP securitization for Sukuk is needed to encourage Sukuk for financing creativity and innovation development, because IP securitization makes an important contribution to creating a new option of financial aid for supporting innovation development. The use of IP assets to back Sukuk should be promoted since challenges to provide tangibles for underlying assets persist. The common underlying assets for Sukuk, which are mostly tangibles, need to include intangibles in order to provide greater opportunities for companies to issue Sukuk.

Although it is possible to structure IP securitization for Sukuk, and this has great prospects which are promising, it is very important to address the set of challenges from a doctrinal/Shariah perspective and at the regulatory and practical level. From the Shariah doctrinal perspective and taking account of the AAOIFI arrangement, IP rights assets as intangible objects, especially in the form of claims/royalties, cannot be used as underlying assets for Sukuk. However, when compared with the practice in Malaysia and several other Sukuk issuances, as well as the provisions in Indonesia's SBSN Law, intangible assets are allowed as underlying assets for Sukuk. Thus the intangible asset of IP can be used to back Sukuk. From a regulatory perspective, most countries still do not regulate IP securitization for Sukuk issuance, which can lead to legal uncertainty for IP securitization practise. From the technical perspective the system and infrastructure of IP securitization have not been well developed. The acceptance of IP as a new class asset for Sukuk is also challenging because Sukuk still focuses on using tangible assets rather than intangible assets such as IP. The intrinsic nature and unique attributes of IP also create some challenges, mostly on the valuation, uncertain economic benefit risks because of massive infringements of IP, and the limited duration of IP protections.

References

Ahmed, M. (2015). Islamic Project Finance: A Case Study of the East Cameron Project. *The Journal of Structured Finance, 20*(4), 120–135.

Al Bashir, M., & Al Amin, M. (2009). Sukuk Market: Innovations and Challenges. In S. S. Ali (Ed.), *Islamic Capital Markets: Products, Regulation & Development*. Islamic Development Bank.

Alam, N., Kabir Hassan, M., & Haque, M. A. (2013). Are Islamic Bonds Different From Conventional Bonds? International Evidence From Capital Market Tests. *Borsa Istanbul Review, 13*, 22–29.

Arif, M. I. A. M. (2017). The Concept of Intellectual Property As Al Mal: An Islamic *Perspective Approach. International Journal of Educational Best Practices, 1*(1), 102–108.

Bennett, S. (2006). The IP Asset Class: Protecting and Unlocking Inherent Value. *John Marshall Review of Intellectual Property Law, 5*, 402–430.

Borrowers, is This 1998's Biggest Show in Town?. (1998, June 10). *Euromoney*.

Chu, N. (1998). Bowie Bonds: A Key To Unlocking The Wealth of Intellectual Property. *Hastings Communication and Entertainment Law Journal, 21*, 469–499.

Culver, P. F. (1994). The Dawning of Securitization. *Probate & Property, 8*, 36.

Davies, S. (1998). PolyGram bond issue to raise US$650m. *Financial Times*.

Deacon, J. (2004). *Global Securitization and CDO's*. Wiley.

Fairfax, L. M. (1999). When You Wish Upon a Star: Explaining The Cautious Growth of Royalty-Backed Securitization. *Columbia Business Law Review, 441*(3), 441–488.

Fitch, T. P. (2006). *Dictionary of Banking Terms.* Barrons Educational Series, United States.
Gabala, J. M. (2004). Intellectual Property Alchemy: Securitization of Intellectual Property as an Innovative Form of Alternative Financing. *John Marshall Review of Intellectual Property Law, 3*, 307–330.
Garner, B. A. (Ed.). (2009). *Black Law Dictionary.* West Publishing Co, Thomson Reuters, United States.
Glasner, A. (2008). Making Something Out of Nothing: The Trend Towards Securitizing Intellectual Property Assets and the Legal Obstacles that Remain. *Journal of Legal Technology Risk Management, 3*(2), 27–72.
Janger, E. J. (2002). Muddy Rules for Securitizations. *Fordham Journal of Corporate & Financial Law, VII*, 301–320.
Klee, K., & Butler, B. (2002). Asset-Backed Securitization: Special Purpose Vehicles and Other Securitisation Issues. *Uniform Commercial Code Law Journal, 35*, 23–67.
Mclean, J. (2008). Finance Nouveau: Prospects for the Securitization of Art. *New Mexico Law Review, 38*, 561–585.
Morris, M. (2009). *Royalty Securitization: Were Bowie Bond Just a Fad?* Capital Formation Institute.
Nikolic, A. (2009). Securitization of Patents and its Continued Viability in Light of the Current Economic Conditions. *Albany Law Journal of Science and Technology, 19*(2), 394–420.
Nimmer, R. T. (2001). Revised Article 9 and Intellectual Property Asset Financing. *Maine Law Review, 53*(2), 288–359.
Pandey, R. (2006). *Intellectual Property Valuation: a Critical Aspect of IP Securitization.* SSRN. https://doi.org/10.2139/ssrn.904604
Rahmah, M. (2015). Promoting Intellectual Property Securitization for Financing Creative Industry in Indonesia: Challenges and Solutions. *International Journal of Indonesian Studies, 1*(2), 110–127.
Robert, A. (1997). *David Bowie to Securitize Royalties: Ziggy Plays the Markets.* ECON. & FIN.
Rosly, S. A., & Sanusi, M. M. (1999). The Application of Bay' Al-'Inah And Bay' Al-Dayn in Malaysian Islamic Bonds: An Islamic Analysis. *International Journal of Islamic Financial Services, 1*, 2.
Schoon, N. (2008). *Islamic Banking and Finance.* Spriramus Press.
Scott, D. L. (2003). *Wall Street Words: An A To Z Guide to Investment Terms for Today's Investor.* Houghton Mifflin Company.
Securities Commission Malaysia. (2009). *Islamic Securities (Sukuk) Market.* Lexis Nexis.
Serwer, A. (1998, June 8). Sequel to Bowie Bonds: Supreme Securities. *Fortune.*

Shaw, G. M. (1990). Developments in Securitized Markets: Selected Legal Considerations Relating to Asset Backed Securities. *Practicing Law Inst./ Corp., 712*, 247.
Sylva, J. (1999). Bowie Bond Sold For Far More Than a Song: The Securitization of Intellectual Property as a Super-Charged Vehicle for High Technology of Financing. *Santa Clara Computer & High Technology Law Journal, 15*, 195–230.
Tosato, A. (2010). Security Interests Over Intellectual Property. *Journal of Intellectual Property Law & Practice, 6*(2), 93–104.

CHAPTER 7

Tapping Malaysian Intellectual Property Islamic Financing

Noor Suhaida Kasri

1 Introduction

The world has shifted towards a more knowledge-based economic activity. The presence of intellectual property, a major component of intangible assets in businesses, is becoming prominent and significant relative to tangible and fixed assets. The ubiquity of intellectual property (IP) has proliferated from the developed economies to the developing economies, particularly in the East Asia region. The Global North, particularly the USA, led on international patent filing application; however, from 2010, China emerged as a global leader in patent development. This has led to a knowledge-based transformation in the Global South and diversification of the economy (Ibrahim, 2014).

IP in Malaysia has seen positive growth, at a steadfast pace. As of March 2023, the Intellectual Property Corporation of Malaysia (MyIPO) has received 1782 Patent and Utility Innovations, 12,264 Trademarks, 423

N. S. Kasri (✉)
ISRA Institute, INCEIF University, Kuala Lumpur, Malaysia
e-mail: noor-isra@inceif.edu.my

N. Naim et al. (eds.), *Intellectual Property and Innovation*, The Political Economy of the Middle East,
https://doi.org/10.1007/978-981-96-4020-1_7

Industrial Designs, and 4 Geographical Indications. This reflects the rising interest in, appetite for, and awareness of IP among some sectors in Malaysia (MyIPO, 2023).

The growth of the IP sector is said to be supported by the emergence of innovative start-ups and small and medium-size (SME) enterprises that tend to be closely linked with IP. These enterprises form the backbone of most economies in the world. To support the development of these enterprises, funding/financing is key. However, IP funding/financing is a perennial problem in the IP industry, particularly in emerging economies. Despite the intangible asset value of IP to businesses, many developing economies have yet to grasp its importance and relevance. Not enough efforts and resources have been devoted to accelerating the growth of this increasingly critical sector, due to a lack of understanding of how to leverage value from IP assets (Ibrahim, 2014).

To facilitate the IP sector, financial institutions must reassess their existing funding practices. The current financial valuation structures and risk measures decide how IP fits into decision making. The banking system highly ranks the interest of depositors and would have robust risk measuring in place when deciding on whether a venture is low or high risk. The research contends that, due to the lack of understanding of how IP can be valued, many SMEs with high potential for growth on the basis of their IP value are required to provide alternative collateral. The value of the IP from SMEs can be leveraged more effectively to accurately reflect the value of the business (Ibrahim, 2014).

Recognising IP as an important asset class and its potential economic value to Malaysia, the Government of Malaysia (Government) has rolled out key building blocks to grow the nascent IP sector. Working together with the relevant ministries, agencies, market regulators, financial and Islamic financial markets, and IP market players, tailor-made initiatives have been launched that offered funding/financing to IP-related enterprises. Supporting infrastructure has been a critical need and the Government has prioritised creating new infrastructures specifically for the IP industry to support financing decision making.

This chapter deliberates on these key initiatives and infrastructures that have been made available for the IP market players in Malaysia. While it attempts to cover specifically IP Islamic financing and highlights the existing Islamic financing products, due to the dual nature of the existing initiatives offered to the IP industry, the description of this financing will include conventional financing. The chapter is divided into six sections.

Section 1 introduces the context of the chapter. Section 2 describes the position of the Malaysian IP industry as measured by the global benchmark, namely the World Intellectual Property Organization's (WIPO) Global Innovation Index. Section 3 showcases case studies on existing IP financing initiatives in Malaysia, which examine the two main categories of financing models for the IP sector, namely the traditional financing model represented by debt-based financing and the alternative financing model reflected by equity-based funding and innovative funding. Following the debt-based financing division, the following financing schemes are discussed: the Intellectual Property Financing Scheme (IPFS) provided by the MOSTI; the Intellectual Property Guarantee Scheme (IPGS) provided by the Syarikat Jaminan Pembiayaan Perniagaan (SJPP) under the Minister of Finance; and the IPFS provided by Malaysia Debt Ventures Berhad.

Three critical enablers that facilitate the implementation of the IP financing initiatives are also discussed, namely, IP valuation, IP assets as collaterals, and the Incentives Coordination and Collaboration Office. Under the alternative financing category, three interesting initiatives have been selected and showcased, namely the MTDC-pitchIN ECF, the MyCreative funding, and the Mat Daud Kilau Gold Wafer initiative. Then Sect. 4 discusses the case for Malaysia as a potential country model for the UAE in growing its IP financing sector and illustrates the nascent IP financing initiatives in the UAE. Section 5 focuses on lessons for the UAE to learn in developing financing for its IP industry.

2 Malaysia's Intellectual Property World Ranking

WIPO publishes the Global Innovation Index (GII) report. The WIPO's GII is essentially a league table that measures the innovation outputs of national economies. The criterion for analysis is under certain key categories that are centred on how innovative a country is. It has human capital and the research capabilities of a country as a core metric, evidence of infrastructure for innovation, intangible asset-based knowledge management, growth, and analysis of creative outputs. Due to its robust measurement, the GII is being recognised as a leading reference for measuring and assessing, including improving countries' innovation ecosystems and economic policy planning (WIPO, 2022a).

Table 7.1 Malaysia's strengths and weaknesses in innovation

Strength			*Weaknesses*		
Code	*Indicator name*	*Rank*	*Code*	*Indicator name*	*Rank*
2.2.2	Graduates in science and engineering, %	3	1.2.3	Cost of redundancy dismissal	104
2.3.4	Quacquarelli Symonds (QS) university ranking, top 3	16	2.1.3	School life expectancy, years	79
3.1.1	ICT access	19	2.3.3	Global corporate R&D investors (Top 3)	38
4.1.1	Finance for startups and scaleups	2	3.2.3	Gross capital formation, % GDP	94
4.1.2	Domestic credit to private sector, % GDP	16	3.3.2	Environmental performance	91
4.2.1	Market capitalization, % GDP	11	5.1.2	Firms offering formal training, %	83
5.3.2	High-tech imports, % total trade	4	5.3.5	Research talent, % in businesses	57
6.3.3	High-tech exports, % total trade	1	6.1.3	Utility models by origin/bn PPP$[a] GDP	56
7.1.3	Global brand value, top 5000, % GDP	10	7.1.2	Trademarks by origin/bn PPP$[a] GDP	93
7.2.5	Creative goods exports, % total trade	1	7.1.4	Industrial designs by origin/ bn PPP$[a] GDP	81

Source: WIPO (2022b) p. 6

[a] bn PPP$ GDP: The GDP of a country expressed in billions of US dollars, adjusted for Purchasing Power Parity (PPP), which accounts for differences in the cost of living and inflation between countries

In the recent WIPO GII 2022 report, Malaysia ranked 36 out of the 132 economies worldwide. By income group, Malaysia ranked at third position among the 36 upper middle-income group economies and ranked at eighth position among the 17 economies in South East Asia, East Asia, and Oceania. Malaysia's strengths and weaknesses in innovation have been assessed using specific indicators (see Table 7.1).

The strength of Malaysia in the criteria of finance, credit, and investment under the Market Innovation indicator is further dissected into the following scoring and ranking (see Table 7.2).

Based on Table 7.2, it is observed that there is a wide gap between the scores of the domestic credit to the private sector (134.0) with the finance for start-ups and scale-ups (60.6). This signals the need for the Government and market regulator to create appropriate initiatives and incentives to

Table 7.2 Malaysia's scoring and ranking for credit and investment

		Score	*Rank*
4.1	**Credit**	**55.7**	**10**
4.1.1	Finance for start-ups and scale-ups	60.6	2
4.1.2	Domestic credit to private sector, % GDP	134.0	16
4.1.3	Loans from microfinance institutions, % GDP	n/a	n/a
4.2	**Investment**	**16.2**	**40**
4.2.1	Market capitalization, % GDP	117.0	11
4.2.2	Venture capital investors, deals/bn PPP$ GDP	0.0	54
4.2.3	Venture capital recipients, deals/bn PPP$ GDP	0.0	61
4.2.4	Venture capital received, value, % GDP	0.0	46

Source: WIPO (2022b) p. 70

boost the appetite of capital providers or funders to provide funding to these underserved sectors.

This funding gap echoes the plight of the start-ups and scale-ups in accessing intellectual property-based funding. Based on the funding/financial institutions, the lack of funding to this sector is due to the following factors.

Irregular income flows experienced by the underserved led to them being categorised as risky. Conventional debt-based financing fits businesses with regular repayments where their credit patterns are considered well understood. Such irregular income flows, as experienced by the underserved, led to them being categorised as risky. Start-ups or scale-ups do not have the same credit patterns. They are commonly seen in emerging areas of commerce and, due to this, often are not able to establish the long-standing credit patterns of businesses relying on conventional debt-based financing. With no proven credit patterns, the underserved face difficulties in obtaining financing, and even if financing is granted, the profit can go as high as 10% (MDV, 2014; OECD, 2015).

2.1 *Lack of Tangible Collateral and Valuation Mechanism*

Increasingly, the profile of such firms is often 'asset-light' as they invest more in IP and software, compared to tangible assets, which are often traditionally used as collateral for financing from banks. A key challenge to accepting IP as collateral is its valuation. Hence many banks do not have the experience, expertise, or capability to assess the viability of IP as well as its valuation as collateral (Adrian, 2015; BNM, 2022).

There is an urgent need for a more varied scope of funding mechanisms that match the diverse needs across the business's funding lifecycle, which is key in supporting the growth of underserved firms. This eventually promotes longer-term financial stability (BNM, 2022). Section 3 captures this in more detail using selected case studies, which reflect the initiatives taken and driven by the Government in tailoring IP financing in line with the requirements of the underserved businesses.

3 Intellectual Property Financing Initiatives in Malaysia

The trend of financing/funding has evolved globally. Today, the traditional finance models, which are represented by the mainstream debt-based model of financing, are complemented by an alternative avenue of financing, coined as alternative finance. Traditional and alternative financing models are widely recognised as important avenues for the growth of the IP market.

In Malaysia, IP financing has evolved mainly through traditional finance models. This is demonstrated by the financing packages offered by the Government, including the relevant Ministries and Agencies that act as the intermediary in ensuring the funds from the government are distributed to the right recipients and targeted at a certain business development stage. The private sectors, like banks and financial institutions, have also played a critical role in assisting the distribution of the Government's financing package to the eligible recipients in the IP sector.

Having said that, at this juncture, it is worth noting that the Government also provides grants. For instance, to date, there are more than 80 grants and incentives under the Government that have been awarded through the MOSTI. The distribution of government grants is facilitated through the involvement of more than 13 fundraising organisations, such as MDV and SME Corporation. These funds spurred Malaysian start-up companies to consider being innovative, having the financial support to use emerging technologies to create new IP asset-based technological outputs.

The advent of technology and the changes brought on by the global COVID-19 pandemic have accelerated the movement of alternative finance alongside the traditional debt-based financing offering. The presence of alternative financing helped in narrowing the financing gap in the IP sector. Through this channel and aided by advanced technology tools, alternative financing providers are able to offer loans/financing at a lower rate to businesses with IP rights due to their low financing cost. Rapid application processing and approvals have boosted the popularity of alternative financing, which may potentially, in the long run, outperform the mainstream financing model.

Premised on the above setting, this section attempts to examine the two main categories of financing models for the IP sector in Malaysia, namely:

1. The traditional financing model represented by debt-based financing;
2. The alternative financing model as reflected by equity-based funding and innovative funding.

Due to their vital contribution to the development of the IP market in Malaysia, two IP financing schemes and a guarantee scheme have been selected to be part of the case studies under the debt-based financing category. These schemes are known as:

1. the Intellectual Property Financing Scheme (IPFS) provided by the MOSTI;
2. the Intellectual Property Guarantee Scheme (IPGS) provided by the Syarikat Jaminan Pembiayaan Perniagaan (SJPP) under the Minister of Finance; and
3. the Intellectual Property Financing Scheme (IPFS) provided by Malaysia Debt Ventures Berhad.

As part of the IP enabling ecosystem, three critical enablers facilitating IP financing initiatives are showcased in this section, namely the IP valuation, the IP collateral assets, and the Incentives Coordination and Collaboration Office.

Though alternative financing is still at the embryonic stage, three interesting initiatives are worth mentioning: the MTDC-pitchIN ECF, the MyCreative funding, and the Mat Daud Kilau Gold Wafer initiative. The emergence of these two models on the landscape of IP financing reflects the seriousness, commitment, and political will of the Government, regulator, and market players in addressing the financing gap and growing the local IP market at par with their international IP peers.

3.1 The Traditional Financing Model Represented by Debt-Based Financing

3.1.1 Intellectual Property Financing Scheme (MASTIC IPFS)

The IPFS was launched in 2013 by the Malaysian Science and Technology Information Centre (MASTIC), a division under the MOSTI. As of February 2015, RM200 million has been allocated for IPFS as part of the initiatives under the 'Industrial Technology Development: A National Plan of Action'. The idea of IPFS is to encourage innovation in the country through technopreneurs and tech companies. This will help elevate the tech sector and, in turn, generate positive growth for the economy as Malaysia advances towards achieving high-income nation status (Adrian, 2015).

Under IPFS, companies with IP rights can now use these rights as an additional source of collateral in getting funding. This helps in alleviating the difficulties faced by some technology-focussed companies when they seek funding from financial institutions. Therefore, to be eligible, applicants must:

1. be a Malaysian incorporated company with at least 51% Malaysian shareholding and must have a minimum paid-up share capital of RM100,000;
2. own the IP and the said IP must be registered with MyIPO;
3. have its IP valued with MyIPO or any other valuer approved by Malaysia Debt Venture (MDV).

The IPFS is also applicable to finance all MDV financing products (except post-shipment).

Those eligible will enjoy a financing of up to 80% of the IP value for a tenure of 5 years (including a grace period of up to 12 months) on top of the 50% guarantee provided by the Government as well as another 2% government rebate. The interest/profit rate offered is within the range of 7.5%–9.75% depending on the credit risk associated with the applicants (MASTIC, 2023).

IPFS helps to narrow the funding gap faced by the IP sector, which is dominated by start-ups and SMEs. Despite SMEs in general, forming 98% of the Malaysian economy and contributing to the country's GDP by 37.4% in 2021 (NESDC, 2021), the sector is beset with issues and challenges in getting funding for their businesses. As mentioned earlier, start-ups and SMEs are perceived as high-risk borrowers/customers and lack collateral. With the less rigid financing eligibility requirements afforded by IPFS (unlike the typical banks and financial institutions' rigid financing requirements) and the 50% government guarantee that addresses their credit enhancement issue, IP market players now have better options in searching for funds.

3.1.2 Intellectual Property Guarantee Scheme (IPGS)

IPGS was launched in 2018 by SJPP, a wholly owned company of Minister of Finance Incorporated. In line with the Government Budget 2009, SJPP's main purpose is to administer and manage government guarantee schemes as part of the Second Stimulus Package. The schemes allow SMEs funding opportunities, thus inculcating further innovation and increasing productivity. To be eligible for the IPGS, the applicants must:

1. be registered under the Companies Act 1965 and/or Companies Act 2016 with at least 51% shares held by Malaysian and shareholders' funds below RM20.0 million; and
2. have an IP valued by MyIPO.

Those eligible will enjoy an 80% government guarantee coverage and a guarantee fee of 0.75% per annum payable upfront. To ensure that the financing facilities are eligible for the IPGS, the applicants' financing facility must meet the following conditions:

1. The purpose is to be used for working capital as well as for capital expenditure (CAPEX) and cannot be used to refinance existing facil ities granted by the same or other participating financial institutions. The participating financial institutions and/or SJPP will be responsible for determining the genuineness of the applicants based on their respective credit evaluation procedures;
2. The minimum and maximum financing limit is RM100,000.00 and RM5.0 million respectively;
3. The tenure of financing is for a period of 13 years or until 31 December 2030, whichever is earlier. This is to be in line with the IPGS's limit of the utilisation of up to RM1.5 billion only or upon expiry of guarantee tenure on 31 December 2030, whichever is earlier;

4. The interest/profit rate is as determined by participating financial institutions;
5. The type of facility can be a Term Loan/Term Financing and/or Overdraft;
6. The source of funds is from the participating financial institutions.

To date, there are 32 financial institutions participating in the IPGS, as shown in Table 7.3. These financial institutions include major banks from the domestic and international arena, with 15 of them being registered Islamic banks under BNM.

The Islamic banks that participate in the IPGS offer the following terms as per Table 7.4.

The offering of IPGS by the Government helped to spur the appetite of the participating financial institutions to offer finance to SMEs that would have more attractive rates and contractual terms. This creates collaboration opportunities between the Government and the participating banks and financial institutes in providing SMEs with a more fit for purpose

Table 7.3 IPGS participating financial institutions

Conventional banks	*Islamic banks*
Affin Bank	Affin Islamic
Agro Bank	Al Rajhi Bank
Alliance Bank	Alliance Islamic Bank
AmBank	AmBank Islamic
Bank Rakyat	Bank Islam
BSN (Bank Simpanan Nasional)	Bank Muamalat
CIMB Bank	CIMB Islamic
EXIM Bank	Hong Leong Islamic Bank
Hong Leong Bank	HSBC Amanah
HSBC	Maybank Islamic
Maybank	MBSB Bank
MIDF (Malaysian Industrial Development Finance)	OCBC Al-Amin
OCBC	Public Islamic Bank
Public Bank	RHB Islamic Bank
RHB Bank	Standard Chartered Saadiq
Standard Chartered	
UOB (United Overseas Bank)	

Source: SJPP (2023)

Table 7.4 Participating Islamic banks in the IPGS

Bank	*Product*	*Financing details*	*Shariah contract*
Affin Islamic Bank	Automation & Digital Guarantee Scheme (ADGS-i)	Up to RM10 million, Halal businesses only	No info
	High-tech Facility, national aspirations	Up to RM800 million; 3.5% (without guarantee), 5% (with guarantee)	Tawarruq
Maybank Islamic Berhad	SME digital financing	RM3000–RM500,000; Base Financing Rate (BFR): 6.65% (as of 8/5/2023)	Commodity Murabahah, Tawarruq
CIMB Islamic Bank Berhad	Automation & Digital Guarantee Scheme-i	RM100,000–RM10 million	No info
Bank Islam Malaysia Berhad	SME Automation & Digitalization Facility (ADF)	Up to RM3 million per SME; 4% per annum	Tawarruq
	Start-up financing program	Min RM100,000; Max RM5 million	Tawarruq
Hong Leong Islamic Bank	SMEElite	Up to RM5 million; IFR: 1.00%–2.25%	Commodity Murabahah, Tawarruq
AmBank Islamic Berhad	Fund for SMEs, ADF	Up to RM3 million per SME; 4% per annum	No info
	Fund for SMEs, high tech and green facility	Up to RM10 million; 3.5%–5% per annum	No info

Source: Created by the author

solution to meet their demands for collateral, consequently meeting the funding needs of SMEs (SJPP, 2023).

3.1.3 Malaysia Debt Venture's Intellectual Property Financing Scheme (MDV IPFS)

Another IPFS was launched in 2013 by MDV. MDV was established by the Government in 2002 with the objective of providing flexible and innovative financing facilities to develop the Information and Communications Technology (ICT) area. In terms of its value to growth and innovation, the Government aims for the ICT to act as a catalyst for economic growth (MDV, 2023).

Sharing similar motives to MASTIC IPFS, MDV IPFS offers financing for IP-rich businesses to leverage their IP rights as collateral. This generates an influx of capital investments to tech-focussed businesses and gives them the financial resources to innovate. It addresses the funding gap difficulties encountered by technology-rich businesses when applying for loans against their IP value from financial institutions.

MDV IPFS afforded similar financing eligibility requirements to MASTIC IPFS, though with some additions as follows:

1. The company must fall within MDV-mandated sectors, i.e. ICT, Biotechnology, Green Technology, and other high-growth sectors; and
2. The stage of business must be at the growth level.

Those eligible for MDV IPFS will be offered the following terms:

1. Quantum/Margin of Financing: Up to RM10 million or 80% of valued IP, whichever is lower;
2. Tenure: 5 years financing tenure (inclusive of a grace period of up to 12 months);
3. Guarantee: 50% guarantee provided by the Government; and
4. Interest/Profit Rate: 2% per annum interest/profit equalisation payment (MDV, n.d.).

3.2 *Supporting Infrastructure for IP Financing*

3.2.1 *IP Valuation*

One of the key infrastructures supporting the growth of the IP financing sector is the establishment of IP valuation. Realising the importance of IP valuation, the Government mandated MyIPO to drive a series of initiatives to establish IP valuation in Malaysia. Shouldering this national mandate, MyIPO carried out the following tasks.

MyIPO conducted an extensive training programme on IP valuers and valuation practice in 2013 with the help of local and international WIPO-linked IP experts, the University of Berne, and the World Trade Institute. As part of the programme, participants were required to pass the examination before being conferred with the certification. From 53 participants, only 23 passed and the successful participants are now part of Malaysia's pool of IP Valuators. These qualified IP Valuators continued to partake in a series of capacity-building programmes, for instance, participating in several practical trainings related to the IPFS scheme and actual valuation. Acknowledging the diversity in the methods that can be used in the valuation standard, MyIPO developed the National IP Valuation Model (IPVM). The development of the IPMV was benchmarked against international standards, for example the International Financial Reporting Standards (IFRS), the International Valuation Standards, and the International Organization for Standardization (ISO). As a result, the IPVM became the reference for financial institutions that provides a standardised, Malaysia-centric, and widely accepted valuation method in IP valuation (Asia-Pacific Economic Cooperation, APEC, 2018).

3.2.2 *IP Assets as Collateral*

The creation of the IPVM, which enables IP rights to be valued, commercialised, and used as collateral to obtain financing from financial institutions, catalysed several IP-based statute amendment initiatives. From 2013, three important IP-related legislations have been promulgated and amended as follows:

1. The Industrial Designs (Amendment) Act 2013 was approved and came into operation on 1 July 2013;
2. The Trademarks Act 2019 came into force on 27 December 2019;
3. The Patents (Amendment) Act 2022 came into force together with its implementing Regulations on 18 March 2022.

By virtue of these amendments, registered trademarks, industrial designs, and patents are now being recognised as security interests.

Through these amendments, explicit provisions are being provided, particularly in the Trademarks and the Industrial Designs legislations, that stipulate standardised practices or procedures for creating security interests over their respective IP rights. For instance, the Trademarks Act 2019 stipulates on the granting requirements for a security interest. To register, a transaction must be either a fixed or floating charge over the registered trademark. According to the Industrial Designs (Amendment) Act 2013, a person becomes entitled to a registered industrial design through a security interest transaction. The Registrar of Industrial Designs records their industrial design in the official register. Once recorded, the registered industrial design is effective against third parties.

Similar recognition is echoed in the Companies Act 2016 which requires a company that creates a charge over its property or any of its undertakings to register the said charge at the Registrar of Companies. The requirement for the registration of a charge includes a charge on:

1. Goodwill;
2. A patent or licence under a patent;
3. A trademark;
4. A copyright or a licence under copyright.

Charges that are notified to the Registrar of Companies are then reflected in the relevant company's search reports (Charmayne et al., 2023). The statutory recognition of IP rights as a security interest helps to transform IP into a more valuable financial asset due to the greater credibility and transparency accorded to the IP rights (WIPO, 2015).

The recognition of IP rights as collateral can also be seen in the recent Financial Sector Blueprint 2022–2026 (Blueprint) of the Central Bank of Malaysia (CBM). The envisioned centralised collateral registry, an initiative of the CBM, together with the Registrar of Companies and the relevant agencies, is aimed at expanding the collateral base for SME financing. This is done by centralising the registration for all secured interests. In essence, the registry offers greater transparency, screening for potentially conflicting or competing security interests before making a decision. This helps in lowering any incidences of disputes over rights to the assets. The assets that are pledged as collateral would offer more reliable credit appraisals for funders (BNM, 2022).

3.2.3 *Incentives Coordination and Collaboration Office*

The Incentives Coordination and Collaboration Office (ICCO) was set up by the Government in 2015. It is mandated to coordinate and monitor all incentives across the economic sectors in the Twelfth Malaysian Plan. To ensure its mandates are effectively implemented, the Malaysian Ministry of Domestic Trade and Consumer Affairs' current state and district offices are being used as a single point of contact for SMEs seeking services. The services that ICCO renders include assisting with IP registration, licence and permit applications, as well as financial support information. The establishment of ICCO has helped to improve the industrial value chain and IP commercialisation and, in turn, solidified Malaysia as the regional centre for digital content (Ministry of Economy, 2021).

3.3 The Alternative Financing Model via Equity-Based Financing and Innovative Financing

Alternative financing is recognised as a vehicle that is able to attend to the distinct and non-conventional business needs when assessing the businesses financial lifecycle, especially in technology-intensive industries (see Table 7.5). As emerging industries appear in the field of business, many businesses do not have established credit patterns, which often limits their finance options. The profile of these firms is often 'asset-light' as they tend to invest more in their research and development than tangible assets. Their core assets are predominately in their IP, such as their copyright in software.

Given its importance, alternative financing is part of the strategic focus in the CBM's Blueprint, for the country to transform into a high-income nation. To achieve this status, firms need to be nurtured and supported with the right ecosystem and infrastructure. However, the alternative financing market in Malaysia is currently underdeveloped as compared to its peers (see Table 7.6). More effort and dedication, as well as stronger willpower, are required from all stakeholders to boost this sector to be at par with its counterparts.

The Malaysian SMEs' heavy reliance and concentration on traditional financing with financial institutions, as shown in Table 7.6, is a worrying sign. This, in the long run, requires attention as there is a danger of

Table 7.5 Available funding sources for businesses by stage of development

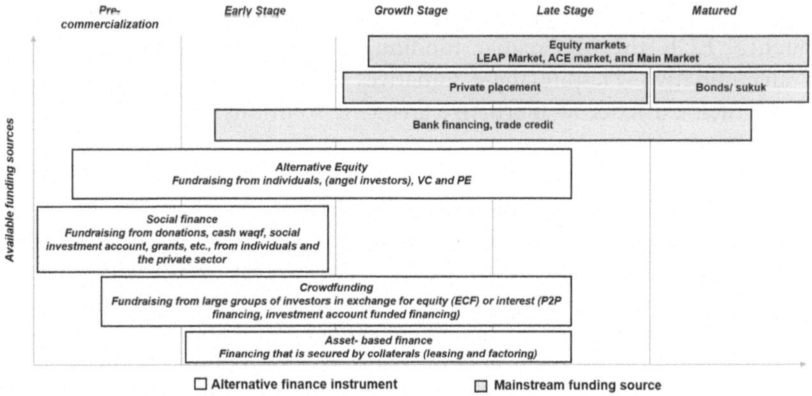

Source: BNM (2022) p. 43

Table 7.6 Malaysia's alternative financing market vis-à-vis other countries as of 2018

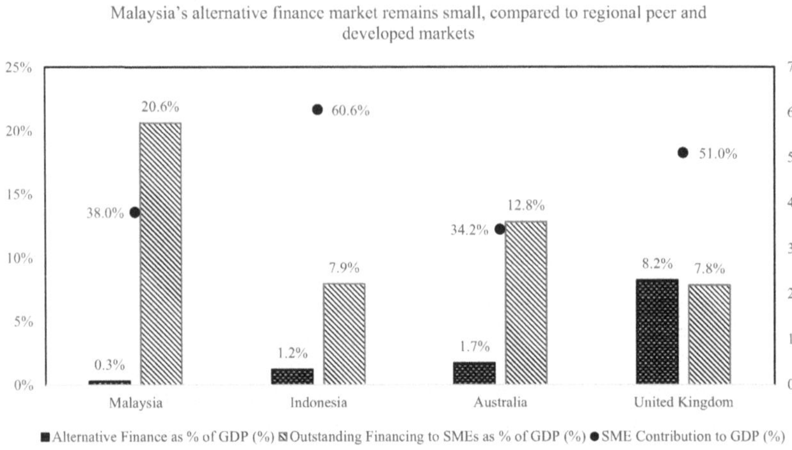

Source: BNM (2022) p. 43

excessive risk, leading to detrimental impact. This evergreen issue can be tackled by reforming the ecosystem surrounding traditional financing. In cognisance of this need, the CBM indicated its stance in the Blueprint that it would further develop new supporting and enhancing existing infrastructures. This will provide the essential scaffolding that could exponentially grow the underdeveloped alternative finance ecosystem (BNM, 2022).

Against that background, this sub-section looks into IP's alternative finance solutions through the selected case studies, namely the MTDC-pitchIN ECF, the MyCreative funding, and the Mat Daud Kilau Gold Wafer initiative. Despite these initiatives still being at their embryonic stage, their existence as alternative financing solutions for the IP market is worth mentioning.

3.3.1 MTDC-pitchIN Equity Crowdfunding

The MTDC-pitchIN ECF Programme was launched in 2020 by the MTDC in collaboration with pitchIN. The MTDC was established in March 1992, with the mandate to build world-class technology-based Malaysian companies through its integrated offerings: Strategic Investments, Centre of 9 Pillars (Co9P™) focusing on Industry 4.0, Technopreneur Training Academy, MTDC's Technology Centres and

Advisory, and Value-added services which focus on SME companies in the technology sector (LinkedIn, 2023). MTDC's "*ECF partner, pitchIN (Pitch Platforms Sdn Bhd), is a Recognised Market Operator by the Securities Commission of Malaysia and operates an Equity Crowdfunding platform for companies to raise their funding from the public*" (MASTIC, 2023).

The ECF programme provides technology-rich businesses with an online platform for equity-based financing investment from a substantial base of public investors. To be eligible, applicants must:

1. be a Malaysian incorporated company with majority shares owned by Malaysian shareholding;
2. have IP-backed technology;
3. have commercial ready prototype; and
4. be qualified to launch fundraising campaign through crowdfunding platform (i.e. pitchIN) (MASTIC, 2023).

3.3.2 MyCreative Funding

To spur the capacity of the Malaysian creative industry, in September 2012, the Government launched MYCREATIVE VENTURES Sdn. Bhd. (MyCreative). Being owned by the Minister of Finance Inc. and the investment arm of the Government, MyCreative is mandated to support the local creative industry through strategic and innovative funding initiatives, particularly for those that are still at a preliminary stage and require timelines to build better profit margins. Since its inception, RM200 million has been allocated to boost the contribution of the creative industry to the Malaysian economy (MyCreative Ventures, 2023a). This is at the back of the industry's "*contribution towards the country's GDP at 1.9% for the last five years, according to the Department of Statistics Malaysia*" (Malaysiakini, 2021; MyCreative Venture, 2018).

The funds allocated for MyCreative are distributed by way of grants, equities investment, and loans to viable Malaysian creative businesses, which is expected to make the following impact:

1. Enhancing the attractiveness of the domestic creative industry, thus creating more jobs;
2. Increasing the gross income of the creative industry, which results in an increase in its contribution towards the country's GDP;
3. Elevation of reputation through enhanced public recognition and social impact.

To be eligible for MyCreative funding, a pre-requisite condition is an extensive short- and long-term business plan spanning five years. Additionally, the applications must meet requirements from the eligibility criteria that include incorporation, Malaysian shareholder majority, and RM 20,000 minimum capital, and they must fit into one of the 10 categories within the definition of creative industries such as music, literature, and fashion. Those eligible for MDV IPFS will be offered financing from the fund; it has an upper limit of RM5 million with a cost range of 6 to 8%, across a maximum five-year term. For guarantee and collateral, shareholders and directors are required to give a hybrid of personal and/or corporate guarantees, as well as debentures on the company and/or IP collateral (MyCreative Venture, 2023b).

3.3.3 Mat Kilau *Gold Wafer Initiative*

In 2022, Co-opbank Pertama (CBP) launched a special edition gold wafer featuring the star of the famous movie *Mat Kilau*. CBP is a cooperative bank established under the Co-operative Act 1993 under the supervision of the Co-operative Commission of Malaysia. *Mat Kilau* was selected as the subject of the gold wafer as the film created an extraordinary phenomenon. After 33 days of screenings in Malaysia, Singapore, and Brunei, it made RM90 million in ticket sales (Sok, 2022). Being a heroic and important warrior in the history of Malaysia, Mat Kilau instils a sense of determination and commitment within the nation. These factors influenced CBP to honour the success of the film and capture its essence in the special edition gold wafer. The special edition *Mat Kilau* gold wafers were made available to CBP's valued customers. A total of 2000 gold wafers were produced that were priced at RM350 per gram. These gold wafers were made available for purchase across 29 CBP branches nationwide (Izz, 2022).

4 Islamic Finance and Intellectual Property in the United Arab Emirates

Islamic finance is a significant game player in its contribution to the global economy. Despite the impact of the COVID-19 pandemic on the global economy, Islamic finance has shown resilience and a growth trajectory. The global total Islamic finance industry assets reached almost US$4 trillion in 2021 with a growth of 17%, up from 14% in 2020 (ICD and

Refinitiv, 2022). Malaysia and the United Arab Emirates (UAE) are two leading jurisdictions that contribute significantly to the growth of Islamic finance. This is shown in Malaysia's total Islamic finance assets, which accounted for US$650 billion, while the UAE's accounted for US$252 billion (ICD and Refinitiv, 2022).

Besides Islamic finance, these two countries have exhibited similar competitive traits in the IP sector. In the 2022 WIPO's GII report, the UAE ranked 31st among the 132 economies, the highest of all the Gulf Cooperation Council states, compared to Malaysia's 36th rank. Against the high income group, the UAE ranked 30th and regionally, it ranked 3rd. The UAE's strengths and weaknesses in innovation lie in the following indicators (see Table 7.7).

Table 7.7 UAE's strengths and weaknesses in innovation

Strengths			*Weaknesses*		
Code	*Indicator name*	*Rank*	*Code*	*Indicator name*	*Rank*
1.2.3	Cost of redundancy dismissal	1	2.1.1	Expenditure on education, % GDP	84
1.3.1	Policies for doing business	6	5.1.5	Females employed with advanced degrees, %	80
1.3.2	Entrepreneurship policies and culture	1	6.1.1	Patents by origin/bn PPP$ GDP	113
2.2.3	Tertiary inbound mobility, %	1	6.1.3	Utility models by origin/bn PPP$ GDP	76
3.1.1	ICT access	3	6.1.4	Scientific and technical articles/bn PPP$ GDP	88
3.2.1	Electricity output, GWh/mn pop.	8	6.2.1	Labor productivity growth, %	71
3.2.2	Logistics performance	11	6.3.2	Production and export complexity	80
5.1.4	GERD financed by business, %	5	7.1.2	Trademarks by origin/bn PPP$ GDP	110
5.2.2	State of cluster development and depth	3	7.1.4	Industrial designs by origin/bn PPP$ GDP	115
5.3.5	Research talent, % in businesses	2	7.2.2	National feature films/mn pop. 15–69	63
7.2.5	Creative goods exports, % total trade	11			

Source: WIPO (2022c) p. 6

Table 7.8 UAE's scoring and ranking for credit and investment

		Score	*Rank*
4.1	**Credit**	**40.8**	**27**
4.1.1	Finance for startups and scaleups	48.9	16
4.1.2	Domestic credit to private sector, % GDP	88.4	34
4.1.3	Loans from microfinance institutions, % GDP	n/a	n/a
4.2	**Investments**	**35.8**	**20**
4.2.1	Market capitalization, % GDP	65.4	28
4.2.2	Venture capital investors, deals/bn PPP$ GDP	0.2	19
4.2.3	Venture capital recipients, deals/bn PPP$ GDP	0.1	18
4.2.4	Venture capital received, value, % GDP	0	11

Source: WIPO (2022c) p. 123

While the strength of IP innovation in the UAE is shown to lie mainly in Institutions, Infrastructure, and Business Sophistication, its weaknesses lie mainly in Knowledge and Technology Output and Creative Output. Nonetheless, the UAE's criteria on Market Innovation are not reflected in its strengths or weaknesses. Nonetheless, the state of UAE's Market Innovation can be ascertained based on Table 7.8, which indicates the scoring and ranking for its IP credit and investment.

Malaysia, on the other hand, enjoyed a heavy scoring on its Market Innovation criteria. Its main strengths lie in its IP funding and financing including Islamic financing for its IP SMEs and start-ups. It garnered a score of 60.6 for the finance for start-ups and scale-ups indicator, while the score for the domestic credit to the private sector is 134 (see Table 7.2). Given this scenario, there is a clear case for Malaysia to be an optional country model for the UAE in developing the appropriate building blocks for the country's IP financing ecosystem.

4.1 IP Financing Initiatives in the UAE

Compared to Malaysia, IP financing in the UAE is still at a nascent stage. Nonetheless, several initiatives and ongoing discussions worth mentioning are evidence of the continuous effort of the UAE government in building a funding system for the IP sector. Among them are the following.

4.1.1 *The Mohammed Bin Rashid Fund for SMEs*

The Fund aims at financing innovative pilot projects for SMEs. It focuses on key relevant areas of the UAE's National Innovation Strategy, such as renewable energy, transportation, education, health, water, and technology.

To qualify for the Fund, the project and the applicant are required to meet the following criteria:

1. The project idea must be unique and innovative;
2. The project must be registered as the IP of its respective owner, and the initial stage of the project must have already been established;
3. The applicant must be a resident, individual, or a company registered in the UAE. This includes all companies in the region, Emirati and non-Emirati companies;
4. The applicant needs a business plan that can give long-term projections using a business-specific, tailored feasibility study.

Up to 94% of the SMEs operating in the UAE can access the funding, which equates to over 86% of the private sector workforce size and over 60% of the UAE's GDP (Invest in Dubai, 2023).

4.1.2 *The Science, Technology, and Innovation Policy (STIP)*

The STIP is focussed on preparing for the post-oil era and investing in science and technology-based sustainable innovation and boosting a knowledge-based economy in the UAE. It renders support by making available research and development (R&D) facilities. Besides that, the STIP helps in identifying the conditions and tests that can befall the researchers and technicians. These include the limited access to specialised R&D, infrastructure, high laboratory costs, and prototyping facilities (Nadde, 2021).

4.1.3 *IP Finance Project*

With the support of WIPO, the UAE will be developing a project on IP finance that will allow local businesses and entrepreneurs to use their IP to secure financing. Key building blocks for IP financing, namely IP valuation and IP collateral, may also be considered in the project. This will allow innovative entrepreneurs and businesses to unlock new avenues of financing for growth using their most valuable IP assets (WIPO, 2023).

These IP financing initiatives align with the UAE national vision 'We the UAE 2031'. It envisaged a 10-year national developmental plan, i.e.

from 2021 to 2031, "*with a focus on social, economic, investment and development aspects. The plan seeks to enhance the UAE's position as a global partner and an attractive and influential economic hub in the future*" (U.ae, 2023).

5 Lessons Learned

The Malaysian case study demonstrates the drive and the will of the Government and CBM to grow the IP sector in Malaysia, particularly IP financing. The building blocks and structural changes implemented, though average relative to the advanced and matured IP market, are important for high-income group economies like the UAE. Several lessons can be learned from the journey of developing IP financing in Malaysia, among them:

1. Developing an IP valuation framework will help in measuring and valuing IP for financing. This initiative should be led by the government or market regulator;
2. Developing an IP valuation framework will facilitate financial institutions to build their respective internal IP financing framework. The framework may include "*practical guidance for both businesses and financial institutions in identifying, managing and valuing IP assets, and a way to include such assets within an institution's existing credit assessment procedures*" (Ibrahim, 2014);
3. Incorporating IP as security interest in one's legal framework is essential. In addition, the legal documentation that relates to a charge over IP rights will promote certainty, clarity, and consistency and will lead to cost-effective streamlined processes (Ibrahim, 2014);
4. Developing processes that embed transparency as a form of continuous audit and assessment on the performance of the assets will aid in providing early signals of potential trouble (BNM, 2015);
5. Getting the government to start building the right enabling ecosystem will spur the growth of the IP, which includes building supportive initiatives and incentives;
6. Extending tax incentives for IP companies. For instance, in the recent Budget 2023, the Government announced tax breaks for companies that do research and development for promoted items and IP creation in Malaysia. Under this initiative, companies are

excused from paying income taxes for a period of up to 10 years (Ministry of Economy, 2021);

7. Creating awareness of IP and IP financing will help to lower hindrances to funding;
8. Building capacity and expertise among the financiers will equip them with the changes and development of the IP market. This helps in positioning them at par with their peers in the international advanced IP market.

These key takeaways require strategic planning and implementation by the governing stakeholders. However, for them to be effectively implemented, mindset shift and strategic collaboration and engagement among the government, market regulators, funding providers, and IP industry players are key.

6 Conclusion

This chapter discussed IP financing, a perennial problem engulfing the IP industry, particularly in emerging IP economies. Despite the critical contribution of IP towards one's economy, IP issues are still not well understood; hence, less effort and fewer resources are being invested to grow this critical sector. Although IP financing in Malaysia has yet to reach the advanced level enjoyed by the advanced economies, the Government has established key building blocks and launched tailor-made funding/financing schemes to assist the IP-related enterprises.

The chapter highlighted several funding/financing schemes established by the Government, and the reason for their selection is based on the impact they made on the IP industry. These funding/financing schemes were divided into two main categories of financing models: the traditional financing model represented by debt-based financing and the alternative financing model reflected by equity-based funding and innovative funding. Under the debt-based financing division, the following financing schemes were discussed: the IPFS provided by the MOSTI; the IPGS provided by the SJPP under the Minister of Finance; and the IPFS provided by Malaysia Debt Ventures Berhad financing schemes. MTDC-pitchIN ECF, MyCreative funding, and Mat Daud Kilau Gold Wafer initiatives were studied under the alternative financing category. In addition to the above, the chapter also examined three critical enablers that facilitate the implementation of these IP financing/funding initiatives, namely, IP valuation, IP assets as collateral, and the Incentives Coordination and Collaboration Office. The examination of these case studies presented a good example for the United Arab Emirates to emulate, particularly in developing IP financing for its IP sector. The common trait shared by Malaysia and the UAE—being an OIC member country and home to a growing Islamic finance and IP sector—made Malaysia a good country model for the UAE. The chapter is timely as the global economy is searching for exemplary financing/funding models that are inclusive and sustainable and promote healthy and quality growth for the IP industry.

References

Adrian, W. (2015). *Finance: Banking on intellectual property. The Edge Markets Malaysia*. https://theedgemalaysia.com/article/finance-banking-intellectual-property%C2%A0

Asia-Pacific Economic Cooperation (APEC). (2018). *Best practices on intellectual property (IP) valuation and financing in APEC*. https://www.apec.org/docs/default-source/publications/2018/4/best-practices-on-ip-valuation-and-financing-in-apec/218ctibest-practices-on-intellectual-property-ip-valuation-and-financing-in-apec.pdf?sfvrsn=e235ee10_1

Bank Negara Malaysia. (BNM). (2015). *Financial stability and payment systems report 2014*. Bank Negara Malaysia. https://www.bnm.gov.my/documents/20124/856377/fs2014_book.pdf/b2fea510-2443-d705-ec06-39b307c993dd?t=1585724965224

Bank Negara Malaysia (BNM). (2022). *Financial sector blueprint 2022–2026*. https://www.bnm.gov.my/documents/20124/5915429/fsb3_en_book.pdf

Charmayne, O., Jillian, C., Melissa, L., & Gooi, Y. S. (2023). *Intellectual property transactions in Malaysia: Overview*. Thomson Reuters. https://uk.practicallaw.thomsonreuters.com/w-018-1360?contextData=(sc.Default)&transitionType=Default&firstPage=true

Ibrahim, M. (2014). *Deputy governor welcoming remarks at the Intellectual Property Financing Conference 2014*. Bank Negara Malaysia. https://www.bnm.gov.my/-/deputy-governor-welcoming-remarks-at-the-intellectual-property-financing-conference-2014

Invest in Dubai. (2023). *Funding opportunity*. https://invest.dubai.ae/funding-opportunities

Islamic Corporation for the Development of the Private Sector & Refinitiv. (2022). *ICD—Refinitiv Islamic Finance Development Report 2022: Embracing change*. https://www.refinitiv.com/content/dam/marketing/en_us/documents/gated/reports/ifdi-report-2022.pdf

Izz, L. H. (2022). *Co-Op Bank Pertama lancar wafer emas Mat Kilau. Harian Metro.* New Straits Times Press (M) Bhd. https://www.hmetro.com.my/bisnes/2022/12/913590/co-opbank-pertama-lancar-wafer-emas-mat-kilau

LinkedIn. (2023). *Company profile: Malaysian Technology Development Corporation (MTDC),* https://www.linkedin.com/company/mtdcmalaysia/?originalSubdomain=my

MalaysiaKini. (2021). *Anticipating 2022 for the creative industry.* https://www.malaysiakini.com/advertorial/600310

Malaysian Debt Venture. (2014). *Monetizing intellectual property.* https://www.mdv.com.my/v3/monetising-intellectual-property/

Malaysian Debt Venture (MDV). (2023). https://www.mdv.com.my/v3/

Malaysian Debt Venture (MDV). (n.d.). https://internaldev.smecorp.gov.my/smecorp/ProgrammeDetails2.php?programme=62

Malaysian Science and Technology Information Centre (MASTIC). (2023). *Strategic Data and Foresight Technology Division, Ministry of Science Technology and Innovation.* https://mastic.mosti.gov.my/sti/incentives/intellectual-property-financing-scheme-ipfs

Ministry of Economy. (2021). *12th Malaysian Plan (RMK12) 2021–2025: A prosperous, inclusive, sustainable Malaysia.* Percetakan Nasional Malaysia Berhad. https://rmke12.epu.gov.my/en

MyCreative Venture. (2018). *MyCreative Ventures approves RM34million financing to 19 successful creative companies.* http://www.mycreative.com.my/news_events/mycreative-ventures-approves-rm34million-financing-to-19-successful-creativ

MyCreative Venture. (2023a). *What is MyCreative.* http://www.mycreative.com.my/about

MyCreative Venture. (2023b). *How it works? How does MyCreative's funding work?* http://www.mycreative.com.my/how

MyIPO. (2023). *Statistic-Application & Registration.* https://www.myipo.gov.my/en/statistic-application-registration/#toggle-id-1

Nadde, S. I. (2021). *Study of the intellectual property protection regulatory frameworks of the GCC.* https://www.eeas.europa.eu/sites/default/files/documents/IPR%20regulatory%20frameworks%20in%20the%20GCC%20Report%202021%2004.pdf

National Entrepreneur & SME Development Council (NESDC). (2021). *MSME Insights 2021: MSMEs towards sustainable recovery.* https://www.smecorp.gov.my/images/Publication/MSME_Insights/SME_Insight_2021_1_English_Full_Version.pdf

Organisation for Economic Co-operation and Development (OECD). (2015). *Review of Malaysia's national intellectual property system.* Directorate for Science, Technology and Innovation Committee for Scientific and Technological Policy. https://one.oecd.org/document/DSTI/STP(2015)8/en/pdf

Sok. (2022). *Mat Kilau earns RM90 million, beating Avengers: Endgame record!*. https://en.syok.my/entertainment/mat-kilau-rm90-million-beating-avengers-endgame

Syarikat Jaminan Pembiayaan Perniagaan Berhad (SJPP). (2023). https://www.sjpp.com.my/schemes/archive/intellectual-property-guarantee-scheme-ipgs

U.ae. (2023). *'We the UAE 2031' vision*. https://u.ae/en/about-the-uae/strategies-initiatives-and-awards/strategies-plans-and-visions/innovation-and-future-shaping/we-the-uae-2031-vision

World Intellectual Property Organization (WIPO). (2015). *Global Innovation Index 2021: Country Statement, 55th Series of Assemblies of WIPO Member States*. https://www.wipo.int/edocs/mdocs/govbody/en/a_55/a_55_my.pdf

World Intellectual Property Organization (WIPO). (2022a). *Global innovation index 2022: What is the future of innovation-driven growth?* WIPO. https://oacps-ri.eu/wp-content/uploads/wipo-pub-2000-2022-section1-en-gii-2022-at-a-glance-global-innovation-index-2022-15th-edition.pdf

World Intellectual Property Organization (WIPO). (2022b). *Global innovation index 2022: Malaysia*. https://www.wipo.int/edocs/pubdocs/en/wipo_pub_2000_2022/my.pdf

World Intellectual Property Organization (WIPO). (2022c). *Global innovation index 2022: United Arab Emirates*. https://www.wipo.int/edocs/pubdocs/en/wipo_pub_2000_2022/ae.pdf

World Intellectual Property Organization (WIPO). (2023). *WIPO to support IP projects in the UAE*. https://www.wipo.int/about-wipo/en/dg_tang/news/2023/news_0006.html

CHAPTER 8

AI Innovation, Intellectual Property Commercialization, and the Rise of the Intellectual Capital Economy: Challenges and Prospects for GCC Economies

Zaid Hamzah

1 Introduction

The Fourth Industrial Revolution has ushered in a new era where intellectual capital, which includes intangible assets and intellectual property (IP), has emerged as a critical driver of economic value. Characterized by digital transformation and disruptive technologies such as artificial intelligence (AI) and machine learning (ML), the rise of the data-driven and AI-enabled economy has underscored the growing significance of intellectual capital and the rise of the emerging intellectual capital economy.

Z. Hamzah (✉)
School of Computing (Advanced Computing for Executives),
National University of Singapore, Singapore, Singapore
e-mail: zaid@u.nus.edu

N. Naim et al. (eds.), *Intellectual Property and Innovation*, The Political Economy of the Middle East,
https://doi.org/10.1007/978-981-96-4020-1_8

Intellectual capital includes intangible assets such as know-how and brand as well as intellectual property rights such as patents, trademarks, copyrights, and trade secrets. The Microsoft definition of "Intellectual capital" refers to the intangible assets a company possesses, including its knowledge, skills, relationships, and innovations. Unlike tangible assets, such as buildings or machinery, intellectual capital resides in the minds of employees and the culture of the organization. It's the collective intelligence that drives a company to innovate, solve problems, and stay ahead of the competition (Understanding Intellectual Capital, 2024). Ocean Tomo's 2020 Intangible Asset Market Value Study reveals that intangible assets now account for over 90% of the S&P 500 market value, underscoring their significance (Ocean Tomo, 2020).

Against the backdrop of the recent phenomenal rise of generative AI, this chapter examines how the Gulf Cooperation Council (GCC) countries member states are positioning their economies amid this market shift. It explores the challenges and prospects associated with driving AI innovation and the commercialization of AI-related intellectual property in the GCC economies. The chapter advocates a niche and leapfrogging strategy tailored to the unique characteristics and advantages of GCC economies. Before going deeper into these issues, first start with some key definitions of the terms that will be used in this chapter. Commercialization in the context of AI innovation refers to the process of taking AI technologies or innovations from research and development stages and bringing them to the market for widespread commercial use (Westgarth et al., 2022). Commercialization must result in the generating of revenue in order to pay for the initial investments made into AI innovation.

Commercialization of AI innovation is sometimes referred to as monetization of AI innovation (Merikanto, 2024). The two terms are often used interchangeably. They refer to the process of bringing an AI-powered product, service, or technology to market and generating revenue from it. This can involve a variety of activities, such as:

- Licensing AI technology to other companies
- Assigning AI IP to another company in exchange for royalties or other payments
- Using AI IP as a capital contribution in a joint venture with another company
- Selling AI-powered products or services directly to customers

The commercialization process involves various steps and considerations (National Science Board, 2020). Here is the breakdown of these key components:

IP Rights: Intellectual property refers to the legal rights that protect AI innovations, including patents, copyrights, trademarks, and trade secrets. Commercialization involves identifying, protecting, and managing these IP assets to secure the competitive advantage of the AI innovation. This can include patenting AI algorithms in products or services with a "technical effect" or protecting proprietary datasets used in AI models.

Licensing: Licensing in AI commercialization involves granting permission to other entities or individuals to use, modify, or distribute the AI technology or IP. This can be done through various types of licences, such as exclusive, non-exclusive, or sublicensing agreements. Licensing allows the AI innovator to generate revenue while enabling others to leverage the technology for their specific purposes.

Assignment: Assignment refers to the transfer of ownership or rights of AI innovations or IP to another party. It is the same as selling something. This may occur through the sale or transfer of patents, copyrights, or other IP assets related to the AI technology. Assignments can be a part of commercialization when an AI innovator decides to exit a project or transfer rights to a larger organization.

Use of IP Rights in Joint Ventures: In some cases, AI commercialization involves forming joint ventures or partnerships with other companies or organizations. IP rights or technology can be used as a capital contribution in these ventures. For example, one company may bring AI algorithms, while another provides access to valuable datasets. The joint venture leverages these contributions to develop and market AI solutions collaboratively. The best commercialization strategy for a particular AI innovation will depend on a number of factors, such as the type of innovation, the target market, and the innovator's resources and goals. Here are three examples of how the commercialization strategies described above can be used to commercialize AI innovation.

Example 1 is a company that develops a new AI algorithm for predicting customer churn and could license the algorithm to other companies in exchange for royalties. Google licenses its AI-powered speech recognition technology to other companies, who use it to power their own voice assistants and other applications (Google Cloud, 2024). Example 2 is a company that develops a new AI-powered medical diagnostic tool and could assign the patent for the tool to a pharmaceutical company in exchange for upfront payments and royalties on future sales. IBM assigned the patent for its Watson AI technology to the University of Texas, who used it to develop new cancer treatments (Ross & Swetlitz, 2017). Example 3 is two companies that are developing complementary AI technologies that could form a joint venture to develop and market a new AI-powered product or service. Microsoft and Nokia formed a joint venture to develop and market AI-powered smartphones (Baker, 2011). By understanding the different ways to protect and commercialize AI IP, innovators can maximize their chances of success in bringing their AI innovations to market. Commercialization in AI innovation is a multifaceted process that involves not only developing the technology but also navigating the legal and business aspects of protecting, licensing, assigning, and leveraging IP rights to bring AI innovations to market successfully. It requires a strategic approach to maximize the value of AI innovations while ensuring legal compliance and protecting the innovator's interests.

The key thing to note is that the ownership of the IP rights is ultimately not as critical as the ability to extract value from such ownership. When any organization invests in AI innovation, they typically spend vast amounts of money, often running into millions of dollars. If these organizations are not able to secure their returns on investment, then their investments are fruitless.

1.1 Rise of the Intellectual Capital Economy

The evolving marketplace has seen a substantial shift in value from tangible to intangible assets, with intangibles now driving the majority of corporate value. Ocean Tomo's 2020 report highlights the dominance of intangible assets, specifically IP, in the S&P 500 market value. This shift signifies the changing dynamics of economic value creation and necessitates a re-evaluation of traditional economic models.

1.2 AI Is Transforming the World

Against the phenomenal rise of generative AI like ChatGPT, advanced developments in AI and ML are reshaping the global landscape. Against this shift in the marketplace, how are the GCC member states positioning their economies in this new global landscape? This chapter addresses the challenges and prospects of driving AI innovation and the commercialization of AI-related IP in the GCC economies and proposes a niche strategy for them.

1.3 *Shift from Dependence on Oil*

GCC countries have long acknowledged the imperative to diversify their economies and reduce their reliance on oil revenue (World Bank Group, 2023). In this pursuit, they have recognized the value of intellectual capital, encompassing knowledge assets (Saudi Authority for Intellectual Property, 2024), and other intangible assets.

Transitioning to an emerging intellectual capital economy presents numerous challenges for GCC countries. These challenges arise from the need to diversify their economies (Saidi, 2024), overcome historical dependencies, and address systemic barriers that hinder innovation and commercialization (Altiparmak, 2023). Nonetheless, the recognition of these challenges marks an important step forward in the GCC countries' pursuit of economic transformation.

GCC economies face two critical challenges in this endeavour. Firstly, they need to accelerate the pace of innovation, particularly in the realm of AI development. Secondly, they need to develop strategies and programmes to leverage intellectual property as a new driver of economic value through effective commercialization strategies.

Consider the following current situation in selected GCC countries in the area of AI innovation, including the commercialization of intellectual property rights in relation to these AI innovations:

2 Examples of AI Innovation and Commercialization in the GCC

Abu Dhabi is home to several leading healthcare providers, including the Abu Dhabi Health Services Company (SEHA). SEHA has implemented AI-based medical imaging technologies for various applications, such as automated detection of breast cancer and lung disease and improving the accuracy of medical diagnosis. The Abu Dhabi Department of Health has also launched several initiatives to promote the adoption of AI in healthcare, including the development of an AI-based medical imaging centre. This is an example of how AI innovation is being deployed and commercialized. Although no published data is available on how SEHA charges others for the use of its services, it can be assumed that the investments made in AI innovation in this instance have been commercialized either for its own use or by licensing to other entities.

Another UAE-based start-up, Infermedica, has developed an AI-powered diagnostic tool that utilizes natural language processing to assist healthcare providers in making accurate diagnoses. This innovation not only enhances patient care but also opens opportunities for licensing its AI algorithms to healthcare institutions worldwide. In Saudi Arabia, Saudi Aramco, the world's largest oil company, has deployed AI-driven solutions for predictive maintenance, reservoir management, and drilling optimization. These innovations have resulted in significant cost savings and increased efficiency, positioning Saudi Aramco as an industry leader in AI-driven energy solutions.

Fintech companies in the GCC are leveraging AI to revolutionize financial services. Dubai-based robo-advisory platform Sarwa uses AI algorithms to provide personalized investment advice. By securing patents for their algorithms, Sarwa ensures a competitive edge in the rapidly growing robo-advisory market, attracting both local and international investors. In the area of healthcare, for instance, an AI-powered system is being developed to diagnose and treat diseases more accurately and efficiently. In the UAE, the Ministry of Health and Prevention initiated a project called "RoboDoc" in collaboration with IBM Watson Health. RoboDoc is an AI-powered virtual doctor that assists healthcare professionals in diagnosing and treating diseases more accurately and efficiently. It provides real-time information and recommendations based on a vast database of medical literature and patient records.

In the field of education as another example, there are efforts to use AI to develop personalized learning programmes for students. Saudi Arabia has been investing in personalized learning programmes with AI. A start-up called Noon Academy offers an AI-driven platform that tailors educational content to individual students' needs (Noon Academy, 2024). This platform provides personalized lessons and recommendations, helping students improve their academic performance. In transportation, AI-powered self-driving vehicles and traffic management systems have been developed. The UAE has been at the forefront of testing autonomous vehicles. For example, Masdar City in Abu Dhabi has been running pilot projects with autonomous electric vehicles (Masdar, 2016). These self-driving EVs utilize AI and advanced sensors for navigation and safety.

In the oil and gas sector, AI is being used to improve the efficiency of oil and gas production and exploration; Saudi Aramco, one of the world's largest oil companies, has been heavily investing in AI to improve efficiency in oil and gas production. They have developed AI-based systems for predictive maintenance, reservoir management, and drilling optimization. These innovations are aimed at increasing productivity and reducing operational costs.

In agriculture, there is development of AI-powered systems to monitor crop health and predict yields. In Qatar, initiatives like the Qatar Computing Research Institute's (2024) "Qatar Food Security Program" have been working on AI-powered systems to monitor crop health and predict yields. These systems use drones and AI algorithms to analyse data and provide insights to farmers for more efficient crop management. GCC countries are actively seeking opportunities to monetize their AI innovations through licensing agreements and partnerships. For instance, Qatar's Sidra Medicine has partnered with international pharmaceutical compa nies to license its AI-driven drug discovery platform, which accelerates drug development processes.

Investments in people are also being made in the GCC. The GCC is investing in talent development to sustain its AI innovation ecosystem. Initiatives like the Saudi Data & AI Authority's AI Academy and the UAE's AI Institute aim to nurture a skilled workforce capable of driving AI research and development. The GCC economies are witnessing a profound transformation driven by AI innovation. Through strategic investments, robust IP protection mechanisms, and international collaborations, these countries are capitalizing on their AI advancements to diversify their economies and enhance global competitiveness.

It is clear that based on the level of activities described above, the GCC economies are witnessing a profound transformation driven by AI innovation. Through strategic investments, robust IP protection mechanisms, and international collaborations, these countries are capitalizing on their AI advancements to diversify their economies and enhance global competitiveness. However, challenges such as regulatory adaptation and talent development require continued attention to ensure sustainable growth in the AI sector. As GCC countries continue to innovate and commercialize their IP rights, they are poised to play an increasingly influential role in the global AI landscape.

The commercialization of AI innovation in the GCC has the potential to generate significant economic benefits for the region. AI can help to boost productivity, create new jobs, and attract foreign investment. It can also help to improve the quality of life for GCC citizens by providing innovative solutions to challenges in areas such as healthcare, education, and transportation. The GCC governments and businesses will need to continue to accelerate their investments in AI research and development, and to create an environment that is even more conducive to the commercialization of AI innovation. By doing so, the GCC countries can position themselves as major global contributors in the emerging AI economy.

3 The Significance of AI Development in the Global Context

AI has emerged as a transformative technology with the potential to revolutionize various industries and sectors. Its applications range from healthcare and finance to transportation and manufacturing. The growing reliance on AI in research and development has made it a key driver of innovation.

The Stanford University AI Index serves as a valuable benchmark for assessing global AI development and highlights the dominant positions of the United States and China. Their leadership positions underscore the competitive advantage they possess in AI-related research and adoption, driving economic growth and shaping future technological advancements.

The Global Innovation Index (GII) in turn is one of the regular benchmarks that evaluates countries' innovation capabilities. It assesses a wide range of indicators that capture different dimensions of innovation. These indicators include institutions, human capital and research, infrastructure, market sophistication, business sophistication, knowledge and technology outputs, and creative outputs. The GII provides valuable insights into a country's strengths and areas for improvement, serving as a guide for policy formulation and investment decisions.

The Global Innovation Index (GII) 2022 shows the GCC countries' challenges in the innovation landscape. In the GII 2022, the UAE is the highest-ranked GCC country at 31st place, followed by Saudi Arabia at 51st, Qatar at 52nd, Kuwait at 62nd, Bahrain at 72nd, and Oman at 79th. While some GCC countries have shown improvement in their innovation performance, they still lag behind compared to other advanced economies.

With innovation being increasingly driven by AI and ML, it is useful to look at the Stanford University AI Index 2020. China and the United

States are leading the world in AI development, with the United States at the top of the ranking in research and China leading in AI adoption. In contrast, the GCC countries lag far behind. In the same index, Saudi Arabia ranks 50th, the United Arab Emirates (UAE) ranks 57th, Kuwait ranks 79th, Bahrain ranks 86th, Qatar ranks 93rd, and Oman ranks 100th.

The United States and China, as the global leaders in AI development, have capitalized on their advanced capabilities, driving innovation and reaping economic benefits. In contrast, GCC countries face significant challenges in positioning their economies amid this transformation. The combination of both the GII and the Stanford University AI Index sheds light on the GCC countries' current standing in AI development and innovation performance. The rankings reveal that GCC countries, while making some progress, lag behind their counterparts in AI development and innovation metrics. To compete effectively, GCC countries must prioritize AI innovation and specifically the commercialization of AI-related IP.

In the latest 2023 AI Index Report published by the Stanford Institute for Human-Centered Artificial Intelligence, the United Arab Emirates ranks 16th in the world in AI innovation, followed by Saudi Arabia at 22nd, Qatar at 31st, and Kuwait at 42nd. Bahrain and Oman were not included. Based on the latest data points, the GCC countries are making significant progress in AI innovation, but they still lag behind the world's leading AI innovators, such as the United States, China, and the United Kingdom. These rankings suggest that the GCC countries are still in the early stages of AI innovation, but they are making progress. As can be seen in the examples highlighted earlier, the GCC countries are investing heavily in AI, and they have a growing number of AI start-ups and research projects. However, the GCC countries also face a number of challenges, such as a lack of skilled AI talent and a relatively small domestic market. We will now cover these challenges and what can be done to deal with them.

To set the larger context in this review of innovation and AI, the GCC countries could focus their efforts to improve both their innovation and AI index ranking for several reasons:

1. Economic Competitiveness: The AI index ranking indicates a country's ability to drive innovation and reap economic benefits from AI development. GCC countries' low rankings suggest they may struggle to compete with global leaders in AI development, potentially impacting their economic growth and competitiveness.

2. Innovation Gap: The significant gap between GCC countries and global leaders in AI development indicates a need to bridge the innovation gap. Failing to do so may result in GCC countries missing out on opportunities to drive economic growth, improve productivity, and enhance their global standing.
3. IP Commercialization: The AI index highlights the importance of commercializing AI-related IP. GCC countries' low rankings suggest they may not be effectively leveraging their AI research and development to drive innovation and economic growth.
4. Global Influence: A strong AI index ranking can contribute to a country's global influence and reputation as a leader in innovation. GCC countries' low rankings may impact their ability to shape global AI agendas and standards.
5. Future Readiness: The AI index ranking can be seen as a proxy for a country's readiness for future technological advancements. GCC countries' low rankings may indicate a need to invest in developing their AI capabilities to ensure they are well prepared for future technological disruptions.

3.1 *Challenges Faced by GCC Countries in the GII Rankings*

A range of factors contribute to the challenges faced by GCC countries in the GII rankings including limited research and development investment, insufficient funding for innovation initiatives, and a shortage of skilled human capital which can impede progress.

Other factors include inadequate institutional support, including IP protection and regulatory frameworks, which can also hinder innovation. Additionally, limited collaboration between academia, industry, and government entities restricts knowledge sharing and stifles innovation ecosystems. The lack of diversified economies and over-reliance on traditional sectors pose further challenges to innovation-driven growth in the GCC countries.

3.2 *Strategies to Foster Innovation in GCC Countries*

To improve their positions in the GII rankings and foster innovation, GCC countries can adopt several strategies:

1. Enhancing R&D investment and allocating resources to support innovation initiatives is crucial. This includes funding for research institutions, innovation clusters, and start-ups.
2. Fostering collaboration between academia, industry, and government entities can promote knowledge exchange and facilitate technology transfer. Public–private partnerships, incubation programmes, and innovation hubs can stimulate innovation ecosystems.
3. Investing in human capital development and education, with a focus on science, technology, engineering, and mathematics (STEM), can cultivate a skilled workforce capable of driving innovation.
4. Strengthening IP protection and enforcement frameworks can incentivize research and protect the rights of innovators. Finally, promoting entrepreneurship, supporting start-ups, and creating a favourable regulatory environment can spur innovation-driven economic growth.

3.3 Policy and Regulatory Frameworks

Establishing effective policy and regulatory frameworks is crucial for fostering AI development in GCC countries. Clear guidelines for data privacy, protection, and security are necessary to build trust in AI technologies. IP rights protection and enforcement frameworks should be strengthened to encourage innovation and incentivize research and development. Flexible regulations that accommodate technological advancements while ensuring ethical AI deployment are paramount. Additionally, facilitating cross-border collaborations and knowledge-sharing platforms can contribute to the acceleration of AI development in the region.

The GCC countries face significant challenges in AI development and adoption, as evidenced by their rankings in the Stanford University AI Index. However, the gap presents opportunities for growth and transformation. By addressing the challenges through strategic investments, fostering collaborations, and implementing supportive policies and regulatory frameworks, GCC countries can bridge the AI development gap and harness the transformative potential of AI. Embracing AI as a key driver of innovation and economic diversification will position GCC countries as players in the global AI landscape, enabling them to drive sustainable economic growth, enhance competitiveness, and pave the way for a technologically advanced future.

3.4 Leapfrogging Innovation in Niche Sectors: Opportunities for GCC Countries

In the pursuit of economic diversification and growth, GCC countries face the challenge of catching up with larger economies. Recognizing the limitations of competing across a broad front, the GCC countries need to adopt a leapfrogging approach by focusing on niche sectors for innovation.

The GCC countries could explore niche areas, particularly in emerging fields such as AI and ML, and renewable energy, agritech in harsh hot climates, and smart cities are identified as potential niche sectors for GCC economies. By leveraging their unique strengths and opportunities, GCC countries can foster innovation, overcome developmental constraints, and position themselves as global leaders in these specialized sectors.

4 Lessons from Singapore

The GCC countries may find useful lessons from smaller but high-value economies like Singapore, which relies solely on people and the creation of intellectual capital to drive commercial value. AI innovation is increasingly being positioned as the newest commercial and economic value driver (Ministry of Digital Development and Information, 2024). For decades, Singapore has embarked on transforming its economy into an innovation-driven one. In the last five years, efforts to ramp up AI adoption especially among the small to medium-sized enterprises have been intensified.

Today, Singapore is positioning itself to be an AI-first nation. AI innovation is given top priority today. At the same time, the management and commercialization of intangible assets including IP rights has been intensified at the national level with new strategies (Intellectual Property Office of Singapore, 2025).

Singapore has given innovation top national priority for decades. Singapore ranks first in the Asian region and fifth globally in the 2023 Global Innovation Index, beating even some larger economies. It has achieved this by consistently investing in education, research and development, and building a supportive business environment. For instance, Singapore has focused on developing niche areas like biotech, advanced manufacturing, and fintech, where it has a comparative advantage.

Singapore's focus on education, research and development, and fostering a supportive business environment, along with its emphasis on niche sectors, offers insights that can inform the strategies of GCC countries. By adopting Singapore's approach and tailoring it to their unique strengths and opportunities, GCC countries can enhance their innovation ecosystem, strengthen their intellectual capital, and position themselves as leaders in specialized industries.

4.1 *The Power of Intellectual Capital in Singapore's Success*

Singapore's remarkable rise as an innovation-driven economy can be attributed to its reliance on intellectual capital. Recognizing the limitations of traditional resources, Singapore strategically focused on nurturing its human capital and creating a knowledge-based economy. By investing in education, research and development, and human capital development, Singapore has built a highly skilled workforce capable of driving innovation, creativity, and entrepreneurship. The emphasis on intellectual capital has allowed Singapore to attract global talent, foster knowledge-intensive industries, and generate high-value economic output.

4.2 *Consistent Investments in Education and Research*

One of Singapore's key strengths lies in its deep commitment to education and research. The government has consistently allocated significant resources to develop a world-class education system and support cutting-edge research institutions. By prioritizing STEM (science, technology, engineering, and mathematics) education and promoting interdisciplinary collaboration, Singapore has nurtured a talent pool equipped with the skills needed to excel in emerging fields. Moreover, the country has established research centres and technology hubs that facilitate collaboration between academia and industry, leading to the translation of research outcomes into commercial applications.

4.3 *Fostering a Supportive Business Environment*

Singapore's success also stems from its efforts to create a supportive business environment that encourages entrepreneurship and innovation. The government has implemented pro-business policies, streamlined bureaucratic procedures, and provided incentives to attract investments and foster the growth of start-ups and small and medium-sized enterprises (SMEs). Additionally, Singapore has developed a robust ecosystem of venture capital firms, incubators, and accelerators that provide financial support, mentorship, and networking opportunities to budding entrepreneurs. This supportive ecosystem allows ideas to flourish, facilitates the commercialization of IP, and promotes collaboration between local and international firms.

4.4 *Niche Sector Development for Comparative Advantage*

Singapore's focus on developing niche sectors where it has a comparative advantage has been instrumental in its success. The country has strategically identified and cultivated industries such as biotechnology, advanced manufacturing, and fintech, leveraging its expertise, infrastructure, and regulatory frameworks to become a global leader in these areas. This targeted approach enables Singapore to concentrate resources and expertise, fostering specialization and innovation in sectors where it can excel and create economic value.

GCC countries can similarly identify niche sectors that align with their unique strengths and market opportunities. By concentrating their efforts on these specialized areas, GCC countries can leverage their resources, talent, and competitive advantages to drive innovation, attract investments, and establish themselves as global leaders in these sectors. Singapore's experience could serve as a compelling blueprint for GCC countries seeking to harness intellectual capital and drive economic growth.

4.5 *Embracing a Niche Approach: Unlocking Economic Value in GCC Economies*

A niche approach is probably the best way for the GCC economies. It is important to build the "soft" infrastructure and the capabilities to commercialize and extract economic value, as owning IP assets such as patented technologies is not as critical as the ability to commercialize such assets. To overcome the challenges associated with transitioning to an intellectual capital economy, GCC countries must adopt a focused approach. Recognizing that competing across too broad a front is not feasible against larger economies like the United States and China, GCC economies need to identify and excel in niche sectors. By strategically selecting areas where they possess a comparative advantage, such as renewable energy, agritechnology in harsh hot climates, and smart cities, GCC countries can leverage their unique strengths and regional needs. This focus enables targeted investments, concentrated expertise, and a greater likelihood of success in innovation and commercialization efforts.

4.6 Building Capabilities for Effective Intellectual Property Commercialization in GCC Countries

While creating and owning IP assets is essential, the ability to effectively commercialize and extract economic value from these assets is even more critical. GCC countries must invest in building the capabilities required for successful commercialization. This includes developing a skilled workforce, fostering entrepreneurship, and cultivating robust innovation ecosystems.

Investing in education and vocational training programmes that focus on areas like AI, ML, and technology commercialization will create a talent pool equipped with the knowledge and skills to translate ideas into marketable products and services. Moreover, fostering collaboration between academia, industry, and government is vital to establishing a supportive ecosystem that encourages knowledge transfer, accelerates innovation, and facilitates commercialization.

In the era of the knowledge-based economy, the ability to commercialize IP assets is crucial for driving economic growth and creating sustainable competitive advantages. This requires investments in human capital development, the establishment of robust innovation ecosystems, and the creation of an enabling regulatory environment. By focusing on these critical factors, GCC countries can transform their IP assets into tangible economic outcomes, fostering innovation, and driving their transition from oil-dependent economies to knowledge-driven economies.

4.7 Building Soft Infrastructure for Effective Commercialization

GCC countries need to develop the necessary soft infrastructure, including legal frameworks, supportive policies, and robust innovation ecosystems, to facilitate the commercialization process. This entails creating an environment that encourages entrepreneurship, provides access to funding and resources, and fosters collaboration between academia, industry, and government. By strengthening these elements, GCC countries can overcome the challenges associated with IP commercialization and unlock the full economic potential of their intellectual capital.

4.8 Developing Capabilities for Effective Commercialization

To effectively commercialize IP assets, GCC countries must invest in developing the necessary capabilities. This includes building a skilled workforce equipped with the knowledge and expertise to transform ideas into marketable products and services. Investing in education and vocational training programmes that focus on relevant areas such as AI, data analytics, and technology commercialization will be essential. Additionally, fostering entrepreneurship and providing support mechanisms for start-ups and SMEs will stimulate innovation and enhance the commercialization ecosystem. GCC countries can also establish technology transfer offices and innovation hubs to facilitate the transfer of research outcomes to the marketplace, promoting collaboration between academia and industry.

4.9 Emulating Successful Models for IP Commercialization

GCC countries can learn from successful models of IP commercialization implemented by countries like Singapore. Singapore's emphasis on people and the creation of intellectual capital has driven its commercial success. By consistently investing in education, research and development, and fostering a supportive business environment, Singapore has nurtured a culture of innovation and successfully commercialized IP assets. GCC countries can adopt similar strategies by aligning their investments in education and research with market needs, providing incentives for entrepreneurship, and building strong partnerships between academia, industry, and government. Furthermore, leveraging the experiences and lessons learned from successful IP commercialization initiatives in other countries can help GCC countries develop tailored approaches that suit their unique contexts.

4.10 Investment in Human Capital

Developing the necessary human capital is a critical component of building capabilities for IP commercialization. GCC countries should invest in education and training programmes that nurture a skilled workforce with expertise in innovation, technology transfer, entrepreneurship, and IP management. By equipping individuals with the knowledge and skills required to identify, protect, and commercialize IP assets, these countries can foster a culture of innovation and entrepreneurship. Moreover, fostering collaboration between academia, research institutions, and industry can facilitate the transfer of knowledge and expertise, leading to more effective IP commercialization.

4.11 Building Robust Innovation Ecosystems

Creating a robust innovation ecosystem is essential for facilitating the commercialization of IP assets. GCC countries should establish innovation hubs, research centres, and technology parks that provide the necessary infrastructure, resources, and support for entrepreneurs, start-ups, and researchers. These ecosystems should foster collaboration, knowledge sharing, and networking opportunities to bridge the gap between academia and industry. Furthermore, fostering partnerships between local and international firms can facilitate technology transfer and access to global markets. Additionally, providing funding mechanisms, such as venture capital funds and grants, can fuel innovation and support the commercialization of IP assets.

4.12 Fostering an Enabling Regulatory Environment

An enabling regulatory environment is crucial for promoting and protecting IP rights, facilitating technology transfer, and incentivizing innovation and entrepreneurship. GCC countries should establish comprehensive IP laws and regulations that protect the rights of innovators and provide a clear framework for IP commercialization. Additionally, streamlining bureaucratic procedures, reducing red tape, and creating incentives such as tax breaks or subsidies can encourage businesses to invest in research and development R&D and IP commercialization. Furthermore, fostering a culture of respect for IP rights through awareness campaigns and enforcement measures can create a conducive environment for innovation and encourage local and foreign investments.

4.13 Integrating IP Commercialization with Niche Sector Innovation

To maximize the economic value of IP assets, GCC countries should integrate IP commercialization efforts with their focus on niche sector innovation. By aligning IP strategies with the targeted niche sectors identified earlier, such as renewable energy, agritech in harsh hot climates, and smart cities, GCC countries can create a synergistic approach that accelerates innovation and enhances the commercialization potential of their IP assets. This integration allows for a strategic focus on areas where the countries have unique strengths and competitive advantages, enabling them to differentiate themselves in the global market and capture higher economic value from their IP assets.

Building capabilities for effective IP commercialization is crucial for the economic transformation of GCC countries. By investing in human capital, building robust innovation ecosystems, and fostering an enabling regulatory environment, these countries can unlock the economic potential of their IP assets. By integrating IP commercialization with niche sector innovation, GCC countries can leverage their unique strengths to drive growth, attract investments, and position themselves as leaders in specific industries. Embracing IP commercialization as a strategic imperative will enable GCC countries to harness the full economic value of their intellectual capital and drive sustainable economic development in the knowledge-based economy.

5 Conclusion

The GCC countries recognize the value of AI innovation and the importance of finding new alternative growth sources including the commercialization of IP rights of products and services which are AI-enabled. The GCC countries recognize the value of transforming their economies into knowledge or intellectual capital economies, where knowledge assets, IP, and other intangible assets become the cornerstone of economic growth. However, this transition presents a complex array of challenges that the GCC countries must navigate with strategic foresight.

The transition to the emerging intellectual capital economy, however, will not be an easy one for the GCC countries. The region faces several hurdles that must be overcome to successfully shift from a resource-based to an intellectual capital-based economy. One of the most significant challenges is the need to develop a highly skilled workforce that can drive innovation and create IP. The current education systems in many GCC countries need to be reformed to focus more on STEM (science, technology, engineering, and mathematics) education, critical thinking, and creativity. There is also a need to foster a culture of lifelong learning to ensure that the workforce remains adaptable to the rapidly changing demands of the global economy.

Building an intellectual capital economy requires robust institutional and legal frameworks to protect IP rights and encourage innovation. While some progress has been made in this regard, there is still a need for stronger enforcement of IP laws, the establishment of more research and development institutions, and the creation of incentives for private sector investment in innovation. The shift from an oil-dependent economy to one based on intellectual capital also requires a cultural transformation. This includes changing societal attitudes towards entrepreneurship, innovation, and risk-taking. In many GCC countries, there is still a preference for stable, government jobs over entrepreneurship and private sector careers. Encouraging a culture of innovation and entrepreneurship is crucial for the success of this transition.

While diversification is necessary, GCC countries also need to identify and specialize in niche areas where they can build a competitive advantage. This might involve focusing on sectors such as renewable energy, financial technology (fintech), AI, and biotechnology, where the region can leverage its existing strengths and resources. Developing expertise in these areas will require significant investment in research and development R&D, infrastructure, and human capital. Even with a strong focus on innovation and knowledge creation, the GCC countries will need to develop capabilities to effectively commercialize intellectual capital. This involves building ecosystems that support start-ups and SMEs, facilitating access to venture capital, and fostering collaborations between academia, industry, and government. The ability to translate IP into commercially viable products and services will be key to extracting economic value from knowledge assets. The experience of Singapore offers valuable lessons for the GCC countries as they seek to transition to an intellectual capital economy. Like the GCC, Singapore faced significant challenges in diversifying its economy away from a reliance on trade and manufacturing. However, through strategic planning, investment in education and research and development, and the creation of a conducive business environment, Singapore has successfully transformed into a global hub for innovation and knowledge-based industries.

Key aspects of Singapore's success that could serve as a blueprint for the GCC include the focus on AI Innovation and Intellectual Capital Strategy. With its limited resources, Singapore has identified innovation, especially AI innovation and intellectual property monetization, as a new growth driver. Singapore's success in commercializing its intellectual capital is partly due to its vibrant innovation ecosystems, which include partnerships between government, academia, and the private sector. The GCC countries should focus on building similar ecosystems that support start-ups, encourage collaboration, and provide access to financing and markets. Singapore has consistently prioritized education and skills development, with a strong emphasis on STEM fields, vocational training, and continuous learning. The GCC countries can emulate this approach by investing in educational reforms that equip their populations with the skills needed for the knowledge economy. Singapore's well-established legal frameworks for intellectual property protection and business regulation have created a stable environment for innovation and entrepreneurship. The GCC can learn from Singapore's example by strengthening their legal systems and creating clear, transparent regulations that encourage investment and innovation. Singapore identified key sectors where it could excel, such as biotechnology, financial services, and digital innovation, and directed resources towards building competitive advantages in these areas. The GCC countries should similarly identify niche sectors aligned with their strengths and develop targeted strategies to excel in these areas.

The GCC economies are at a critical juncture as they seek to transition from a reliance on oil revenues to becoming intellectual capital-driven economies. While the challenges are significant, the potential rewards are substantial. By focusing on education, building robust legal frameworks, encouraging cultural shifts towards innovation, and learning from successful models like Singapore, the GCC can navigate the complexities of this transition and secure a prosperous future driven by intellectual capital.

References

Akkas, E., & Altiparmak, S. O. (2023). Innovation, Technology Transfer, and Endogenous Growth in the GCC Countries. In M. M. Rahman & A. Al-Azm (eds) *Social Change in the Gulf Region. Gulf Studies* (8), Springer, Singapore. https://doi.org/10.1007/978-981-19-7796-1_24

Baker, R. (2011, February 11). Nokia to partner with Microsoft under new structure. https://www.marketingweek.com/nokia-to-partner-with-microsoft-under-new-structure/

Commercialization of Artificial Intelligence, National Science Board | Science & Engineering Indicators | NSB-2020-5 (2020). https://www.google.com/search?q=commercialization+of+AI+innovation&rlz=1C1CHBF_enSG918SG918&oq=commercialization+of+AI+innovation&gs_lcrp=EgZjaHJvbWUyBggAEEUYOTIHCAEQIRigAdIBCTY2ODNqMGoxNagCCLACAQ&sourceid=chrome&ie=UTF-8

Computing Research Institute. (2024). *Hamad bin Khalifa University (Qatar)*. https://www.hbku.edu.qa/en/qcri

Google Cloud. (2024). Turn speech into text using Google AI. https://cloud.google.com/speech-to-text

Masdar. (2016. December 4). Masdar City's PRT System Celebrates Milestone with 2 Millionth Passenger. https://masdar.ae/en/news/newsroom/masdar-citys-prt-system-celebrates-milestone-with-2-millionth-passenger

Merikanto, J. (2024). Monetizing AI—Disruptive Shifts in Business Models and Monetization. https://www.linkedin.com/pulse/monetizing-ai-disruptive-shiftsbusiness-models-jari-merikanto-au2kf/

Ministry of Digital Development and Information (Singapore). (2024, March 1). Artificial Intelligence (AI) Initiatives Launched to uplift Singapore's Economic Potential. https://www.mddi.gov.sg/media-centre/press-releases/ai-initiatives-launched-to-uplift-sg-economic-potential/

Noon Academy. (2024). https://www.learnatnoon.com.

Ocean Tomo. (2020, March 30). Intangible Asset Market Value Study. https://oceantomo.com/intangible-asset-market-value-study/

Ross, C., & Swetlitz, I. (2017, September 5). IBM pitched its Watson supercomputer as a revolution in cancer care. https://www.statnews.com/2017/09/05/watson-ibm-cancer/

Saidi, N. (2024, May 9). Economic Diversification is the GCC's Top Priority. Middle East Council on Global Affairs. https://mecouncil.org/blog_posts/economic-diversification-is-the-gccs-top-priority/#:~:text=Robust%20and%20extensive%20economic%20diversification,macroeconomic%20stability%20and%20job%20creation

Saudi Authority for Intellectual Property. (2024, June). The Intangible Assets in the Kingdom of Saudi Arabia 2023. https://externalportal-backend-production.saip.gov.sa/sites/default/files/2024-06/The%20Intangible%20Assets%20in%20the%20Kingdom%20of%20Saudi%20Arabia%202023.pdf

'Singapore IP Strategy (SIPS) 2030', Intellectual Property Office of Singapore (2025, March 25), singapore-ip-strategy-report-2030-18May2021.pdf

Smart Nation Singapore. (2023, December 4). National Artificial Intelligence Strategy 2 to uplift Singapore's Social and Economic Potential. https://www.smartnation.gov.sg/media-hub/press-releases/04122023/

'Understanding intellectual capital, *Microsoft*' (2024). https://www.microsoft.com/en-us/microsoft-365-life-hacks/organization/intellectual-capital#:~:text=Unlike%20tangible%20assets%2C%20such%20as,stay%20ahead%20of%20the%20competition

Westgarth, T., Chen Wen, H. G., & Heath, R. (2022, May). *Understanding UK Artificial Intelligence R&D Commercialisation and The Role of Standards.* https://oxfordinsights.com/projects/understanding-ai-rd-commercialisation

World Bank (2023, November 22). *Economic Diversification Efforts Paying Off in GCC Region but More Reforms Needed.* https://www.worldbank.org/en/news/press-release/2023/11/22/economic-diversification-efforts-payingoff-in-gcc-region-but-more-reforms-needed

CHAPTER 9

Distributed Ledger Technology as an Innovative Collective Management Tool for the GCC Music Industry

Zi Yang and Anthony O'Dwyer

1 Introduction

The Gulf Cooperation Council (GCC) region has become an increasingly popular place for global tourism. However, according to Forbes Middle East (2024), despite the region's strong economic position, only one singer from the GCC is listed among the top 10 Arabic musicians. In this sense, the GCC musicians' world impact is limited. It has been said that music and art are key to society and culture. For DJ and musician Gilbert Galindo:

Z. Yang (✉)
School of Law, Queen's University Belfast, Belfast, Northern Ireland, UK
e-mail: zi.yang@qub.ac.uk

A. O'Dwyer
School of Law and Humanities SETU, South East Technological University (SETU), Waterford City, County Waterford, Ireland
e-mail: anthony.odwyer@setu.ie

N. Naim et al. (eds.), *Intellectual Property and Innovation*, The Political Economy of the Middle East,
https://doi.org/10.1007/978-981-96-4020-1_9

> Art and music are basic human functions. Humankind and art cannot function without one another. … [t]he interaction with sound is unavoidable, … [p]eople have always found music significant in their lives, whether for enjoyment … emotional response, … or creating. (Galinado, 2009)

The continued development of the music industry is therefore crucial, not only to the well-being of GCC creators but also to the social and cultural fabric of the region. Building on the authors' academic and industry experience in the global music industry, this chapter proposes using distributed ledger technology (DLT) as a possible addition to traditional collective management organisation (CMO) structures, which currently allow artists to license their work, manage their revenue, and promote the ethno-musicological importance of the region.

CMOs are organisations authorised to manage the copyright and related rights of rights-holders, whether these be musicians, songwriters, publishers or recording labels (EU Directive 2016, Part 1, 2). Authors assign CMOs their copyright and in return CMOs collect revenues from the exploitation (radio play, public performance, etc.) of the author's work in jurisdictions around the world. CMOs are intrinsic to the workings of the industry as it would be impossible for rights-holders to access the full extent of their revenues otherwise. Nevertheless, these organisations face ongoing criticism for a perceived lack of transparency, high transaction costs and a failure in certain situations to pay artists (Tresise et al., 2018, 144). Accordingly, there may be scope for technical and structural improvement via DLT.

DLT has been described as a '… technical protocol to create a secure, transparent ledger that reports transactions to everyone within the network' (Tresise et al., 2018, 144; see also Wright, 2019). In this decentralised system, information is shared across the system in real time and verified by users. Therefore, it provides an alternative model for financing and management of intellectual property rights.

This chapter argues that a public distributed ledger could resolve many of these issues, foremost the transparency and cost elements via self-executing smart contracts. It provides an additional tool to the aforementioned CMO model, and in turn provides musicians with improved control, transparency and access to the Web 3.0 ecosystem. As the technological innovation is still at its early stage, there are legitimate concerns over DLT energy consumption and environmental impact. But attempts have been made to advance the technology and increase efficiency.

Moreover, employing DLT in music management is a meaningful usage of the technology which could benefit musicians and the Web 3.0 movement. Based on lessons from the financial sector, the chapter then highlights that traditional CMOs shall play a role in leading this innovation to overcome technological barriers and reduce fraud risk, while emphasising that musicians shall be treated fairly for sustainable development (Chomsky et al., 2017). Overall, this chapter acts as an exemplar for meaningful engagement with distributed ledge technology across the world. As an energy-rich region with a rich Arab music heritage, GCC is in a unique position for pioneering this innovation.

2 Recent Developments in the Music Industry

As an attempt to overcome CMOs' limits, a Silicon Valley start-up, InMusik, provided one 'proof-of-copyright' service to musicians. For a small fee, users could access the InMusik portal and create a hash that represented their musical work. The hash was unique to the uploaded piece of music which represented the artist's contribution to a collaborative or solo work. By combining the unique hash number or identifier with a timestamp, artists could prove that they created X work at Y time. And if the work had been altered in any way, then when the hash was run again, it would produce a different alphanumerical string. This service allowed musicians to verify their contribution to a sound recording or song.

CMOs may be unable to pay musicians royalties where their work has not been formally or accurately registered and therefore cannot be identified. A system based on DLT/blockchain technology has the capacity to record all of the aforementioned transactions, thus making it easier to trace the origin of works that are later designated as 'orphan works' (EU Intellectual Property Office Observatory, n.d.). Accordingly, musicians found InMusik's service valuable as it created a space where artists internationally could collaborate on new and innovative music without being limited by time and geographic location.

That said, musicians were initially concerned that their creative input might be misappropriated by other collaborators, which raised the question of how they might protect their work. Anyone familiar with the creative process will know that as time passes it becomes more difficult to accurately identify where one's own contribution ends and a collaborator's contribution begins. The timestamping service provided the peace of mind necessary to allow creativity on the platform to flourish. For just

€1/$1, creators could timestamp what their contribution was at a specific time. Where disputes later arose, a mediator could run the hashing algorithm to establish each creator's contribution. If the algorithm returned a different alphanumerical sequence to the original hash, then this indicated that the file/song, etc. had been modified in some way. It was then for the expert witness/mediator to determine how much the additional contribution actually made to the song by comparing each collaborator's timestamped track (or song version). Was the contribution an entirely new chorus or a simple flourish on a melody? While the work of the mediator was critical to the process, the timestamping not only provided the initial peace of mind to create but also an accurate reminder of what one's contribution was despite what one might later have thought to be the case.

Having provided one case example of the potential benefits of a DLT model for CMOs, the following section further elaborates on the impact of a number of DLT systems with disparate applications.

3 DLT Addresses Existing Problems Within CMOs

Against the need to reform collective management in the music industry, DLT has the potential to increase transparency and information accuracy for music collective management in Web 3.0.

3.1 DLT and Transparency

The most well-known DLT system, Bitcoin, was first revealed in late 2008 in response to public anger over lack of transparency in the traditional banking system (Bondarev, 2020). Thus, studying the mechanism of Bitcoin is important for understanding DLT's potential in increasing transparency. As Chen et al. (2018) recognised, since the foundation laid out by Bitcoin is followed by other blockchain innovations, including smart contracts, understanding Bitcoin is also crucial for understanding the wider Web 3.0 ecosystem.

The traditional centralised payment system relies heavily on commercial banks as information intermediaries. On one hand, banks record, verify and execute payment information on behalf of their customers (Ali et al., 2014). On the other hand, banks also take deposits from the public and then lend those deposits to industries and households (Stiglitz, 2010). During the lending process, banks gather crucial information on currency demands and supplies, including who needs the money and at what cost.

Such information is shared with central banks, so the latter can stabilise prices by adjusting banknote supply and interest rates. In other words, this traditional layout concentrates information, wealth and power in banks. Subsequently, when the financial crisis hit in 2007/2008, central banks and governments were forced to bail out commercial banks to save the economy (Fitzpatrick, 2016).

Against this background, the concept of Bitcoin was first revealed in late 2008 by an online figure who went by the name Satoshi Nakamoto, a Japanese equivalent of 'John Smith'. Each Bitcoin is a chain of digital signatures (Wright, 2019). When transferring a Bitcoin to another user, the payer adds his/her unique signature to the chain. This process takes place through the Central Processing Unit (CPU) of the computer. The CPU is the processor in the compute that executes instructions of a computer program (Li et al., 2019). After verifying a transaction, one CPU can add one block to the chain. This block generated is known as Proof-of-Work. Once added to the Bitcoin, this block cannot be changed. Since transactions are publicly announced, the longest chain is verified by the most Bitcoin users and assumed to be the first and valid transaction. Therefore, this mechanism provides transparency to everyone connected in the network. The first CPU to add the block is rewarded with a new Bitcoin for verifying the transaction. This reward motivates more users to participate in the verification process, which subsequently makes the blockchain longer and Bitcoins safer. Thus, the Bitcoin payment system is a peer-to-peer support network, where information is shared in public.

In addition to transparency, blockchain also overcomes the centralised system's inefficiency in detecting errors (Wright, 2019). In September 2018, Deliveroo, the online food delivery platform, experienced an error on its app (Knapman, 2018). Even though Deliveroo was receiving and processing information as usual, the app misinformed customers. Based on this incorrect information, some customers placed multiple orders and were charged multiple times. This example suggests that centralised systems can be inefficient in detecting errors. Alternatively, in the Bitcoin system, transactions are announced publicly, where only the longest chain is accepted by all users as a valid transaction. Therefore, parties to a transaction (customers and restaurants; musicians and fans) could directly confirm orders, and therefore avoid intermediary error. For music management, such accuracy reduces the risk of musicians not getting paid properly due to inaccurate registration.

3.2 *DLT and the Web 3.0 Ecosystem*

Following the basic principle established in Bitcoin, Ethereum (ETH) further advances blockchain technology. The concept of Ethereum was first created in 2013 by Vitalik Buterin, a 19-year-old Russian-Canadian programmer (TechCrunch, 2018). After developers weakened Buterin's character in an online game, Buterin started asking the crucial question: Why should big tech companies control the Internet? In Dhillon, Metcalf and Hooper's words (2021), Ethereum represents the transfer from Web 2.0 to Web 3.0. During Web 2.0, people's social interactions with each other on the Internet created huge commercial profits. Ethereum asks a crucial question about Web 2.0: Why should big tech companies profit from other people's creative work? Ethereum believes that the distribution system is unfair and so long as people rely on the platforms as intermediaries, the unfair exploitations will continue (Fridman, 2021). While the way in which DLT could provide an alternative distribution model, hence challenging music platforms' (e.g. Spotify) dominance, will be not be discussed here, this section perceives the smart contract as a transparent collective management tool embedded in the innovative Web 3.0 ecosystem.

Instead of simply sharing information with the public, such as the blockchain system discussed earlier, Ethereum further opens its code, and hence, shares knowledge on DLT design with the public (TechCrunch, 2017). Ethereum proposes a de-centralised solution, by opening its code and allowing the public to create their own de-centralised apps (DApps). Such DApps are created via smart contracts. A well-known analogy for smart contracts is a vending machine (TechCrunch, 2017). Each vending machine stores products, such as bottled water or snacks. The machine is pre-programmed to give customers the selected product after payment is made. Similarly for smart contracts, no agency is required to execute the transaction, which could reduce the agency fee for musicians.

The same automatic process applies to smart contracts. Each smart contract is programmed to execute itself when a pre-determined condition is made. The codes of existing smart contracts are all open. Thus, the technology barrier to creating a DApp is low. Therefore, the public as content creators can set up their own vending machine-like DApp based on existing DApps' codes at a relatively low cost. Through the example of Steem, the following paragraphs also highlight the user's increased capacity to ditch poorly managed platforms.

Launched in 2016, Steem is a distributed ledger alternative for social media platforms like YouTube (O'Neal, 2020). The network adopted the Proof-of-Stake verification method, over which the creator, Ned Scott, had significant voting rights. In February 2020, Scott decided to transfer his right to an investment firm, the Tron. The takeover was resisted by some Steem users. Eventually, the commercial takeover was complete. However, since all Steem's code was open resource, those against the takeover created a duplicate of Steem. Subsequently, users were able to move to new Hive at little cost. Therefore, opening all codes on Ethereum empowers users and content creators. To regain customers in this emerging market, CMOs should treat musicians with fairness.

Nevertheless, the chapter recognises that, people's capacity to interpret smart contracts and other cryptographic data still varies. As will be demonstrated in Sect. 5, this new knowledge gap is abused by some DLT developers to exploit novice users. Against this background, this chapter argues that established CMOs could lead the innovation to reduce musicians' exposure to online fraud risk, while emphasising the need to treat musicians fairly to maintain the market.

Furthermore, as demonstrated in Sect. 2, for music collective management, a major flaw of the World Intellectual Property Organization (WIPO) verification system is that the system was moot without a wider ecosystem. In contrast, DApps have great potential to be implemented across wider areas in the public's life (Park & Li, 2021). One restriction for smart contracts being widely adopted in the real world is that smart contracts can only process digital codes (Chainlink, n.d.). Thus, if a smart contract states the CMO should pay musicians for using their music, the contract still relies on someone (an oracle) to translate the information into the digital code, before triggering the payment. Then, the advantages of smart contracts, such as reducing human error, counterparties' default risk and even de-centralisation, are diminished. Ethereum solves this problem via chainlinks (Lex Clips, n.d.). Chainlinks can be perceived as a blockchain of oracles. When importing real-world information into the smart contract, the information will first be translated into codes. Then, chainlinks verify the information through a distributed ledger. Similar to Bitcoin, the longest block is the most valid information. This information is then passed on to the smart contract. Through this mechanism, smart contracts can bridge the digital world and the real world while maintaining de-centralisation. This innovation is the foundation of

Web 3.0, a metaverse where people live in a mixture of the real world and digital world.

Building on this argument, open-source coding can reduce the barrier for musicians to be involved in music colleague management such as peer-support networks. While some may argue that a live DLT system which allows musicians to see all transactions relevant to their work is unrealistic, de-centralised applications (DApps) can employ smart contracts to streamline and improve the system's performance. In this sense, blockchain may provide a more suitable framework for high-volume, transparent, accurate and both time-sensitive and non-time-sensitive CMO management tools. In this sense, this research provides a template for the wider adoption of DLT in management.

Nevertheless, there are potential concerns for content creators with open-source coding. While the underlying code of a blockchain platform is protected under the *Berne Convention for the Protection of Literary and Artistic Works* and other international treaties as an authorial work, these organisations may decide to adopt the Creative Commons licensing approach and offer users a free licence to use this code in limited ways (Creative Commons, n.d.). Currently, GCC signatories to the Berne Convention include all GCC member states, namely, Bahrain, Kuwait, Oman, Qatar, Saudi Arabia and the United Arab Emirates. Bahrain implemented the Convention in 1997, Oman in 1999, Qatar in 2000, the UAE and Saudi Arabia in 2004, and Kuwait in 2014 (IPRO, n.d.-a, n.d.-b, n.d.-c, n.d.-d, n.d.-e, n.d.-f). How the GCC should respond to open-source coding is, however, beyond the remit of this current chapter.

A typical Creative Commons licence states that the use must not be for profit and must attribute the work to the original author; however, blockchain companies are not limited by these agreements. There is, however, a security concern in building a 'trusted' hashing system, blockchain, Di-fi or DAO network on code created by others. In many ways, relying on such 'public code' is like giving everyone access to one's house keys; trust in the other users/creators on the network is a necessity, and that may not be possible or desirable.

Furthermore, for ordinary users, announcing real-world information publicly through blockchain could cause privacy concerns. In the science fiction novel *Snow Crash*, this privacy concern in the digital world is expressed when the main character, Y. T., is racing in the metaverse:

> It takes half a second. They are scanning the many bar codes mounted on her chest. They are finding out who she is. The Mafia now knows everything about Y.T.—where she lives, what she does, her eye colour, credit record, ancestry, and blood type. (Stephenson, 2011)

The metaverse imagined in this 1990s book is now a burgeoning reality in the Metaverse proposed by Facebook (Meta, n.d.). How users' privacy ought to be protected in the Metaverse is already an important topic for researchers and regulators.

To conclude, DLT has many potential applications in the intellectual property sphere from creating registries such as the InMusik example above, to licensing and digital rights management. Blockchain and smart contracts can be used to increase transparency and accuracy in collective management. In return, being able to provide such meaningful services would then encourage more people to engage with blockchain, which benefits the development of the technology (Bonadio & Sganga, 2024).

4 Addressing the Energy Consumption and Environmental Concern over DLT

Despite its potentials, using DLT in collective management can be slow. Consequently, verifying transactions via blockchain can be inefficient. Where a traditional payment system like Visa handles over 300 million transactions per day (Statista, 2021a, 2021b), the Bitcoin system only has 300,000 transactions (Bitcoin.org, n.d.). As all information is announced publicly and the valid transaction should contain the longest blockchain, the Bitcoin system can take an average of 10 minutes to confirm a transaction (Parkin, 2020). In this sense, the DLT-based Bitcoin system is significantly slower than the traditional payment system. Therefore, even though transparency in the Bitcoin payment system can avoid centralised errors as in the Deliveroo example, the Bitcoin payment system needs more than two days to confirm Deliveroo users' daily orders. In other words, users can only get their lunch tomorrow or later. Thus, the Bitcoin payment system is inefficient. This inefficiency also means blockchain can be extremely energy consuming (Bondarev, 2020). In 2021, China banned crypto, criticising crypto mining as excessively energy consuming without serving a meaningful economic purpose or meeting the country's net zero plan (National Development and Reform Commission, 2021). This chapter recognises these legitimate concerns but justifies using DLT in collective management from the following three perspectives.

4.1 *Ongoing Technological Updates to Increase Efficiency*

Several changes have been made with the Ethereum system to improve efficiency, which echoes the public's rising consciousness around the environment (Ethereum.org, 2024). To begin with, Ethereum puts unverified transactions automatically in a pool (Ethereum.org, 2024). Inside the pool, transactions are allocated into blocks. Instead of verifying each individual transaction, Ethereum miners verify blocks. The blocks are connected as a chain. The chain increases efficiency, thereby reducing energy consumption of running the blockchain.

Furthermore, Ethereum is also gradually replacing Proof-of-Work with Proof-of-Stake (Ethereum.org, 2024). Instead of allowing everyone to mine ETH, Proof-of-Stake restricts miners' mining capacity based on the ETH they hold. The rationale of the decision is that, when more users try to mine, the difficulty of producing a Proof-of-Work is increased to avoid inflation. However, the increased difficulty also means more energy is consumed for verifying the transaction, which leads to serious power supply and environmental concerns. Ethereum tries to mitigate the environmental problem by restricting miners' mining capacity. In the Proof-of-Stake system, one miner can only mine a percentage of the transactions based on the ETH he holds. Therefore, the system is less likely to be overcrowded and forced to increase the difficulty. Thus, this technology could reduce energy consumption in blockchain payment systems.

Nevertheless, transactions still take computer power to process. This leads to a crucial concept in Ethereum, namely, 'gas' (Ethereum.org, 2024). The term is an analogy for petrol/gas consumed in physical transportation. In Ethereum's Web 3.0 ecosystem, one needs Ethereum gas for digital transactions. In the real world, gas price is affected by supply and demand, while gas consumption is related to the speed of delivery and the weight of the goods. Similarly, in Ethereum, gas price is calculated automatically via ETH wallets based on supply and demand, and the gas required for digital transactions is priced based on the speed of the transaction and the size of the smart contract. Interestingly, to get the transaction verified faster, parties to a transaction are also encouraged to add a tip for the miners. To properly calculate the suitable tip, most wallets add the tip automatically. Interestingly, this story resembles Sandel's discussion on the fast pass in New York City (2012). Against heavy traffic, New York City offers several fast passes. Originally, the fast passes were only open to buses. However, in recent years, one can buy the right to use the fast pass. Therefore, instead of waiting in line for hours, those with more money can cut the journey short. Sandel criticises fast passes as they enhance money's dominance in the modern society. Essentially, fast passes undermine the value of equality in the traditional first-come-first-serve system. The chapter has no intention to simplify the moral dilemma involved in DLT innovation. Rather, aims to raise awareness of the moral debates in adopting DLT.

4.2 A Meaningful Innovation

In 2021, Park and Li built a direct connection between distributed ledger technology and morality in studying global supply chain management. They argue that digital ledger technology provides a reliable and traceable tool to store and share environmental and social impact issues related to economic activities, including how pollution generated during production flows into the environment and how the suppliers treat workers and local communities. In traditional contracts, information is exclusively for direct contract parties. Yet, distributed ledger technology allows environmental and social information to be shared with all participants in real time, thus allowing the public to make conscious and informed decisions. Against this background, Park and Li suggest that distributed ledger technology can play a crucial role in achieving the United Nation's sustainable development goals.

In the current market, DLT-based payment innovations like Bitcoin are largely reduced to an asset for financial speculation. As discussed in Sect. 3, the Bitcoin network rewards the first one verifying the transaction with new Bitcoin. The incentive mechanism is known as mining. As revealed in *Commercial Bank PrivatBank v Kolomoisky* [2021] EWHC 403 (Ch), mining requires extremely high investment and energy. In this case, the bank accused a Ukraine oligarch, Igor Kolomoisky, of fraud for his Bitcoin assets disclosure. Kolomoisky had a significant business interest in several Bitcoin mining companies across the world. In one Bitcoin investment in Georgia, Kolomoisky directly invested around $50 million in a Bitcoin farm, another major shareholder of which was a company indirectly associated with him, Georgian Manganese LLC. Personally, Kolomoisky was expected to receive the lesser value of 50,000 Bitcoin or USD 1 billion in

January 2021 from his direct investment. However, the farm was closed in September 2019, with a total of 3533.3 Bitcoin mined. In this case, DLT is not used to increase transparency in the banking market, but as an asset for speculation. Furthermore, as Ngetich (2020) disclosed, listed companies like Fintech Group, Square and MicroStrategy are using Bitcoin as their reserve assets, with expectations that the value of Bitcoin will increase. Whereas Tesla, the electric car manufacturer, accepted Bitcoin as a payment option shortly into 2020, making the company and its owner Elon Musk major holders of Bitcoin (Libich & Lenten, 2021). Institutional investors' dominance suggests that it is impossible for individual musicians to lead such an experiment. Subsequently, Sect. 5 argues that CMOs shall lead the experiment of using DLT in music collective management due to their established financial foundation.

For regional collective music management, the transaction volume may not necessarily need be as time-sensitive, although a more efficient system would ultimately be preferred by musicians. Hooijer and Baloyi (2016) note that a single radio station transmitting music for half of its on-air time will play over eighty thousand tracks in a single year. Accordingly, a single sound recording—the recorded version of the song—may have multiple participating rights-holders—writers, musicians, arrangers, labels and publishers—in the distribution of royalties. The authors note that with less than a dozen licensed radio stations, a CMO will have to process millions of transactions in any one distribution cycle. While Ethereum may be better suited to the fast distribution of royalties by CMOs, better suited DLTs could be tailor-made for this segment of the music industry.

This chapter's proposal of using Blockchain for collective management in the music industry overcomes commercial agency risks under the traditional CMO structure. Using DLT as a collective management tool is a meaningful innovation as it provides musicians a cost-efficient tool to register and distribute their creative work. Therefore, the carbon emission generated during the process is justifiable. By sharing information with musicians in real time, and allowing musicians to be involved in information verification, blockchain technology has the potential to change the power dynamic between the CMO (agent) and the musician (principal).

4.3 The GCC

Finally, while this chapter's discussion of DLT is largely applicable across the board, the GCC is in a unique position to test this innovation. On one hand, the GCC is an energy-rich region with some of the world's lowest carbon content fuels (Al-Sarihi, 2023). According to the International Renewable Energy Agency (2016), GCC proven oil reserves are estimated at 493 billion barrels, representing 29% of the global total, and GCC proven natural gas reserves are estimated at 42 trillion cubic metres, representing 22% of the global total. In contrast, China's decision to ban crypto is also related to its own energy position. Unlike the GCC, China has a significant reliance on coal-fired power, which results in high carbon dioxide (Kao et al., 2024). Therefore, the GCC has a strategic advantage in mitigating the environmental concerns over DLT.

On the other hand, as Mansfeld and Winckler (2008) pointed out, all GCC member states have developed plans to expand their tourism sectors to diversify the oil-based economy since the 21st century. Some of the most famous projects include the Dubai emirate, the Qatar FIFA World Cup 2022, the World Aquatics Championships in 2023 in Qatar, and the Red Sea Project in Saudi Arabia (Saleh et al., 2022). During the process, the GCC member states have emphasised hospitality infrastructure (Farooq et al., 2023; Farooq et al., 2024). However, in addition to massive airport expansions and hotel buildings, GCC member states also benefit from the unique Arab music culture (Plenckers, 2021). As the WIPO (2021) recognised, such culture, including local music and performance, is also a rich resource for the development of the tourism sector, and the effective management of this creative industry is vital to the success of the region's branding strategy.

Yet, the current IP and royalty distribution system historically and concurrently ignores and discriminates against the creation of community art by indigenous communities around the world, including GCC member states, where the single or co-author-centric model of Western Europe (Anglo-American), rather than the collective authorship 'way' of communities in the global south, for example, is not adequately rewarded, remunerated or credited (Simmone, 2019). These systems or ways of creating are effectively round blocks in square holes, pariahs, anathema to Western IP systems, or more comparatively, the theft of art historically—see the 'Elgin Marbles', a collection of Greek architecture looted by Lord Elgin's agents from the Parthenon in Athens, and sold to the British Museum in the early 1800s—and arguably continued by the Berne Convention and its progenies in the way art is valued and what art is considered worthy of protection by an Anglo-European-centric IP system (Hicks, 2020; Riley, 2020). Pioneering DLT music management could give the GCC an opportunity to support local talent against such adversity.

In summary, DLT can be slow in verifying transactions, which causes legitimate concerns over energy consumption and environmental impact. However, these concerns are justifiable, as the technology has been advanced to increase efficiency; using DLT in music collective management is a meaningful engagement of the technology, instead of speculative mining. As an energy-rich region, GCC has the advantage to experiment with blockchain technology in the sphere of music management and enhance cultural tourism in the region.

5 Implementation

Finally, how should the GCC music industry engage with DLT in collective management? Based on earlier experiments in other sectors, this section unveils the practical and moral complexity of engaging with DLT. It subsequently proposes that traditional CMOs take the lead in the innovation and avoid crypto speculation.

In September 2021, Netflix launched the thrilling drama series *Squid Game*, a story about hundreds of cash-strapped people enrolled in deadly games (Netflix, n.d.). While failing the games would cost one's life, the final survivor takes home 45.6 million Korean won (approximately £28.2 million). The drama became a worldwide sensation, with over 142 million household views globally (Rushe, 2021). Inspired by this drama, in October 2021, a crypto, SQUID, was launched, promising holders the opportunity to play the Squid Game online and profit (BBC News, 2021). Such launching is known as an initial coin offering (ICO) (UK Financial Conduct Authority, FCA, 2019). As the recognised ICO is highly risky, but if properly regulated can be used as an alternative funding tool for new and innovative business models. The FCA has been experimenting with ICO regulation via its regulatory sandbox programme (HM Treasury, 2021). The following analysis highlights the ambiguity within the contractual parties' rights and obligations in the IPO market, which is relevant to the GCC member states' financial regulators and legal researchers.

Shortly after the ICO, the SQUID price jumped from less than a cent to over £2000 per coin (BBC News, 2021). Later, as Biance disclosed, all money from SQUID sale was transferred into a wallet called 'Squid Token Rug Pull 2' (Scarcity Studios, 2021). 'Rug pull' is a scam in the crypto industry where crypto developers abandon a project and run away with investors' money. Through the example of the SQUID scam, the following paragraphs highlight an online fraud risk that musicians may face in

DLT collective management. The chapter argues that to reduce this fraud risk, DLT-based collective management should be led by established CMOs.

In the five-page whitepaper, the developer claimed that SQUID will allow users to play thrilling games as in the TV series *Squid Game*, although less deadly, and survivors will be rewarded with more SQUID. This claim is problematic in several aspects:

To begin with, by associating itself with *Squid Game*, SQUID developers (n. d.) created a false sense of connection between the crypto and the drama. Take the BBC report (BBC News (World), 2021) as an example:

> If you're a fan wanting to express your devotion to the hit Korean Netflix show Squid Game - well, there's a cryptocurrency for that.
>
> Gamers have created an online version of the programme, for which you need the Squid cryptocurrency to play.

To make the situation even worse, while the report used the words 'have created', the online game was merely a proposal. No actual game was developed. In the absence of credible information sources, users may wrongly believe that the crypto is associated with Netflix and hence underestimate the risk that the developers could not or would not deliver the proposed online game. Traditionally, this misrepresentation is less likely to happen because contractual parties would need to identify each other. But, instead of a traditional contract, SQUID at least promised to offer digital content (games) to consumers via the de-centralised Binance market, where sellers are kept anonymous. The chapter has no intension to criticise the media's reports on SQUID. Rather, by analysing the event, the chapter demonstrates musicians' potential risk exposure to online misinformation and fraud in the complicated de-centralised channels.

In addition to the anonymous counterparty, a crucial fact about SQUID and covered by the smart contract is the fact that SQUID was not transferable. As the FCA (2019) warned, the terms of ICOs may vary dramatically from crypto to crypto. For instance, SQUID, if actually developed, would have given holders the right to play the exclusive online game without the ability to re-sell. Yet, another smart contract-backed crypto, Gemini Dollar (n.d.), promises to safeguard the value of the crypto with reserved US dollars. Trying to do something different is essential for each new crypto to attract users. Therefore, against the diversity in DLT, it is crucial that buyers do understand their rights and obligations under smart contracts.

Against this backdrop, the SQUID scam should not be easily dismissed as a single event, or an accident caused by social media. Instead, the scam should be studied as a wakeup call for financial regulators and legal researchers to address transparency in smart contracts.

This is not to say smart contracts should be replaced by traditional contracts. As Savelyev (2017) indicated, computer codes largely follow the pattern that if Y happens, Z follows, which is the same logic as a contract. Furthermore, as demonstrated in Sect. 3, smart contracts can reduce human errors by automatic executions and hence can increase certainty in contractual relationships. The problem here is that the absence of a traditional contract hides crucial information through complex codes, which render investors unable to assess risks. As Lord Denning ruled in J Spurling Ltd v Bradshaw [1956] EWCA Civ 3:

> I quite agree that the more unreasonable a clause is, the greater the notice which must be given of it. Some clauses which I have seen would need to be printed in red ink on the face of the document with a red hand pointing to it before the notice could be held to be sufficient.

The ruling is over 60 years old. Yet, for musicians to truly benefit from DLT collective management, smart contracts must be designed in a user-friendly way to accommodate people without much knowledge in computer science (Palladino, 2019).

Such a trick is not news. Take the financial market as an example. As Thompson pointed out, even though people speak English when trading financial derivatives, the conventional meanings of the words are changed dramatically as if it is a different language. Jargon hides and even misleads investors as to risks involved in derivatives products. Except in the crypto market, the jargon is computer codes. Thus, the lack of transparency in the UK crypto market is just a modern example of this historical problem.

In *The Age of Surveillance Capitalism*, Zuboff (2019) also highlighted the difference between technology and surveillance capitalism through the example of the Google search engine's retention of user information. In 2009, the public first became aware that Google collects and store users' search histories for an indefinite period. When questioned about this practice, Google's CEO at that time, Eric Schmidt, claimed that 'the reality is that search engines including Google do retain this information for some time.' The statement sounded as if retaining users' information was an inevitable natural result of technological innovation. In other words, the public was ignorant to even question such practices.

Yet, as Zuboff pointed out, retaining users' information is a deliberate decision of surveillance capitalism. By designing the search engine to retain users' information, Google acquires a database for studying users' behaviours, which then allows Google to influence users for commercial gain. The same logic applies to smart contracts. The lack of transparency in smart contracts is not an inevitable natural result of technology innovation. Rather, it is a strategy to render meme investors incapable of assessing risks involved in the transaction. Therefore, the SQUID scam is not a result of flaws in distributed ledger technology. Rather, it is a modern repetition of the traditional attempt to conceal knowledge, and hence to exploit the vulnerable.

In the book *Snow Crash*, the digital world was almost a rich-only playing field. Hiro was only able to have a place in the Metaverse New York because as a hacker, he got to crypto early. The situation actually coincides with the development of Bitcoin, where it is now impossible for ordinary people to mine. The book describes the rich-only Metaverse New York as follows:

> This is Downtown, the most heavily developed area. If you go a couple of hundred kilometres in either direction, the development will taper down to almost nothing, just a thin chain of streetlights casting white pools on the black velvet ground.
>
> ...
>
> That's why the damn place is so overdeveloped. Put in a sign or a building on the Street and the hundred million richest, hippest, best-connected people on earth will see it every day of their lives. (Stephenson, 2011)

In this sense, the story gives a warning against excluding the public from crypto and Web 3.0. Without the public, the metaverse cannot reach its full potential in the technological and social revolution. The digital world will not be fully built.

6 Conclusion

Music plays a crucial role in the GCC's culture and public life. Building on academic and practical experience, this chapter explores DLT as an alternative collective management tool for GCC musicians to license, manage and profit from their creative work.

Traditionally the tasks are managed under CMOs, who are centralised agents representing musicians across the global market. This centralised approach allows musicians to promote their work overseas. However, such centralised agents have been criticised for a lack of transparency and high transaction costs. More importantly, where some artists fail to register their work properly, royalties remain at CMOs, instead of going to artists. Against these shortfalls, several attempts have been made to provide musicians with additional tools such as the 'Proof-of-Work' mechanism previously provided by InMusik, WIPO and others. However, these services are often short-lived due to high costs and low eco-support. Therefore, there is a need for an alternative CMO eco-system where creators are offered additional tools and services that might help them better exploit their creative works.

DLT is well fitted to address this gap for the following reasons. Firstly, the distributed ledger shares information publicly in real time with network users. Subsequently, it increases transparency in collective management and information accuracy. Secondly, smart contracts allow musicians to better distribute and manage their own creative work in Web 3.0. Together, these technologies have the potential to benefit creatives by mitigating the current CMO model's shortfalls, and subsequently divert more royalties to artists. In return, being able to provide such meaningful services would then encourage more people to engage with blockchain, which benefits the development of the technology. Previous examples from the financial market highlight the heavy investment required and a fraud risk people faced in engaging with DLT. Against this background, traditional CMOs are best positioned to lead the technological innovation due to their strong financial position and established reputation in the industry.

Nevertheless, the technology is far from perfect. On one hand, CMOs will be aware of the moral complexity of the innovation and treat musicians fairly. On the other hand, DLT can be slow in verifying transactions, which causes concerns over energy consumption and environmental impact. In recognition of these concerns, the technology itself has been advanced to increase efficiency. More importantly, using DLT in music collective management is a meaningful engagement of the technology. As an energy-rich region, the GCC has the advantage to experiment with blockchain technology in the sphere of music management and enhance culture tourism in the region.

References

Al-Sarihi, A. (2023) *The GCC and the road to net zero.* Middle East Institute. https://www.mei.edu/publications/gcc-and-road-net-zero

Ali, R., John, B., Roger, C., & James, S. (2014). Innovations in payment technologies and the emergence of digital currencies. Bank of England Quarterly Bulletin, 2014(Q3). Available at SSRN: https://ssrn.com/abstract=2499397

BBC News (World). (2021, October 29). *Squid game cryptocurrency soars 23000% in first few days.* [Twitter]. https://mobile.twitter.com/bbcworld/status/1454175979992199168?ref_src=twsrc%5Etfw

Bitcoin.org. (n.d.). *Frequently Asked Questions.* https://bitcoin.org/en/faq#what-is-bitcoin

Bonadio, E., & Sganga, C. (Eds.). (2024). *NFTs, Creativity and the Law: Within and beyond Copyright.* Routledge.

Bondarev, M. (2020). Energy Consumption of Bitcoin Mining. *International Journal of Energy Economics and Policy, 10*(4), 516.

Chainlink. (n.d.). *Decentralised Oracle Networks for Any Smart Contract.* https://chain.link/use-cases

Chen, S., Chen, C. Y.-H., Härdle, W. K., Lee, T. M., & Ong, B. (2018). Econometric Analysis of a Cryptocurrency Index for Portfolio Investment. In D. L. K. Chuen & R. Deng (Eds.), *Handbook of Blockchain, Digital Finance, and Inclusion* (Vol. 1). Elsevier Inc.

Chomsky, N., Hutchinson, P., Nyks, K., & Scott, J. (2017). *Requiem for the American Dream: The 10 Principles of Concentration of Wealth & Power* (Illustrated paperback edition).

Creative Commons. (n.d.). *Creative Commons.* https://creativecommons.org/

Dhillon, V., Metcalf, D., & Hooper, M. (2021). Unpacking Ethereum. In *Blockchain Enabled Applications.*

Ethereum.org. (2021a, November 11). *Gas and Fees.* Ethereum. https://ethereum.org/en/developers/docs/gas/

Ethereum.org. (2021b, November 5). *Proof-of-Stake.* Ethereum. https://ethereum.org/en/developers/docs/consensus-mechanisms/pos/#top

EU Intellectual Property Office Observatory. (n.d.). *Orphan Works Are Works that Are still Protected by Copyright, but Whose Authors or Other Right Holders Are not Known or Cannot Be Located.* European Union Intellectual Property Office. https://euipo.europa.eu/ohimportal/en/web/observatory/orphan-works-db

Farooq, U., Tabash, M. I., Anagreh, S., Al-Rdaydeh, M., & Habib, S. (2023). Economic Growth, Foreign Investment, Tourism, and Electricity Production as Determinants of Environmental Quality: Empirical Evidence from GCC Region. *Environmental Science and Pollution Research, 30*(16), 45768–45780. https://doi.org/10.1007/s11356-023-25545-0

Farooq, U., Tabash, M. I., Saleh Al-Faryan, M. A., Işık, C., & Dogru, T. (2024). The Nexus between Tourism-Energy-Environmental Degradation: Does Financial Development Matter in GCC Countries? *Tourism Economics, 30*(3), 680–701. https://doi.org/10.1177/13548166231174812

Financial Conduct Authority (FCA). (2019, February 27). *Initial coin offerings.* https://www.fca.org.uk/news/statements/initial-coin-offerings

Fitzpatrick, D. (2016). The global financial crisis: A critical moment, not juncture. In *The politics of regulation in the UK: Between tradition, contingency and crisis.* Palgrave Macmillan.

Forbes Middle East. (2024). *The Top 10 Arab Singers.* Forbes Middle East. https://www.forbesmiddleeast.com/list/the-top-10-arab-singers

Fridman, L. (2021, June 3). *Vitalik Buterin: Ethereum 2.0* [Video]. YouTube. https://www.youtube.com/watch?v=XW0QZmtbjvs

Galinado, G. (2009, July). *The Importance of Music in Our Society.* Gilbert Galinoo. https://www.gilbertgalindo.com/importanceofmusic

Gemini. (n.d.). *Gemini dollar.* Gemini. https://www.gemini.com/dollar

Hicks, D. (2020). *The British Muse.* Pluto Press.

HM Treasury. (2021, January). *UK Regulatory Approach to Cryptoassets and Stablecoins: Consultation and Call for Evidence.* https://www.gov.uk/government/consultations/uk-regulatory-approach-to-cryptoassets-and-stablecoins-consultation-and-call-for-evidence

Hooijer, R., & Baloyi, J. J. (2016). Collective Management Organizations—Tool Kit Neighboring Rights. *WIPO World Journal, 2016*(1), 51. https://www.wipo.int/edocs/pubdocs/en/wipo_pub_emat_2016_2.pdf

IPRO. (n.d.-a). Intellectual Property Rights Office for Bahrain. https://intellectualpropertyrightsoffice.org/Bahrain?v=4A398871-5F09-4FD9-8E73-6856 6D10C591#berne

IPRO. (n.d.-b). Intellectual Property Rights Office for Kuwait. https://intellectualpropertyrightsoffice.org/Kuwait?v=4A398871-5F09-4FD9-8E73-6856 6D10C591#berne

IPRO. (n.d.-c). Intellectual Property Rights Office for Oman. https://intellectualpropertyrightsoffice.uk/Oman?c=United_Kingdom

IPRO. (n.d.-d). Intellectual Property Rights Office for Qatar. https://intellectualpropertyrightsoffice.org/Qatar?v=4A398871-5F09-4FD9-8E73-6856 6D10C591#berne

IPRO. (n.d.-e). Intellectual Property Rights Office for Saudi Arabia. https://intellectualpropertyrightsoffice.uk/Saudi_Arabia

IPRO. (n.d.-f). Intellectual Property Rights Office for the United Arab Emirates. https://intellectualpropertyrightsoffice.org/United_Arab_Emirates?v=4A398871-5F09-4FD9-8E73-68566D10C591#berne

Kao, X., Liu, Y., Wang, W., Wen, Q., & Zhang, P. (2024). The Pressure of Coal Consumption on China's Carbon Dioxide Emissions: A Spatial and Temporal Perspective. *Atmospheric Pollution Research, 15*(8), 102188. https://doi.org/10.1016/j.apr.2024.102188

Knapman, H. (2018, September 18). *Not So Fast: Deliveroo App Crash Leaves Customers Furious as Some Are Charged Seven Times.* The Sun. https://www.thesun.co.uk/money/7284287/deliveroo-app-crash-customers-furious-charged-seven-times/

Lex Clips. (n.d.). *Ethereum and Chainlink Are Complementary | Sergey Nazarov and Lex Fridman* [Video]. YouTube. https://www.youtube.com/watch?v=vpO-KVjlgig

Li, F., Ye, Y., Tian, Z., & Zhang, X. (2019). CPU Versus GPU: Which Can Perform Matrix Computation Faster—Performance Comparison for Basic Linear Algebra Subprograms. *Neural Computing and Applications, 31*(8), 4353–4365. https://doi.org/10.1007/s00521-018-3354-z

Libich, J., & Lenten, L. (2021). Bitcoin, Tesla, and GameStop Bubbles as a Flight to Focal Points. *World Economics, 22*(1), 83. https://econpapers.repec.org/RePEc:wej:wldecn:823

Mansfeld, Y., & Winckler, O. (2008). The role of the tourism industry in transforming a rentier to a long-term viable economy: The case of Bahrain. *Current Issues in Tourism, 11*(3), 237–267. https://doi.org/10.1080/13683500802140307

Meta. (n.d.). *Connection is Evolving and So Are We.* https://about.facebook.com/meta/

National Development and Reform Commission. (2021, September 24). *Notice on Promoting the High-Quality Development of Digital Economy in the New Era.* https://www.ndrc.gov.cn/xxgk/zcfb/tz/202109/t20210924_1297474ext.html

Netflix. (n.d.). *Squid Game.* https://www.netflix.com/gb/title/81040344

Ngetich, D. (2020, October 21). *London Stock Exchange-Listed Company Buys Bitcoin as Reserve Asset.* Crypto.news. https://btcmanager.com/london-stock-exchange-company-bitcoin-reserve-asset/

O'Neal, S. (2020, March 20). *Steem Community Resists Takeover, Hard Fork Launches Hive Network.* Cointelegraph. https://cointelegraph.com/news/steem-community-resists-takeover-hard-fork-launches-hive-network

Palladino, S. (2019). *Ethereum for Web Developers.* Apress.

Park, A., & Li, H. (2021). The Effect of Blockchain Technology on Supply Chain Sustainability Performances. *Sustainability, 13*(4), 176. https://doi.org/10.3390/su13041726

Parkin, J. (2020). Pandora's Blocks. In *The Money Code Space: Hidden Power in Bitcoin, Blockchain, and Decentralisation*. Oxford University Press.
Plenckers, L. (2021). *Arab Music: A Survey of Its History and Its Modern Practice*. Archaeopress. http://www.jstor.org/stable/j.ctv25wxc5k
Riley, C. L. (2020, November 6). The British Museums by Dan Hicks Review—Return Everything. *The Guardian*. https://www.theguardian.com/books/2020/nov/06/the-brItish-museums-by-dan-hicks-review-colonial-violence-and-cultural-restitution
Rushe, D. (2021, October 19). 142m Households Watched Squid Game, Netflix Says as It Adds 4.4m Subscribers. *The Guardian*. https://www.theguardian.com/media/2021/oct/19/netflix-quarterly-results-subscribers-squid-game
Saleh, A. S., Bassil, C., & Safari, A. (2022). Tourism Research for the GCC Region: Current Status and Future Research Directions. *Tourism Economics, 28*(6), 1626–1646. https://doi.org/10.1177/1354816621999968
Savelyev, A. (2017). Contract Law 2.0: "Smart" Contracts as the Beginning of the End of Classic Contract Law. *Information and Communications Technology Law, 26*(2), 116.
Scarcity Studios. (2021, November 3). *"Squid Game Coin" Steals Millions from UK Investors in Latest Crypto Rug Pull* [YouTube]. https://www.youtube.com/watch?v=ed6akzzSubY
Simmone, D. (2019). *Copyright and Collective Authorship: Locating the Author of Collaborative Works*. Cambridge University Press.
Statista. (2021a). *Leading Countries Based on Number of Twitter Users as of July 2021*. https://www.statista.com/statistics/242606/number-of-active-twitter-users-in-selected-countries/
Statista. (2021b). *Number of Daily Bitcoin Transactions Worldwide from January 2017 to September 13, 2021*. https://www.statista.com/statistics/730806/daily-number-of-bitcoin-transactions/
Stephenson, N. (2011). *Snow Crash (First Published 1992)*. Penguin.
Stiglitz, J. E. (2010). The financial crisis of 2007–8 and its macroeconomic consequences. In J. E. Stiglitz, S. Griffith-Jones, & J. A. Ocampo (Eds.), *Time for a visible hand: Lessons from the 2008 world financial crisis*. Oxford University Press.
TechCrunch. (2017, September 18). *Decentralising Everything with Ethereum's Vitalik Buterin* [Video]. YouTube. https://www.youtube.com/watch?v=WSN5BaCzsbo&t=640s
TechCrunch. (2018, July 6). *Fireside Chat with Vitalik Buterin* [Video]. YouTube. https://www.youtube.com/watch?v=OHMjbsKN1p4
Tresise, A., Goldfein, J., & Hunter, D. (2018). What Blockchain Can and Can't Do for Copyright. *Australian Intellectual Property Journal, 28*, 144.
World Intellectual Property Organization, & World Tourism Organization. (2021). *Boosting Tourism Development through Intellectual Property*. World Intellectual Property Organization.

World Intellectual Property Organization (WIPO). (n.d.). *WIPO Proof (Discontinued)*. WIPO. https://www.wipo.int/wipoproof/en/

Wright, C. (2019). Bitcoin: A Peer-to-Peer Electronic Cash System. *SSRN Electronic Journal*. https://ssrn.com/abstract=3440802

Zuboff, S. (2019). Home or Exile in the Digital Future. In *The Age of Surveillance Capitalism: The Fight for a Human Future at the New Frontier of Power*. Profile Books.

CHAPTER 10

Synergising IP and Cryptocurrency: A Roadmap for Knowledge-Based Economic Growth

Shaista Peerzada and Sangeeta Verma

1 Introduction

Synergising intellectual property (IP) and cryptocurrency has the potential to promote knowledge-based economic growth in a rapidly evolving digital economy. This convergence can open new opportunities for innovation, entrepreneurship, and economic development. To achieve this, it is essential to clearly understand the fundamentals of IP, including patents, copyrights, trademarks, and trade secrets, and identify any possible overlaps between IP and cryptocurrency. Blockchain technology can be used to establish a transparent ledger for IP assets, improving management and streamlining licensing. The tokenisation of IP assets can allow for fractional ownership, liquidity, and global trade of IP assets. Smart contracts can automate IP transactions, making negotiating licensing agreements, royalty payments, and IP protection easier.

S. Peerzada (✉) • S. Verma
Department of Law, Ajeenkya DY Patil University, Pune, Maharashtra, India

N. Naim et al. (eds.), *Intellectual Property and Innovation*, The Political Economy of the Middle East,
https://doi.org/10.1007/978-981-96-4020-1_10

Creators could use decentralised IP marketplaces to tokenise and sell their IP assets directly to interested buyers. However, it is important to establish legal frameworks that comply with IP laws and financial regulations. To make this work smoothly, educating people about the potential advantages and risks of integrating IP with cryptocurrency is important, as well as prioritising cybersecurity measures to safeguard IP assets stored on blockchain networks.

Advancing the synergy between IP and cryptocurrency can be achieved through investment in research and development. International collaboration can establish global standards and interoperability for their integration. Monitoring and adapting strategies and policies to address emerging challenges and opportunities is crucial. To foster an ecosystem of innovation and entrepreneurship, start-ups and innovators working on IP-cryptocurrency projects can be offered incentives and support programmes. However, ethical considerations, such as privacy, data security, and social impact, must be addressed. It is also crucial to comply with relevant regulations and engage with regulators to ensure regulatory compliance.

Cryptocurrency has emerged as a new way of conducting financial transactions, storing value, and investing. However, it presents various IP challenges related to technology, business practices, and regulatory compliance (Valdeolmillos et al., 2020). Understanding and tackling these challenges is important to stay ahead in the market, manage risks, and follow legal regulations. When trading cryptocurrency, developing new technologies or finding new uses for existing ones can be innovative. However, obtaining patents for these innovations can be challenging due to technicalities and different patent laws across various jurisdictions. Cryptocurrency heavily depends on software, which is usually protected by copyright. Nevertheless, open-source software is widespread in the world of cryptocurrency.

Misunderstanding or violating licensing terms can lead to legal disputes. Trademarks can protect cryptocurrencies' unique names, logos, and brand identifiers. Bitcoin and Ethereum (ETH) are well-known trademarks in the cryptocurrency industry but enforcing their protection can be challenging (Ofodile, 2019). Trademark squatting is a concern in the crypto trading industry as numerous organisations possess confidential information that can be protected as trade secrets (Guajardo et al., 2007). Navigating regulatory compliance can be a hurdle for those involved in the cryptocurrency industry. Laws and regulations that govern cryptocurrencies can impact various aspects of the business, including its IP strategy. Furthermore, piracy and counterfeiting are on the rise, leading to fake cryptocurrencies, deceitful initial coin offerings, and the piracy of software or technology linked to cryptocurrency trading. Comprehending and tackling these issues as the cryptocurrency market grows is crucial.

Cryptocurrency is a virtual or digital currency that uses cryptography to ensure security. Blockchain, a decentralised technology, manages and records transactions across numerous computers. Bitcoin is the most well-known and first cryptocurrency, while Ethereum (ETH) functions as a cryptocurrency and provides a platform for smart contracts. Ripple (XRP) is a digital payment protocol and cryptocurrency facilitating real-time, international payments. It is worth noting that Bitcoin and Ethereum are the most popular cryptocurrencies (Guadamuz, 2020).

Generating new units of cryptocurrency is achieved through a process called mining. Miners utilise powerful computers to solve intricate mathematical problems that authenticate transactions. The miner is awarded cryptocurrency once the transaction is verified and added to the blockchain. Cryptocurrencies are primarily used as investment instruments, though they facilitate regular transactions in some places. It is crucial to note that investing in cryptocurrency has risks associated with it, including volatility, security, and regulatory risks. It is important to research and comprehend these risks before investing in cryptocurrency.

Cryptocurrencies are digital or virtual currencies that use cryptography for security and leverage blockchain technology to achieve decentralisation, transparency, and immutability (He et al., 2022) Network participants, known as nodes, perform transaction validation through a consensus mechanism. Cryptocurrencies are solely digital and lack a physical equivalent. They utilise cryptographic techniques to secure transactions and regulate the creation of new units. Most cryptocurrencies rely on blockchain technology, guaranteeing transparency and immutability of transactions (Patrickson, 2021).

Cryptocurrency users are somewhat anonymous and do not always reveal their identities when transacting. Many cryptocurrencies have a limited number available, which makes them more valuable. Bitcoin was the first and most popular cryptocurrency, invented in 2009 (Söderberg, 2018). Since then, thousands of unique cryptocurrencies have been developed.

2 The Significance of the Research

The surge in cryptocurrencies and blockchain technology has brought remarkable developments in the financial sector and other industries. However, these advancements have also raised complex IP rights issues. These technologies' decentralised, anonymous, and cross-border nature presents substantial challenges for traditional IP enforcement mechanisms (Raymaekers, 2015). This research suggests that Gulf Cooperation Council (GCC) member states can promote economic growth and diversify their economies by utilising IP and cryptocurrency. This strategy can position the GCC region as a centre for innovation, entrepreneurship, and economic resilience in the twenty-first century.

Blockchain-based innovations like smart contracts and non-fungible tokens (NFTs) have significant potential to transform IP management (Bamakan et al., 2022). However, fitting these ground-breaking technologies into established patent categories and guidelines remains difficult. Conflicts and a lack of clarity surrounding IP rights and protections within this nascent technology could stifle innovation.

The objectives of the research into cryptocurrency as presented in this chapter include the following:

- To investigate and analyse the specific IP issues that arise from using blockchain technology and cryptocurrencies.
- To propose a roadmap to maximise the potential of IP and cryptocurrency in the GCC member states. The goal is to create synergies for knowledge-based economic development and stimulate growth by integrating the two industries.
- To understand the competitive landscape and the extent of IP protection sought for blockchain-related innovations, and to investigate current patents.
- To analyse how these issues will impact IP law and policy in the future and learn about reducing IP risks in cryptocurrency trading with emerging strategies such as blockchain-based IP rights management and smart contracts.
- To recommend policymakers, legal practitioners, and industry participants to navigate these challenges.

Due to the widespread adoption and transformative nature of blockchain technology and cryptocurrency, studying IP challenges in cryptocurrency trading is important for various stakeholders. The report provides a comprehensive overview of the current state of IP and cryptocurrency in the GCC, outlining recommendations for synergising these two domains. It also presents a roadmap for knowledge-based growth, outlining steps and policies for GCC member states, and provides policy recommendations for governments, businesses, and investors to promote innovation and investment in IP and cryptocurrency. By understanding these challenges, legal clarity can be provided for developers, innovators, traders, and businesses operating in the blockchain and cryptocurrency space. It can guide the protection of IP rights and mitigate risks associated with potential infringement, thus promoting a secure environment for innovation and trade. The findings of this study could also be valuable for policymakers in creating regulations that safeguard IP rights while encouraging innovation in blockchain and cryptocurrency technologies. Blockchain technology has the potential to revolutionise how IP rights are stored, managed, and enforced by providing a secure and unchangeable record of IP transactions.

By comprehending the IP issues involved in cross-border transactions, international collaboration and regulations in IP enforcement can be enhanced. This study can promote innovation and strengthen investor trust by clarifying blockchain technology's and cryptocurrencies' IP landscape. Such efforts can contribute to the growth and stability of cryptocurrency markets.

3 Brief History and Growth of Cryptocurrency Trading

In 2008, Satoshi Nakamoto founded Bitcoin as a decentralised digital currency that operates without the need for trust in a central authority. The inspiration behind its creation was the financial crisis of the same year, which prompted concerns about the fairness and stability of the global financial system.

In January 2009, Nakamoto mined the first blockchain block, called the "genesis block" or "Block 0." (van Flymen & van Flymen, 2020). The initial Bitcoin transaction was sent from Nakamoto to Hal Finney, a cryptographic activist (Zaki & Danish, 2020). In May 2010, Laszlo Hanyecz made the first Bitcoin transaction in the real world (Hellwig et al., 2020). He traded 10,000 Bitcoins for two pizzas. Bitcoin's success paved the way for other digital currencies, including altcoins like Namecoin, Litecoin, Ripple, and Ethereum. The cryptocurrency market has grown exponentially since the launch of Bitcoin, with the total market capitalisation of all cryptocurrencies reaching trillions of dollars (Katterbauer et al., 2022). Cryptocurrency exchanges offer spot trading, futures, options, and margin trading services. Despite its short history, cryptocurrency trading is significant.

3.1 Importance and Role of IP in Crypto Innovation

IP is essential for both technology and business, as it is a crucial factor in encouraging innovation, driving economic growth, and maintaining a competitive edge. IP rights motivate inventors and creators to develop and share their work by providing them exclusive rights to use and profit from their inventions or creative works. These rights can also make a company more attractive to investors and can play a significant role in a start-up's ability to secure funding. Trademarks safeguard a company's brand and logo, and businesses often invest heavily in research and development to develop new technologies or services. Due to the complexity of IP law, companies often require expert guidance to manage their IP effectively (Gürkaynak et al., 2018).

IP drives innovation and growth within the cryptocurrency industry, especially in the GCC context. It protects innovative technologies and algorithms, incentivising inventors and companies to invest in research and development. Patents, copyrights, and trademarks are essential for ensuring legal certainty and investor confidence in the GCC region.

Trademarks help establish trust among users by protecting the unique identities of crypto projects and exchanges. IP rights enable licensing agreements and collaborations, fostering partnerships between GCC businesses and global crypto innovators. Trade secrets protect valuable, non-public information, including the know-how behind cryptocurrency technologies. GCC member states can incentivise foreign investment by providing legal protection for trade secrets, attracting international cryptocurrency companies to establish a regional presence (Mogielnicki, 2021).

Building a robust legal framework for IP within the cryptocurrency sector is essential for dispute resolution and regulatory compliance. Governments within the GCC can offer incentives, grants, or subsidies for cryptocurrency projects that develop innovative solutions, encouraging local talent and start-ups to explore blockchain and cryptocurrency technologies (Hub, 2021). IP can promote cross-industry synergy by facilitating collaboration between the cryptocurrency sector and other industries like finance, healthcare, and logistics. GCC member states can leverage IP rights to encourage the development of blockchain-based solutions that benefit multiple sectors, fostering knowledge-based economic growth (Lopez et al., 2020).

Regulatory compliance is another key aspect of IP. IP rights help cryptocurrency businesses navigate regulatory frameworks, ensuring they operate within the legal boundaries set by governments, fostering a stable and predictable business environment. In conclusion, IP is a fundamental catalyst for driving innovation, attracting investment, and ensuring legal and regulatory compliance in the cryptocurrency industry.

The importance of IP cannot be overstated when it comes to promoting and safeguarding innovation in cryptocurrencies. By granting IP rights, developers are motivated to create new blockchain technologies, cryptocurrency protocols, and mining hardware while protecting their investments by preventing unauthorised use of their innovations. IP rights also enable crypto businesses to differentiate themselves in the market, share technologies through licensing, and collaborate with others while helping them navigate regulatory requirements and avoid legal disputes.

IP rights are essential for driving ongoing innovation in the cryptocurrency sector, which benefits developing nations by providing greater economic opportunities and enabling individuals to borrow, save, send, and receive money with greater ease. These currencies operate outside conventional currency markets, allowing individuals to improve their standard of living without disrupting the normal functioning of those markets. Thanks to cryptocurrencies and blockchain technology, we are seeing the formation of new small businesses and the creation of vast quantities of new assets (Pascoe & Scott, 2018).

3.2 IP Challenges in Cryptocurrency Trading

Cryptocurrency trading has been increasingly intertwined with various IP challenges. These include the use of innovative technologies that may be patentable, the use of open-source software, the protection of trademarks, and the protection of proprietary trading strategies or algorithms. The legal and regulatory landscape for cryptocurrencies is complex and constantly evolving. Companies must understand and address these IP challenges to protect their interests and maintain their competitive edge. Additionally, cybersecurity is a significant concern, as hackers or security breaches can lead to the theft of valuable IP. As the cryptocurrency landscape matures, understanding and addressing these IP challenges will be crucial for businesses to protect their interests and maintain their competitive edge.

IP challenges in cryptocurrency trading and the broader synergy between IP and cryptocurrency within the GCC are significant and complex (Papaspyridis & Zalan, 2017). Addressing these challenges is crucial for fostering the region's innovation and knowledge-based economic growth. Key IP challenges include lack of clarity on IP rights, open source and decentralisation, patent trolling, cross-border IP enforcement, rapid technological evolution, securing trade secrets, education and awareness, interdisciplinary collaboration, regulatory alignment, and promoting regulatory cooperation among GCC member states (Al-Shammari et al., 2008).

Lack of clarity on IP rights is a challenge as cryptocurrency and blockchain technologies often involve complex concepts. Establishing clear guidelines and regulations to define what can be protected by IP rights in the context of cryptocurrency and blockchain innovations will provide certainty to innovators and investors. Open source and decentralisation make determining who owns the IP and how to enforce those rights difficult. To address patent trolling, stricter criteria for patent eligibility and mechanisms to challenge patents that are not genuinely used for innovation but rather for litigation purposes should be implemented. Cross-border IP enforcement should be promoted through international cooperation and agreements, with blockchain technology encouraged for IP registration and verification (Liang et al., 2023). Regular review and adaptation of IP laws should be established to keep pace with technological advancements, and collaboration between regulators, innovators, and legal experts should be encouraged to develop agile IP frameworks. Strong legal protections for trade secrets in the GCC region should be provided, including remedies for misappropriation and advanced security measures (Khoja et al., 2017). Addressing these IP challenges in cryptocurrency trading and knowledge-based economic growth is essential to create an environment that fosters innovation, protects the rights of innovators, and attracts investment in the GCC region.

Cryptocurrency technology uses blockchain, a decentralised, distributed ledger that records transactions across many computers so that the recorded transactions cannot be altered retroactively. Companies and individuals have filed patents for various applications, including cryptocurrencies' core mechanics, blockchain functionality improvements, and specific applications like smart contracts and more efficient mining techniques. Trademarks are essential in distinguishing the source of goods or services, and companies may choose to protect their proprietary technology or information as trade secrets. Open-source technology also presents IP challenges, such as misunderstanding the terms of open-source licences (Lindberg, 2008). Balancing IP protection with the ethos of decentralisation and openness that underpins much of cryptocurrency technology is a significant ongoing challenge in this field.

A blockchain is a decentralised, distributed digital ledger that records transactions across multiple computers (or nodes) so that they cannot be altered retroactively. Cryptocurrencies like Bitcoin, Ethereum, and many others use blockchain technology. Each cryptocurrency transaction is recorded in a block, and when a block is completed, it is added to the chain in a linear, chronological order. Blockchain uses advanced cryptography to secure transactions, making it nearly impossible to alter the information inside. Traditional transactions require intermediaries (like banks) to establish trust between parties. However, blockchain's decentralised and transparent nature allows parties to transact directly without needing to trust each other or a third party. It is crucial in cryptocurrencies, where direct, peer-to-peer transactions are one of the main attractions (Gainsbury & Blaszczynski, 2017).

The patent landscape around blockchain technology has been growing rapidly, with several major corporations leading in blockchain-related patent filings. These include IBM, Alibaba, Mastercard, and Bank of America. These patents are related to the application of blockchain technology in various fields, such as supply chain management, finance, and data security, with filings occurring in patent offices worldwide. However, the rate of patent approval and the legal enforceability of patents can vary significantly by country. There is potential for increased patent litigation, with issues such as patent infringement or disputes over patent validity becoming more common (Allison et al., 2013). There is a potential tension between the open-source ethos of many blockchain projects and the exclusive rights granted by patents, with some organisations opting to use open-source licences that require contributors to forego patent rights.

Anonymity is one of the defining characteristics of many blockchain-based applications, including cryptocurrencies. However, this anonymity poses significant challenges to enforcing IP rights. One of the most significant challenges is identifying infringers in the first place due to the pseudonymous nature of blockchain transactions. Even if an infringer can be identified, determining the legal jurisdiction for an IP dispute can be challenging. Once an infringer has been identified and the appropriate jurisdiction has been determined, enforcing IP rights can still be difficult (Hitsevich, 2015). Traditional enforcement actions such as court orders may be less effective in blockchain's decentralised, peer-to-peer context. The tension between the enforcement of IP rights and the preservation of privacy is a significant issue in the context of blockchain. New approaches and tools may be needed. Blockchain technology could be part of the solution, but much research and development is still needed (Yli-Huumo et al., 2016).

4 Jurisdictional Issues in Cryptocurrency Trading

Cryptocurrencies and blockchain technology (Hugendubel, 2021), by their very nature, operate without geographical boundaries, enabling cross-border transactions with ease. However, this global reach also brings about significant jurisdictional issues, especially when disputes arise (Ranganadhan, 2023). Different countries have different regulations and laws related to cryptocurrencies and blockchain, and even if a court can establish jurisdiction over a blockchain-related dispute, enforcing that judgement can be difficult. Therefore, it is often unclear under which country's laws a dispute should be adjudicated. Additionally, data protection and privacy laws vary widely between different jurisdictions, and activities on a blockchain could inadvertently violate these laws. The variance in legal frameworks across jurisdictions may also lead to regulatory arbitrage, where entities choose to operate in jurisdictions with favourable regulations.

Blockchain technology's unique characteristics and wide-ranging applications present challenges when identifying, defining, and protecting blockchain-based innovations. Blockchain technology is complex and relatively new, making it difficult for patent examiners and courts to understand it and its innovative aspects fully. It often involves software or business methods, which face patent eligibility challenges in many jurisdictions. Blockchain technology is designed to be decentralised and pseudonymous, making it difficult to identify and locate infringers to enforce IP rights. Additionally, the global nature of blockchain raises questions about legal jurisdiction and the enforceability of IP rights across different countries. Standardisation in the blockchain field is still in its early stages, which could affect the identification, definition, and protection of blockchain-based innovations (Keohane et al., 2003).

The demographic redistribution of cryptocurrency activities is that Europe has the maximum number of exchanges, followed by Asia-Pacific. Ninety-four per cent of all publicly known ATMs are based in North America and Europe, while Africa, the Middle East, and Latin America possess 2% of those ATMs. With the increasing curiosity for cryptocurrencies, companies have been announced to provide goods and services that facilitate most users' use of virtual currencies. Today, the number of people working full-time in the cryptocurrency business is estimated at 2000 employees in 2017. Two Asian countries that have further interest in cryptocurrencies are Japan and South Korea (Kolesnikova, 2018). People from these two main Asian countries truly accept Bitcoins, and many dealers use them for small businesses. Countries like Australia, Argentina, Brazil, Canada, France, Finland, Germany, Italy, Indonesia, Japan, New Zealand, Nigeria, Poland, Philippines, Russia, South Korea, Malaysia, South Africa, Spain, Switzerland, Sweden, Thailand, United States, and the United Kingdom have varying degrees of adoption (Sulimierska & Sikorska, 2023).

Cryptocurrencies are becoming increasingly popular in the economy, but many issues remain unresolved. To make the trade profitable, traders must understand the cryptocurrency and exchange rates in connection to the Forex markets and brokers involved. Additionally, cryptocurrencies have recently been integrated into the economy, which means they have their method of valuation procedure. By trading Forex with cryptocurrencies, a new intermediate currency is introduced, which can unpredictably impact the profits and losses. Cryptocurrencies are a new technology with a high risk of cyber-attacks from hackers. In 2017, there were many major financial problems due to cyber-attacks. With the introduction of cryptocurrencies, there is always a security risk because hackers and fraudsters can tamper with the entire trading process. As a result, the prices in these cryptocurrencies have very high fluctuations, and they keep moving upwards. Since these cryptocurrencies were introduced, various theft cases have been registered worldwide. Most attacks were recovered, making these transactions risky for the Forex markets, particularly as correlations between asset classes evolve. It can be summarised that the Forex markets have benefited from cryptocurrencies and their trading. However, the risk can be eliminating the benefits of cryptocurrency trading.

The GCC and its member states can leverage the power of IP and cryptocurrency to drive knowledge-based economic growth (Chandra et al., 2019). A strategic approach should be developed, which includes understanding the GCC's economic landscape, emphasising IP protection, fostering innovation and research and development, promoting cryptocurrency and blockchain technology, launching a GCC-backed cryptocurrency or token, establishing technology hubs and incubators, encouraging collaboration between government agencies, academia, and the private sector, investing in education and workforce development programmes, providing regulatory clarity, engaging with international organisations and partners, strengthening cybersecurity and data privacy measures, monitoring and evaluating progress through key performance indicators, risk management, marketing and promotion, and sustainability and inclusivity (Kelaart-Courtney, 2010).

To create a roadmap for this synergy, it is essential to conduct a thorough analysis of the GCC and its member states' economic landscapes, identify existing strengths and weaknesses, strengthen IP laws and regulations, encourage research and development investments, create a regulatory framework for cryptocurrency and blockchain technology, launch a GCC-backed cryptocurrency or token, establish technology hubs and innovation incubators, encourage collaboration between government agencies, academia, and the private sector, invest in education and workforce development programmes, ensure regulatory clarity, engage with international organisations and partners, strengthen cybersecurity and data privacy measures, monitor and evaluate progress, develop risk management strategies, promote the GCC's initiatives and advantages in both IP protection and cryptocurrency, and ensure sustainability and inclusivity (Abazeed, 2022). By integrating IP protection and cryptocurrency into a comprehensive strategy, the GCC or its member states can harness the power of innovation and digital assets to drive economic growth and position themselves as leaders in the knowledge-based economy. This roadmap should evolve and adapt over time to respond to changing technological, economic, and regulatory landscapes.

5 Case Studies in Cryptocurrency Trading

5.1 *Mt. Gox Collapse (Cheung et al., 2015)*

Once handling over 70% of all Bitcoin transactions worldwide, Mt. Gox was the leading Bitcoin exchange. However, in 2014, Mt. Gox filed for bankruptcy following a high-profile hack in which 850,000 Bitcoins (worth approximately $450 million and much more today) were stolen. This case highlighted the risks associated with unregulated exchanges and the need for improved security measures in cryptocurrency trading (Sarra & Gullifer, 2019).

5.2 *Silk Road Seizure (Lane, 2013)*

The Silk Road was an infamous online black market, mainly known for selling illegal drugs. Bitcoin was the primary currency used on this platform due to its perceived anonymity. In 2013, the FBI shut down the Silk Road and seized approximately 26,000 Bitcoins. Later, in 2020, the US government seized over $1 billion worth of Bitcoin associated with the Silk Road, demonstrating that Bitcoin transactions are not completely anonymous and can be traced by law enforcement.

5.3 *EtherDelta Case (Sistoso, 2021)*

In 2018, the US Securities and Exchange Commission (SEC) charged the founder of EtherDelta, a decentralised exchange, for operating an unregistered securities exchange. It was the first case of the SEC charging a cryptocurrency exchange, setting a precedent for decentralised exchanges and their potential regulation under securities laws.

5.4 *Tesla and Bitcoin (Hobbs, 2021)*

In early 2021, Tesla announced it had bought $1.5 billion worth of Bitcoin and planned to accept Bitcoin as payment for its vehicles. It led to a significant surge in Bitcoin's price. However, later in the year, Tesla CEO Elon Musk announced that Tesla would no longer accept Bitcoin due to concerns about the environmental impact of Bitcoin mining, leading to substantial price volatility. This case highlights major corporations and high-profile individuals' influence on cryptocurrency markets.

5.5 *DeFi Flash Loan Attacks (Qin et al., 2021)*

Decentralised Finance (DeFi) platforms, which provide financial services using smart contracts on blockchain networks like Ethereum, have been subject to "flash loan" attacks. Here, a user borrows funds, manipulates the market, and then repays the loan within a single blockchain transaction, often leading to significant financial gains at the expense of other users or the platform itself. This case underscores the potential risks and exploits within the complex DeFi market mechanisms.

5.6 *Craig Wright vs. Various Parties (Ghazi et al., 2022)*

Craig Wright, who claims to be the creator of Bitcoin (under the pseudonym Satoshi Nakamoto), has been involved in numerous legal disputes. In several cases, he has sued individuals who denied his claim to be Satoshi Nakamoto for defamation. Additionally, there have been legal disputes over the ownership of early mined bitcoins and the rights to the Bitcoin whitepaper.

5.7 *Bitmain vs MicroBT (Read, 2022)*

In 2020, Bitmain, a prominent Bitcoin mining hardware producer, filed lawsuits against MicroBTs founder in China, claiming IP theft. The dispute arose over the design of a specific Application-Specific Integrated Circuit used in Bitcoin mining hardware (Mostert & Jue, 2018).

5.8 *Ripple Labs vs R3 (Benji & Sindhu, 2019)*

In 2017, Ripple Labs and R3, two blockchain companies, had a legal dispute over an agreement involving the purchase of XRP tokens at a below-market price. This case highlights the complexity of structuring and enforcing contractual agreements in the rapidly changing cryptocurrency market.

5.9 UAEs Regulatory Framework (Baroudi & Benghida, 2022)

The UAE, especially Dubai, is leading in blockchain and cryptocurrency adoption. In 2020, the UAE introduced regulations for blockchain and various cryptocurrencies, attracting more investors.

5.10 Bahrain's Sandbox Approach (Hassan et al., 2022)

Bahrain has implemented a regulatory sandbox for fintech, which includes cryptocurrency-related businesses. It allows these companies to test their blockchain and cryptocurrency solutions in a controlled setting, encouraging innovation and enticing start-ups to the area. A potential study could analyse the businesses that emerged from the sandbox.

5.11 Saudi Arabia's Blockchain Pilots (Elshity, 2022)

Saudi Arabia has introduced numerous blockchain and cryptocurrency initiatives. One of these is the partnership between the Saudi Arabian Monetary Authority and Ripple, which aims to investigate cross-border payments utilising blockchain technology. A case study could analyse the results of these projects and how they have affected the financial industry.

5.12 Oman's Exploration of Blockchain (Al-Riyami & Nair, 2022)

Oman is interested in blockchain tech and its applications. A case study could analyse pilot projects and collaborations in cryptocurrency and blockchain, revealing Oman's approach to innovation.

5.13 Kuwait's Regulatory Environment (Ozili, 2022)

Kuwait, along with other GCC nations, is exploring cryptocurrency regulations. A case study can examine Kuwait's regulatory advancements and their influence on cryptocurrency trading and innovation.

6 Mitigating IP Risks in Cryptocurrency Trading

Mitigating IP risks in cryptocurrency trading requires a comprehensive strategy, including technical measures and legal considerations. If a company is developing new blockchain or cryptocurrency technologies, consider seeking patent protection for your innovations. Understanding the terms of open-source licences is crucial, as misuse can lead to IP infringement. Conduct regular IP audits to identify valuable IP assets, assess potential risks, and develop strategies for managing these assets and risks. Ensure that agreements with employees, contractors, and business partners include clear provisions on the ownership and use of IP.

Monitor the market for potential infringement of IP rights and be prepared to enforce rights when necessary. Ensure compliance with relevant regulations. Consider obtaining IP insurance to cover the costs of enforcing IP rights and defending against infringement claims. Work closely with legal counsel to navigate cryptocurrencies and blockchain technology's complex and evolving legal landscape (Deepa et al., 2022).

It is important to consider the risks associated with IP when engaging in cryptocurrency trading to promote innovation and preserve the rights of creators and innovators. To mitigate these risks, the GCC and its member states should consider implementing various strategies, including educational initiatives, clear IP policies and agreements, IP audits, due diligence, licensing agreements, prior art searches, defensive patenting, IP enforcement, blockchain technology for IP protection, regulatory compliance, dispute resolution mechanisms, international collaboration, and government support. Various initiatives can be taken to educate cryptocurrency traders and businesses about the importance of IP rights. One such initiative is to conduct awareness campaigns and training programmes that cover IP law and best practices. These training sessions and workshops can benefit both traders and developers. User agreements should include provisions for IP rights and licensing agreements. To ensure that IP policies are clear and well-defined, these agreements should explicitly outline ownership, usage rights, and any restrictions.

Additionally, smart contracts should be implemented with similar provisions. Conducting IP audits can help identify and assess IP assets associated with cryptocurrency projects. Before entering partnerships or investments, it is important to perform due diligence.

Establishing licensing agreements for using IP in the cryptocurrency ecosystem is important to ensure clarity and prevent possible disputes and litigation (Savelyev, 2018). These agreements should cover technology, software, and brand licensing. Collaborative agreements must explicitly define IP ownership and usage rights in writing. Conducting prior art searches and developing defensive patenting strategies can also help protect against possible IP conflicts (Steensma et al., 2015). Enforcing IP rights in cryptocurrency involves monitoring and legal action against infringing parties. Blockchain technology can automate IP-related transactions by timestamping them.

Cryptocurrency businesses and traders must comply with IP laws and regulations in the GCC region to ensure regulatory compliance. Mediation and arbitration are excellent alternative dispute resolution methods that can help avoid costly IP litigation. Moreover, international collaboration and government support can promote IP protection in the cryptocurrency industry.

Crypto-related businesses face unique challenges regarding IP protection due to the inherent characteristics of blockchain technology. Blockchain technology has many patentable aspects, and proprietary software built on blockchain protocols may be protected by copyright (Sung, 2019). Some blockchain-related businesses may opt to protect certain innovations as trade secrets. Trademark business name, logo, and any product names to prevent others from using them and causing customer confusion. Ensure employees, contractors, and business partners sign NDAs to maintain the confidentiality of certain information (Wilson, 2019).

Licence agreements can be a way to monetise IP while retaining ownership. Regularly monitor the market and the activities of competitors to identify possible infringement of IP rights. Engage with legal professionals who understand IP law and blockchain technology's unique aspects. Consider IP insurance, which could protect the business from the financial consequences of defending against IP infringement claims or enforcing IP rights.

Thorough patent research and sound legal advice are essential for businesses operating in the cryptocurrency and blockchain space. Patent research helps to identify existing patents in their area of operation, which can help to ensure that the business's activities, particularly any innovations it develops, do not infringe upon existing patents. It can also identify areas with opportunities for patenting, which can provide a competitive advantage by giving the business exclusive rights to the technology for a certain period.

A lawyer with expertise in patent law and blockchain technology-specific understanding can help an entrepreneur understand the implications of patent research, navigate the patent application process, and avoid legal pitfalls. Legal advice is crucial in responding to infringement allegations and enforcing the business's patent rights.

7 The Future of IP and Cryptocurrency

The intersection of IP and cryptocurrency is likely to become even more significant as blockchain technology continues to evolve and proliferate. It includes using smart contracts for automated licensing and royalty payments and blockchain registries for recording and verifying IP ownership. Non-fungible tokens (NFTs) have already started changing the landscape of digital art and other digital IP rights (Sakız & Gencer, 2021). The tension between the anonymous nature of many cryptocurrencies and the need to identify parties to enforce IP rights will continue to present challenges. Issues of jurisdiction and international cooperation in IP enforcement will be increasingly important.

New mechanisms for dispute resolution may evolve to address IP conflicts in the decentralised and pseudonymous context of blockchain and cryptocurrency. Cybersecurity will become increasingly important as cryptocurrency and blockchain technologies become central to IP strategy (Tredinnick, 2019).

NFTs have been a significant development in the intersection of IP and blockchain technology, opening up new possibilities and challenges (Wang et al., 2021). NFTs use blockchain technology to prove ownership and authenticity of digital artworks, allowing artists to sell their work and retain royalties on future resales. They are also used to create unique virtual goods and collectables, raising questions about IP rights. Musicians and music industry stakeholders are exploring NFTs to sell music, merchandise, and experiences directly to fans, providing new revenue streams and greater control for artists. Various legal issues are yet to be resolved around NFTs, including their status under securities law, the tax implications of buying and selling NFTs, and how traditional contract law applies to these transactions. The environmental impact of NFTs, which typically use energy-intensive proof-of-work blockchains, has also been a topic of concern and discussion (Naqvi, 2018).

The interplay of decentralisation, as embodied by blockchain technology and cryptocurrencies, and IP rights introduces several interesting dynamics. Blockchain enables peer-to-peer transactions and direct ownership of digital assets, reducing the need for intermediaries. Its immutable ledger provides a clear history of transactions, which can serve as proof of ownership and provenance for IP rights. Decentralised technologies inherently operate across national borders, enabling new, global markets for IP rights and raising jurisdictional enforcement challenges. Blockchain's pseudonymous nature can make identifying parties for IP enforcement difficult.

Blockchain, particularly public blockchains, epitomises open innovation to enable contribution or build upon the technology. Smart contracts enable programmable IP rights, providing new ways to manage and monetise IP rights. Balancing the benefits of decentralisation with the need to protect and incentivise innovation will be a key challenge in the future.

8 Future Challenges and Opportunities in Cryptocurrency Trading

The world of cryptocurrency trading presents both opportunities and challenges. More businesses and consumers are likely to adopt cryptocurrencies for everyday transactions, which will drive growth in the trading market (Jothi & Oswalt Manoj, 2022). Cryptocurrencies offer the potential for cheaper, faster, and more efficient transactions, especially across borders. Institutional investors are entering the crypto market, and the DeFi sector is creating innovative new financial products and services. Governments and regulatory bodies worldwide are providing more clarity around the legal status of cryptocurrencies, but regulatory uncertainty remains a significant challenge (Goel & Mittal, 2020).

The regulations surrounding cryptocurrency in the GCC region face various challenges, such as uncertainty in regulatory policies, risks of fraud and security, lack of awareness and education, cross-border transactions, market volatility, and technological hurdles. Collaborating with regulators and promoting international collaboration and compliance standards are essential to address these issues. Risk management strategies, diversified investments, and responsible trading practices are also crucial. Technological advancements in cryptocurrency may seem intimidating for businesses and regulators, but developing a continuous learning and adaptation culture can help. Opportunities in this field include an innovative ecosystem, financial inclusion, blockchain use cases, a digital economy, IP protection and monetisation, environmentally friendly and sustainable cryptocurrency, international collaboration, and fintech hubs. Investing in these areas can attract investment and foster innovation. Additionally, promoting sustainable practices in the cryptocurrency sector can attract local and international talent.

Cryptocurrencies are known for their volatility, providing trading opportunities and posing significant risks. Security will continue to be a major concern, and the environmental impact of cryptocurrencies is a growing concern (Jani, 2018). As the cryptocurrency sector continues to mature, both the opportunities and challenges will evolve. Traders and other market participants must stay adaptable and informed to navigate this rapidly changing landscape. Developing countries can use cryptocurrencies to resolve their difficulties due to their low value and corrupt governments. However, developed nations believe cryptocurrency transactions are expensive and process fees are too high (Fang et al., 2022).

The lack of knowledge about Virtual money in the Real world is the biggest problem causing mathematical differences in any country. Cryptocurrencies are exchanged in an unusual method, and it is essential to understand the features of participating in them (Vandervort, 2014). These include daily trading, volume, and the total market worth. Verification is also important, as verifying a business deal takes time. Additionally, the acceptance of any currency is only valid if it easily moves into the transaction mode. For example, Bitcoin is the most popular form of digital currency, but its acceptability by businesspeople and retailers is lacking (Mujlid, 2023).

9 Conclusion

Cryptocurrency and blockchain technologies have transformed how financial systems and digital property are viewed. They have created new opportunities for innovation, trading, and decentralisation. However, these developments have also introduced unique IP challenges that are still being navigated. These technologies' anonymous and cross-border nature presents substantial difficulties in enforcing IP rights and identifying infringement. The decentralised ethos of the blockchain community clashes with the exclusivity of traditional IP rights. Defining and protecting blockchain-based innovations poses further challenges, requiring fitting ground-breaking technology into established patent categories and guidelines.

Despite these hurdles, blockchain's potential for transforming IP management is considerable. It can provide immutable proof of ownership, automate licensing and royalty payments, and enable direct peer-to-peer transactions. Smart contracts and NFTs are already proving these possibilities and pointing towards a future of programmable, decentralised IP rights (Raman & Raj, 2021).

To ensure economic diversification, the GCC must integrate IP and cryptocurrency instead of relying solely on hydrocarbon resources. It requires establishing regulatory clarity, promoting education, and providing robust IP protection and international collaboration to foster innovation. The GCC must keep up with the rapidly changing cryptocurrency landscape and remain adaptable and agile. The region can lead by building a digital economy hub supporting cryptocurrency trading, blockchain development, and IP protection. Cryptocurrencies can also enhance financial inclusion and access for underserved populations. To achieve local success stories, nurturing a robust innovation ecosystem is vital.

The key to resolving the IP challenges in cryptocurrency trading will be ongoing dialogue and collaboration between tech developers, legal experts, and regulators. As the technology evolves, so too must our legal and regulatory frameworks. Fostering a climate that respects both the open-source ethos of the blockchain community and the need for IP protection will be essential for the continued growth and innovation in this space (Lin et al., 2020).

Cryptocurrencies depend on digital transaction methods, making them vulnerable to hackers, criminals, and other dangers. The cryptocurrency market operates solely on blockchain technology, which facilitates the improvement of future investments (Song et al., 2021). However, investors encounter several obstacles due to the lack of transparency, accountability, and professionalism among cryptocurrency-using organisations. Additionally, there is a liquidity issue concerning cryptocurrency, which is readily manipulable. The greatest disadvantage of the cryptocurrency market is that it is completely unregulated, and the prices of the currencies are used to manipulate each other.

Digital transfers are the quickest transactions, but no agency or authority governs them. Cryptocurrency has the potential to alter people's lifestyles and assist inhabitants of developing nations in participating in the global economy. It has benefited the poor, enabling them to enhance their living standards. It is more effective than traditional paper currency because it operates on a peer-to-peer system, making it easier for the average citizen to control things. It also encourages businesspeople to conduct transactions in multiple currencies, enabling them to utilise these funds within their organisation. Residents of developing nations have reaped long-term benefits, such as creating jobs, expanding the tax base, and contributing to infrastructure funding.

The intersection of IP and cryptocurrencies is a rapidly evolving field. Staying informed about new developments and seeking expert legal advice is crucial for anyone in this sphere. As we continue to explore this new frontier, the lessons learnt will shape the future of IP and cryptocurrency trading.

9.1 Recommendations

- Policymakers must collaborate with international counterparts to harmonise regulations and facilitate cross-border enforcement of IP rights.
- Research and development, international collaboration, sustainable practices, government initiatives, regulation adaptation, digital economy growth, financial inclusion, cybersecurity, and consumer protection with continual monitoring, partnerships, and regulatory sandboxes are necessary.
- The goal is to encourage innovation and growth while protecting investors and promoting environmental sustainability.
- Legal practitioners should stay up-to-date with the latest technological developments, case law, and cryptocurrency regulations and develop expertise in blockchain technology and cryptocurrency.
- Industry participants should prioritise developing a strong IP strategy, including patenting key inventions, ensuring proper licensing agreements, and monitoring potential infringements.
- Legal counsel with expertise in IP law and cryptocurrency must advocate for balanced and fair IP policies protecting innovators' rights while fostering a healthy environment for continued development and growth in the cryptocurrency sector.

References

Abazeed, K. A. (2022). *The Impact of Open Banking on the Islamic Financial Industry*. Doctoral dissertation, Hamad Bin Khalifa University (Qatar).

Allison, J. R., Lemley, M. A., & Schwartz, D. L. (2013). Understanding the realities of modern patent litigation. *Texas Law Review, 92*, 1769.

Al-Riyami, S. S. S., & Nair, S. S. K. (2022). Blockchain for Technological and Mindset Revolution: A Qualitative Study in the Sultanate of Oman. In *Blockchain and Deep Learning: Future Trends and Enabling Technologies* (pp. 221–250). Springer International Publishing.

Al-Shammari, B., Brown, P., & Tarca, A. (2008). An investigation of compliance with international accounting standards by listed companies in the Gulf Co-Operation Council member states. *The International Journal of Accounting, 43*(4), 425–447.

Bamakan, S. M. H., Nezhadsistani, N., Bodaghi, O., & Qu, Q. (2022). Patents and intellectual property assets as non-fungible tokens; key technologies and challenges. *Scientific Reports, 12*(1), 1–13.

Baroudi, S., & Benghida, S. (2022). Blockchain in Dubai: Toward a Sustainable Digital Future. In *Contemporary Research in Accounting and Finance: Case Studies from the MENA Region* (pp. 253–271). Springer Nature Singapore.

Benji, M., & Sindhu, M. (2019). A Study on the Corda and Ripple Blockchain Platforms. In *Advances in Big Data and Cloud Computing: Proceedings of ICBDCC18* (pp. 179–187). Springer.

Chandra, G. R., Sharma, B. K., & Liaqat, I. A. (2019). UAE's strategy towards most cyber resilient nation. *International Journal of Innovative Technology and Exploring Engineering (IJITEE), 8*(12), 2803–2809.

Cheung, A., Roca, E., & Su, J.-J. (2015). Crypto-currency bubbles: An application of the Phillips–Shi–Yu (2013) methodology on Mt. Gox bitcoin prices. *Applied Economics, 47*(23), 2348–2358.

Deepa, N., Pham, Q.-V., Nguyen, D. C., Bhattacharya, S., Prabadevi, B., Gadekallu, T. R., Maddikunta, P. K. R., Fang, F., & Pathirana, P. N. (2022). A survey on blockchain for big data: Approaches, opportunities, and future directions. *Future Generation Computer Systems, 131*, 209–226.

Elshity, E. (2022). Acceptance and use of cryptocurrency in Saudi Arabia: A case study of bitcoins. الحاسبات وتكنولوجيا المعلومات لنظم المصرية الجمعية مجلة, 29(29), 97–117.

Fang, F., Ventre, C., Basios, M., Kanthan, L., Martinez-Rego, D., Wu, F., & Li, L. (2022). Cryptocurrency trading: A comprehensive survey. *Financial Innovation, 8*(1), 1–59.

Gainsbury, S. M., & Blaszczynski, A. (2017). How blockchain and cryptocurrency technology could revolutionize online gambling. *Gaming Law Review, 21*(7), 482–492.

Ghazi, B., Kreuter, B., Kumar, R., Manurangsi, P., Peng, J., Skvortsov, E., Wang, Y., & Wright, C. (2022). Multiparty reach and frequency histogram: Private, secure, and practical. *Proceedings on Privacy Enhancing Technologies, 2022*(1), 373–395.

Goel, S., & Mittal, H. (2020). Economic, legal and financial perspectives on cryptocurrencies: A review on cryptocurrency growth, opportunities and future prospects. *World Review of Entrepreneurship, Management and Sustainable Development, 16*(6), 611–623.

Guadamuz, A. (2020). Smart Contracts and Intellectual Property: Challenges and Reality. In *Intellectual Property and the 4th Industrial Revolution*. Kluwer International Law.

Guajardo, J., Kumar, S. S., Schrijen, G.-J., & Tuyls, P. (2007). Physical Unclonable Functions and Public-Key Crypto for FPGA IP Protection. In *In 2007 International Conference on Field Programmable Logic and Applications* (pp. 189–195). IEEE.

Gürkaynak, G., Yılmaz, I., Yeşilaltay, B., & Bengi, B. (2018). Intellectual property law and practice in the blockchain realm. *Computer Law & Security Review, 34*(4), 847–862.

Hassan, M. K., Jreisat, A., Rabbani, M. R., & Al-Mohamed, S. (2022). Islamic FinTech and Bahrain: An Opportunity for Global Financial Services. In *FinTech in Islamic Financial Institutions: Scope, Challenges, and Implications in Islamic Finance* (pp. 65–87).

He, M. D., Kokenyne, A., Lavayssière, X., Lukonga, M. I., Schwarz, N., Sugimoto, N., & Verrier, J. (2022). Capital flow management measures in the digital age: Challenges of crypto assets. *International Monetary Fund, 2022*(5).

Hellwig, D., Karlic, G., Huchzermeier, A., Hellwig, D., Karlic, G., & Huchzermeier, A. (2020). Blockchain in Action: Real-World Applications. In *Build Your Own Blockchain: A Practical Guide to Distributed Ledger Technology* (pp. 173–183).

Hitsevich, N. (2015). *Intellectual property rights infringement on the internet: An analysis of the private international law implications*. Doctoral dissertation, City, University of London.

Hobbs, A. (2021). Analyzing the Tesla–Bitcoin Investment: What's Next for Cryptocurrencies? In *SAGE Business Cases*. SAGE Publications: SAGE Business Cases Originals.

Hub, Q. F. (2021). From Qatar to the World: A report on the state of FinTech in Qatar (2021).

Hugendubel, J. (2021). *Blockchain technology and intellectual property–A basic introduction*. Available at SSRN 3917801.

Jani, S. (2018). *The Growth of Cryptocurrency in India: Its Challenges & Potential Impacts on Legislation*. Research Gate Publication.

Jothi, K. R., & Oswalt Manoj, S. (2022). A Comprehensive Survey on Blockchain and Cryptocurrency Technologies: Approaches, Challenges, and Opportunities. In *Blockchain, Artificial Intelligence, and the Internet of Things: Possibilities and Opportunities* (pp. 1–22).

Katterbauer, K., Syed, H., & Cleenewerck, L. (2022). The impact of the legalization of Bitcoin in the Central African Republic—A legal analysis. *Cuadernos de Economía, 713*, 746.

Kelaart-Courtney, G. P. (2010). *A model of consumer eService adoption within Dubai*. Doctoral dissertation, Curtin University.

Keohane, R. O., Moravcsik, A., & Slaughter, A. M. (2003). Legalized Dispute Resolution: Interstate and Transnational. In *Power and Governance in a Partially Globalized World* (pp. 152–189). Routledge.

Khoja, T., Rawaf, S., Qidwai, W., Rawaf, D., Nanji, K., Hamad, A., & Khoja, T. (2017). Health care in Gulf Cooperation Council countries: A review of challenges and opportunities. *Cureus, 9*(8).

Kolesnikova. (2018). *VCRIX—Volatility index for crypto-currencies on the basis of CRIX* (pp. 7–38). Master Thesis Submitted to Humboldt University of Berlin 30 May.

Lane, J. (2013). Bitcoin, silk road, and the need for a new approach to virtual currency regulation. *Charleston Law Review, 8*, 511.

Liang, H. W., Chu, Y. C., & Han, T. H. (2023). Fortifying health care intellectual property transactions with blockchain. *Journal of Medical Internet Research, 25*, e44578.

Lin, J., Long, W., Zhang, A., & Chai, Y. (2020). Blockchain and IoT-based architecture design for intellectual property protection. *International Journal of Crowd Science, 4*(3), 283–293.

Lindberg, V. (2008). *Intellectual Property and Open Source: A Practical Guide to Protecting Code*. O'Reilly Media, Inc.

Lopez, C., Bendix, J., & Servin, C. (2020). *Bahrain and the Fourth Industrial Revolution*. Milken Institute.

Mogielnicki, R. (2021). *A Political Economy of Free Zones in Gulf Arab States*. Springer Nature.

Mostert, F., & Jue, W. (2018). The application and challenges of blockchain in intellectual property driven businesses in China. *Tsinghua China Law Review, 11*, 13.

Mujlid, H. (2023). A Survey on Machine Learning Approaches in Cryptocurrency: Challenges and Opportunities. In *2023 4th International Conference on Computing, Mathematics and Engineering Technologies (iCoMET)* (pp. 1–6). IEEE.

Naqvi, S. (2018). Challenges of Cryptocurrencies Forensics: A Case Study of Investigating, Evidencing and Prosecuting Organised Cybercriminals. In *Proceedings of the 13th International Conference on Availability, Reliability and Security* (pp. 1–5).

Ofodile, U. E. (2019). The intersection of FinTechs and trademark law: Focus on cryptocurrency. *UC Davis Law Review Online, 53*, 141.

Ozili, P. K. (2022). Decentralized finance research and developments around the world. *Journal of Banking and Financial Technology, 6*(2), 117–133.

Papaspyridis, A., & Zalan, T. (2017). Accelerating innovation in the UAE: The 3i framework. In *Global opportunities for entrepreneurial growth: Coopetition and knowledge dynamics within and across firms* (pp. 355–391). Emerald Publishing Limited.

Pascoe, L., & Scott, J. (2018). Identifying and dealing with cryptocurrency assets in corporate insolvency. *Australian Restructuring Insolvency & Turnaround Association Journal, 30*(3), 18.

Patrickson, B. (2021). What do blockchain technologies imply for digital creative industries? *Creativity and Innovation Management, 30*(3), 585–595.

Qin, K., Zhou, L., Livshits, B., & Gervais, A. (2021). Attacking the Defi Ecosystem with Flash Loans for Fun and Profit. In *Financial Cryptography and Data Security: 25th International Conference, FC 2021, Virtual Event, March 1–5, 2021* (Revised Selected Papers, Part I) (pp. 3–32). Springer Berlin Heidelberg.

Raman, R., & Raj, B. E. (2021). The World of NFTs (Non-fungible Tokens): The Future of Blockchain and Asset Ownership. In *Enabling Blockchain Technology for Secure Networking and Communications* (pp. 89–108). IGI Global.

Ranganadhan, R. (2023). E-Commerce & jurisdiction: An ongoing tussle. *Indian Journal of Law and Legal Research, 5*(1).

Raymaekers, W. (2015). Cryptocurrency bitcoin: Disruption, challenges and opportunities. *Journal of Payments Strategy & Systems, 9*(1), 30–46.

Read, C. L. (2022). Bitcoin Goes Corporate. In *The Bitcoin Dilemma: Weighing the Economic and Environmental Costs and Benefits* (pp. 69–76). Springer International Publishing.

Sakız, B., & Gencer, A. H. (2021). Blockchain beyond cryptocurrency: Non-fungible tokens. *On Eurasian Economies, 2021*, 144.

Sarra, J., & Gullifer, L. (2019). Crypto-claimants and bitcoin bankruptcy: Challenges for recognition and realization. *International Insolvency Review, 28*, 233.

Savelyev, A. (2018). Copyright in the blockchain era: Promises and challenges. *Computer Law & Security Review, 34*(3), 550–561.

Sistoso, R. (2021). Post-etherdelta: Clarifying liabilities for cryptocurrency exchanges and market participants. *Cardozo Arts and Entertainment Law Journal, 39*, 343.

Söderberg, G. (2018). Are bitcoin and other crypto-assets money? *Economic Commentaries, 5*, 14.

Song, H., Zhu, N., Xue, R., He, J., Zhang, K., & Wang, J. (2021). Proof-of-Contribution consensus mechanism for blockchain and its application in intellectual property protection. *Information Processing & Management, 58*(3), 102507.

Steensma, H. K., Chari, M., & Heidl, R. (2015). The quest for expansive intellectual property rights and the failure to disclose known relevant prior art. *Strategic Management Journal, 36*(8), 1186–1204.

Sulimierska, M., & Sikorska, A. (2023). The Cryptoassets Market in the United Kingdom: Regulatory and Legal Challenges. In *The Fintech Disruption: How Financial Innovation Is Transforming the Banking Industry* (pp. 215–242). Springer International Publishing.

Sung, H.-C. (2019). Prospects and challenges posed by blockchain technology on the copyright legal system. *Queen Mary Journal of Intellectual Property, 9*(4), 430–451.

Tredinnick, L. (2019). Cryptocurrencies and the blockchain. *Business Information Review, 36*(1), 39–44.

Valdeolmillos, D., Mezquita, Y., González-Briones, A., Prieto, J., & Corchado, J. M. (2020). Blockchain Technology: A Review of the Current Challenges of Cryptocurrency. In *Blockchain and Applications: International Congress* (pp. 153–160). Springer International Publishing.

van Flymen, D., & van Flymen, D. (2020). Blockchains. In *Learn Blockchain by Building One: A Concise Path to Understanding Cryptocurrencies* (pp. 29–38).

Vandervort, D. (2014). Challenges and Opportunities Associated with a Bitcoin-Based Transaction Rating System. In *Financial Cryptography and Data Security: FC 2014 Workshops, BITCOIN and WAHC 2014, Christ Church, Barbados, March 7, 2014* (Revised Selected Papers 18) (pp. 33–42). Springer Berlin Heidelberg.

Wang, Q., Li, R., Wang, Q., & Chen, S. (2021) Non-fungible token (NFT): Overview, evaluation, opportunities and challenges. arXiv preprint arXiv:2105.07447.

Wilson, C. (2019). Cryptocurrencies: The Future of Finance?. In *Contemporary Issues in International Political Economy* (pp. 359–394).

Yli-Huumo, J., Ko, D., Choi, S., Park, S., & Smolander, K. (2016). Where is current research on blockchain technology? A systematic review. *PLoS One, 11*(10), e0163477.

Zaki, A., Danish, A., & Jamia Millia Islamia. (n.d.). Great crypto expectations: The road to blockchain and intellectual property rights. In *JUSCHOLARS, 1*(3), 12–15. https://lawbhoomi.com/wp-content/uploads/2020/10/176c0-414130_7626247ac6724473b7bc594f49845afd-1.pdf

CHAPTER 11

Liability Gap, Personhood Theories and Effective AI Legal Framework in the GCC Countries: Shariah as the Thread That Binds

Ida Madieha Abdul Ghani Azmi
and Mahyuddin Daud

1 Introduction

The rapid transformation of the GCC countries is now being supported with ambitious national plans to deploy AI and emerging technologies. The Saudi's Vision 2030 that has been cited as a model for other GCC countries, for example, outlines several key initiatives including the setting up of institutions to oversee the development and governance of AI in the country. They include setting up a national centre for AI, an AI regulator, a national data management office and AI college (Hanafi et al., 2021).

Ida Madieha Abdul Ghani Azmi (✉) • M. Daud
Civil Law Department, International Islamic University Malaysia,
Kuala Lumpur, Wilayah Persekutuan, Malaysia
e-mail: imadieha@iium.edu.my

N. Naim et al. (eds.), *Intellectual Property and Innovation*, The Political Economy of the Middle East,
https://doi.org/10.1007/978-981-96-4020-1_11

Saudi's National Strategy for Data and AI (NSDAI), dubbed ASPIRE, aimed to contribute to the Kingdom's effort to move their economy from fuel-based exports to AI-based products and services. Qatar introduced the National AI Strategy which is focussed on six pillars: education, data access, employment, business, research and ethics to spearhead its AI initiatives (Hanafi et al., 2021). The UAE, through its Artificial Intelligence Strategy 2031, intends to deploy the application and incorporation of AI and emerging technologies in transforming its business, government and society, most prominently the transportation industry, where they conducted trials for Alibaba Cloud's 'City Brain', a system that incorporates AI in traffic management (Hanafi et al., 2021).

The GCC countries have embarked on significant investments in AI, hoping to harvest substantial benefit from it. One core area is to create an attractive environment for tech companies to invest in the AI sector (Hanafi et al., 2021). It is foreseen that the economic gain from such investments will be astronomical with figures ranging from billions to half a trillion dollars. The creation of value from AI technologies, however, hinges on several factors: supportive legal framework, effective governance, leading institutions as well as talent acquisition. For example, a total of 20,000 data and AI specialists are targeted to be trained as well as 300 active data and AI start-ups are planned to be trained in 2020 to fuel the AI industry growth (Hanafi et al., 2021).

One of the key components of all these national strategies is the regulatory ecosystem. As Shariah is the foundation of the legal regulation in the GCC countries, this chapter explores the personhood of AI from the perspective of Shariah. As international practice factors heavily in all these GCC countries, Saudi Arabia, for example, aims to create a regulation that fosters a business-friendly environment, and based on international practice, the debate within contemporary scholarship on such matter is also examined.

Principle 7 of the Kingdom's AI Ethics Principles is accountability and responsibility. This principle puts the responsibility to those persons responsible in the designing and developing of the AI systems and oversee the smooth running of the system, as well as the potential risk and negative effects on users of such systems (Saudi Data and AI Authority, 2023). Attribution of liability to the designers and developers of the AI systems requires a clear exposition of the legal status of the artificial intelligence, i.e. the personhood theories, on which this chapter is focussing.

As Shariah is the golden thread that binds the GCC countries (Price & AlDebasi, 2017), an exposition of legal personhood within Shariah perspectives is imperative. On this, the argument is that the transformation that is currently taking place must be embedded together with Shariah laws and value (Naim, 2019, 2021).

As such, this chapter aims to provide a preliminary analysis of the following:

1. importance of legal personhood in determining rights and obligations;
2. the philosophical discourse of 'personhood' from the Orthodox, Hohfeldian and Bundle of Rights perspective, as well as contemporary discourse; and
3. the ontological status of 'personhood' within Muslim scholar's discourse.

2 Importance of Legal Personhood

Legal personhood is important for three separate purposes. First is the determination of responsibility (Smith, 1928). As many autonomous devices, vehicles, apparatus and devices may cause accidents, it has been argued that AI, or the human beings behind the development and design of the AI system, be considered responsible for the ensuing consequences. The second purpose is the determination of rights. As these autonomous systems can complete many human tasks and transactions with perfection, it is argued that the AI, or the individuals behind the AI, should be able to claim certain rights over the outcome of the task (Kurki, 2019a, 2019b). Some examples here are Dall E and ChatGPT, AI platforms that are known for generating content. Although, the ensuing issue is whether these AI systems can claim copyright or patent over the outcome by claiming itself to be authors and inventors. Lastly, legal personhood is important for commercial purposes (Kurki, 2019a, 2019b). If the content created by AI cannot be owned, then it is free for all to use. The analogy is like 'terra nullius', i.e. common resources that are part of public domain and not subjected to private ownership. The notion of 'nobody's land' may pose problems for commercialisation and may lead to over utilisation. Common ownership may also undermine the investment placed in the development of the AI system in the first place.

The European Parliament alluded to the notion that transactions and activities involving AIs and robots require legal certainty in the form of regulation involving legal status for purposes of attribution and responsibility in 2017. The proposal at that time was to come up with 'electronic personality', a hybrid form of personality akin to corporate personality. In a study by the European Parliament in 2020 (Bertolini, 2020), the notion of electronic personality entails two different notions. The first notion envisions the legal status of AI and robots to be in between things and human beings. Such endowment of legal status is predicated on the basis that these autonomous systems are sufficiently intelligent, capable of learning and self-determining. The second alternative interpretation endows AI and robots with artificial personality only for purposes of functionality. The responsibility that accrues from transactions conducted through them requires legal certainty in terms of attribution that some form of artificial personality be conferred to them. The EU AI Act seeks to resolve that issue by instead focussing on the 'risk' posed by using the AI systems, emphasising on data documentation, traceability and human oversight on high-risk AI systems. The target of the Act is to limit the risks of violation of fundamental rights in the usage of AI systems.

The discourse on 'electronic personality' would have to be seen from the decades-long discourse on the other non-human entities, to which this chapter turns.

2.1 Debates on Personhood of Non-human

The debates as to whether a non-human can be bestowed 'personhood' are nothing new. For decades, scholars and courts alike have been grappling with the issue as to whether other entities besides humans can be considered as 'legal-persons'. Some scholars believe that it is not yet appropriate to grant AI full legal personhood as the potential consequences of granting such status to AI could have unintended consequences, and there is often confusion between legal agenthood and legal personhood of the AI (Pagallo, 2018). Since the existing legal framework for AI is still inadequate, a hybrid model of corporate legal personhood was proposed as it can provide a more effective solution to the issue (Raskulla, 2023). Apart from that, other scholars believe that granting AI the ability to be an inventor does not mean that AI is a legal person (Thaldar & Naidoo, 2021).

Animal rights have been the subject of significant debates and even court litigation. A significant decision was entered into in 2014 in relation to animal rights (in this case chimpanzees) in *People ex rel. Nonhuman Rights Project, Inc. v. Lavery, p. 1, henceforth Nonhuman* (998 N.Y.S.2d 248 (2014)). Even though the New York State Supreme Court, Appellate Division endorsed the position that chimpanzees should not be physically restrained, this right is not equivalent to that conferred to a human being in the context of habeas corpus. The court ruled that the notion of 'legal personhood' in its full sense must embody both rights and corresponding duties. As it is impossible to expect some form of fulfilment of these duties from animals, it defeats the purpose of conferring them with the right of legal personhood. The court stated that animals should not have the same legal rights as human beings because they cannot meet all of society's obligations. The term 'person' is frequently used to refer to a human being in legal texts, as well as other texts and everyday speech, but the precise definition of a 'person' is a topic of legal rights and obligations, according to the New York Supreme Court (*People ex rel. Nonhuman Rights Project, Inc. v. Lavery* (998 N.Y.S.2d 248 (2014))).

Beside animals, the position of the unborn could equally be useful in this discourse. Kurki, in his work, investigates the legal status of the animals, artificial intelligence and the unborn by having a broad look at the basic idea of rights and duties (Kurki, 2019a, 2019b). The most important inquiry is the basic notion of legal right and the status of legal person (Afrouzi, 2020). The prevailing assumption is that a legal person would be subjected to legal rights and responsibilities, which creates a nexus between being the status of a legal person and being able to have a legal role in any transactions and activities. On this basis, only humans can be capable of exercising both rights and responsibilities, thus deserving of its legal status as persons in the eyes of the law.

3 Legal Person as the Bearer of Rights and Duties

Bearing the importance of rights and duties to personhood, one can still draw a distinction between passive rights and active rights. Infants, for example, enjoy full legal status even though they are not capable of responding to events happening to them. Adults, on the other hand, enjoy full legal status as they can respond and act against any incidents that occur to them. Regardless, infants are deserving only passive rights as they cannot act on the rights, whilst a full adult will enjoy full active rights.

Any discourse on personhood often starts from the Orthodox Roman view. The Roman jurist Gaius divides components of laws into three categories: persons (personae), things (res) and actions (actiones). In that sense, Gaius visualise persons to be the entire opposite of things (Trahan, 2006). According to Cicero, humans have four distinct personas: reason, personal characteristics, position and occupation (Gill, 1988). The personae, according to Boethius, are 'the unique substance of rational nature' (Kurki, 2019a, 2019b). This concept is essential for establishing that only humans have legal personhood as personhood is seen as the persona needed to play a legal role in this world. The Roman conception of 'persona' remains influential to the modern day and has resulted in the notion that personhood is synonymous to 'right holding and duty bearing' (Wieacker, 1995).

The strict traditional view on personhood leaves 'non-human' entities in a no-zone position in legal theories. Kurki questions the wisdom of the Roman theories and moves to analyse Hohfeldian analysis, to determine whether such analysis will grant a better position to non-human entities. He concedes that Hohfeld also held the view that only humans are legal beings and bearers of legal positions (Kurki, 2019a, 2019b). However, Hohfeldian analysis can be distilled into five formulations and if correctly applied would not preclude entitlement of non-humans to legal relations (Kurki, 2019a, 2019b).

The first formulation is the Rights-or-Duties position, where a legal person can be any entity that holds at least one right or bears at least one duty. The second formulation is the Rights-and-Duties position that warrants a person to hold at least one right and bear at least one duty (Pratama & Rizkiyah, 2022). The third formulation is the Capacity for Rights position where the capacity to exercise rights is the foundation of legal status (Wise, 2015a, 2015b). The fourth formulation focuses on the capacity to participate in legal relations. The fifth formulation looks at the whole combination of rights and obligation as a bundle, also known as the bundle theory (Kurki, 2019a, 2019b).

Further unbundling of the correlation of rights and duties or interests leads to several conceptions. The interest theory right, for example, could be applied to foetuses, animals and enslaved people. The interests possessed by these entities hold rights that are enforceable in a court of law, although such rights are not enforceable by them but rather against them. The will theory, on the other hand, looks at rights as being enforceable if the right-holder possesses the will to do so. On this basis, newborns, animals and persons with mental disorders are not considered to have rights as they have no will to act on or exercise these rights. The last theory is the 'anything beneficial theory', which predicates on the premise that 'any beneficial legal position is a right' (Kurki, 2019a, 2019b).

Applying the bundle theory, Kurki opined that AI is of ultimate value; therefore, AI deserves to be protected along the same line as human children. This notion is considerably contentious as the AI in its current state is nowhere in the position of human children. Furthermore, the consequences of the activities undertaken by AI may create difficulties in the human world as some form of responsibilities and accountabilities may accrue. Finally, as these transactions may also pertain to the commercial context, some legal rights ancillary to issues such as ownership and transfer of rights would arise. In Kurki's opinion, the interest deserved by AI can be classified as claim-rights, i.e. AI may enjoy certain claims that can be considered as correlatives to rights. In that sense, there are two prevailing assertions at each end of a spectrum, one which considers AI as nothing more than a mere tool where its designer is held responsible, and at the other end, AI should be held responsible for its own actions. In the final analysis, in the case of strong AIs, there may be a necessity to endow it with legal personhood in certain incidents, only to recognise its function as an independent commercial actor, along the same line as corporations (Kurki, 2019a, 2019b).

Unlike Kurki that focuses on 'interest-right' as being an essential component of 'personhood', others cast their attention to 'free will, intelligence and consciousness' as the essence of a 'person'. Taking the premise that a legal person is essentially 'a subject of legal rights and duties', this does not naturally mean that only a natural person enjoys such status. The most fundamental question would be 'should' an entity be subjected to legal rights and duties and 'what' type of entity enjoy such status? In that sense, the 'person' only exists in relation to an abstract capacity to function in law, due to a special status created by law to serve certain functionalities (Van Genderen, 2018).

4 AI as Legal Persons?

For supporter of 'sui generis' standard for autonomous technologies, the concept of 'personhood' is a notional one, a bit like the 'Cheshire Cat', depending on the degree of autonomy and societal needs (Van Genderen, 2018). This notion is absent of any moral or ethical ground. In relation to

AI, the purpose could be in the economic benefit derived from the transactions carried through or for the social welfare of the society. The main argument is that there should be departure from the strict traditional theory of personhood to one pragmatic notion that serves economic benefits and brings certainty in a court of law. The lack of consciousness and free will means that the AI is yet to function as a responsible and rational actor to be eligible for full legal personhood. On that basis, there is a need for a framework in which legal consequences of AI activities are framed to give certainty to the society.

A 'truncated' form of legal personhood, one which is more nuanced than legal ontology, is an alternative argument. The preferred view is that instead of personhood, one should look at agenthood instead to give legitimacy to the transactions undertaken by an AI platform in civil law (Van Genderen, 2018). The most important point is to make someone or something accountable and liable to the contracts and businesses conducted by the AI. The truncated form of legal personhood is not only limited to civil liability but also restricted to the scope, capabilities and functions of an AI system. Proper regulations must be set pertaining to the direction of the development of AI. If any AI is perceived to be dangerous, then it should not be released to the public. This is also the main thrust of the EU AI Act that seeks to keep the high-risk AI systems away from public consumption. The suggestion is to come up with a form of compulsory insurance to cover losses arising from the use of AI platforms. The last suggestion is to have a registration system, even if it is an international one, for AI technologies which are dangerous and harmful as early warning to users would be useful (Militsyna, 2022).

With the elaborate discussion on the concept of personhood in contemporary literature, the discussion now moves to the exposition of the personhood concept in Muslim scholarship.

4.1 *Personhood of AI Within the Sharia Legal Framework*

Could AI make autonomous decisions independent of human beings? Is it entitled to being conferred a legal status, just like human beings? In legal parlance, the question of legal status needs to be determined first before such entity can be afforded legal rights and obligations. There has been a plethora of discussions regarding personhood, in which the conclusions are branched into two: (1) an entity who fulfils the criteria of personhood deserves to be treated as a human and (2) no matter how similar it is to the constitution of a human being, the entity cannot be conferred personhood.

4.2 *Personhood in Islam*

The question of 'personhood' in Islam revolves around the issue of when ensoulment happens and when a human can be considered old enough to bear some responsibilities. In religious parlance, central to the foundation of personhood is the process of ensoulment. The Quran speaks in clarity the process of ensoulment as the initiation and the source of personhood. The sole objective of the religious prescription of ensoulment is the noble belief the result would be that the lineage (*nasb*) of a person is protected. Ensoulment is described clearly in the Quran as follows:

> And certainly, did We create man from an extract of clay. Then We placed him as a drop of sperm, firmly fixed. Then We made the sperm into a clot of congealed blood, and of that clot We made an embryo; then We made of that lump, bones, and clothed the bones with flesh. Then We developed another creation out of it. So blessed is God, the best of Creators. (Qur'an 23: 12–14)

Opinions from other Muslim scholars seem to suggest that the main distinction between a human apart from other creations of any sort is the mental and rational element (Latif, 2022). The theory of personhood in Islam is grounded in its religious prescription that personhood is not limited to just cognitive abilities but a combination of a soul and thinking abilities (Rohman et al., 2022).

Like the Western view of personhood, once a person is endowed with legal status, all rights and obligations from his conduct accrue. Therefore, what follows is the question of sins and accountability for one's actions. On this point, Hasan Al-Basri propounded that personhood means the ability to live one's life according to his free will (Riddell, 2019). Although in the Islamic world, a man is to live his life based on Allah's guidelines and laws, he finds that human beings are afforded a certain degree of free will in determining their lives trajectory (Riddell, 2005). Therefore, with this comes another requirement of personhood, i.e. free will.

The discussion on free will is extremely crucial as it is the main prerequisite for someone to be a 'legal person'. A legal person therefore has the right to sue and be sued in law and can have their rights enforced in courts. Hence, the notion of legal personality is derived from moral agency which is regarded as having the cognitive function, autonomy and intention to act in free will. A person is allowed to make moral judgements based on their free will (Almajid, 2010) and in the same token will be equally accountable for his choice and action.

The famous Muslim philosopher, Muhammad Iqbal, posits that what distinguishes a human from others is the human soul. He considers the sole guide or source of power to the human soul to be the revelation, i.e. religious guidance from the Quran and Sunnah. Therefore, revelation serves as the compass to assist humans in navigating their daily journey to submit themselves to the Almighty. For Iqbal, the notion of personhood stems from human agency and that human agency is only realised when one acts on intuition. In describing intuition, Iqbal use words like faith, love and certainty. Iqbal views that a human life journey is to perfect himself and to better know, and serve, his Creator (Hillier & Koshul, 2017). That is one key notion of personhood, the purpose in which a person is created is to get closer to his Creator and to obtain more knowledge of his Lord.

Furthermore, the notion of personhood bears more significance in the Islamic religious world than just financial responsibility akin to corporate responsibility, or to determine culpability in criminal trials or abortion cases. Personhood is highly relevant in defining a person as Allah's servant and therefore must live their lives in full compliance with His laws. In Islam, the purpose of a personhood is to worship Him. This is as defined by the Islamic scholar Abu-Saud, who identifies three primary characteristics of personhood. The first and foremost is to worship God, second is so that mankind can be endowed with the obligations and responsibilities of being the vicegerent of Allah on earth. Man is best suited for this role as only man is recognised as the perfect creation. Moreover, mankind is created to make a living on earth and prosper as a form of stewardship to his Creator (Riddell, 2005).

In Islam, personhood can also be viewed in legal parlance in the forms of legal capacity which come in two forms. The first is termed as full capacity (أهلية الوجوب الكاملة), which entails that the person is endowed with both the legal rights to be treated as a human as well as the religious obligations to Allah and other human beings. The other type of capacity is the incomplete capacity (أهلية الوجوب الناقصة). This form of capacity is associated with infants and those without the ability to have normal cognitive thinking abilities (Bar'I, 2022). For these people, it is mandatory that they be afforded the rights to be treated as a human being, but they are not imposed the full obligation as a Muslim with complete capacity, such as to pray five times daily, or to give alms (Zakah), or to perform the other obligatory supplication.

In terms of the obligation to perform certain mandatory supplication including the five daily prayers, the main criteria that render a person obliged to perform such physical supplications or) (عبادة, will be the performance capacity (أهلية الأداء). This type of capacity comprises two main requirements that must be fulfilled before a Muslim is imposed with the obligation to execute their religious duties. The first is that there must be the ability to understand the Shariah discourses or the reasoning behind the mandatory nature of the religious duties. This remains the most important aspect as in cases of children, they can fulfil the second requirement which is to have the ability to perform the religious duties, but they do not have the cognitive ability to understand why these duties are obligated to them. Therefore, on the same argument, any contractual transaction with them is completely void as their mental capacity is not fully developed. The only exception would be in relation to mumayyiz (مرحلة التمييز). These are children who are yet to attain puberty but have developed the required mental capacity to understand the nature of their religious obligations (Bar'i, 2022).

On this note, Almajid espouses that the terminology in *fiqh* closest to the concept of 'legal personality' as '*dhimmah*' (الذمة) (Almajid). The term that refers to legal capacity is *ahliyyah* (الأهلية), being the prerequisite for having any rights or duties, whether religious or financial. The source of these obligations stems from the fundamental view that humans are created in this world to be vicegerents of God. In that sense, the concept of *dhimmah* is broader than legal capacity as it also extends to obligations in the hereafter, not only of this world. By using this concept, automatically electronic agents would be excluded as they, being non-living matter, are not accountable for their deeds in the hereafter. In the same token, the concept of *dhimmah* cannot be attributed to corporations, as they are not accountable for their deeds in religious manner. However, many Muslim scholars have accepted the conferment of legal status on corporations for functional reasons taking into analogy of the case of *waqf* administrator (Almajid, 2010). Among others, this is to ensure that responsibilities out of transaction carried by the corporations can be carried through by the directors of the corporations, regardless of how many times the directorship has changed. Al Majid views the *dhimmah* which was conferred on '*waqf*' is akin to *ahliyyah al-wujub* and not *ahliyyah al ada* as these *waqfs*, as well as corporations, do not have the capacity to perform and conduct affairs. Instead, these conducts are done by the directors and those running the corporations (Almajid, 2010).

5 Capacity for Legal Rights, Duties or Legal Relations

Within Islamic scholarship, the proposition is that legal personhood relates to the capacity to hold legal rights or to be a party of legal relations. According to a strict traditional view, legal rights are not plucked from the air, or simply exist or created. The official view from Muslim scholars is that legitimate rights are those stemming from and supported by textual provisions from the Quran and Sunnah. Al Zarqa stresses that the term legal right or '*haqq*' refers only to express power or obligation recognised by the Shariah. In the same tone, Al Ibadi reiterates the importance of explicit textual authority from the Creator lawgiver (*alkhatib*) either in the form of mandate or proscription (Al Ibadi, 1974). Such a view restricts the creation of new rights to those only with the textual support of the primary sources of the Shariah (Al-Zarqa, 1946).

In discussing the rights and obligations, the traditional view is that human should be the 'subject' of rights and duties, in the sense of being capable of holding rights, and 'object' of rights as being the recipient of such legal rights? Abdul Salam Daud Al Ibadi (1974) stresses that both the right-holder (*sahib al-haqq*) and the recipient of the right, i.e. party to whom the *haqq* is addressed or the '*mukallaf*', must be natural humans. In that sense, both the giving and the receiving end must be natural persons. As to the argument as to whether rights and duties can exist separately, one well-known Muslim scholar Prof Hashim Kamali disagreed vehemently. His view is that a legal right cannot be detached from the corresponding duty as they are like two sides of a coin. But most importantly, rights supersede duty and is emphasised more in legal obligations and always seen as subservient to duty. The emphasis on textual evidence means that in the 'original absence of liability' maxim (*bara'ah al-dhimmah al-asliyyah*), no legal rights can accrue (Kamali, 1993).

The traditional equation of personhood with legal capacity in transactions manifests in many old fiqh treatise. One of it is the *Mejelle*, which is officially known as *Majallat al-Ahkam al-Adliyyah*, a codification of

Islamic law (Shariah) principles related to civil matters. The *Mejelle* was adopted during the Ottoman Empire and is still used in some jurisdictions influenced by Islamic law. The Code spells out certain rights and responsibilities of individuals, inter alia, in Part II under the heading of maxims of Islamic Jurisprudence. Article 89 of the *Mejelle* stipulates that:

> The responsibility for an act falls upon the author thereof; it does not fall upon the person ordering such act to be performed, provided that such person does not compel the commission thereof. (Al Majalla 1302H, n.d.)

The Article expressly imposes an obligation upon the author and not on some other person even if the act committed by that author was instructed or ordered by other individuals, with the condition that it was done with free will.

From the Article, it could also be observed that the *Mejelle* generally embraces the provisions relating to rights and liabilities of an individual, ranging from the rights to personal safety, property, contractual freedom, legal representation, as well as the rights to due process. In relation to the discussion on personhood and legal rights, the rights to property would be relevant. The Code enumerates that individuals have the right to own, possess and dispose of property in accordance with the principles of Islamic law. This includes rights related to ownership, use, enjoyment and transfer of property. In this context, if an AI were to fit into this description, it would be required to be able to own, possess, enjoy, use and dispose of the property owned freely, and in the context of intellectual property, it refers to intangible property.

Legal duties and responsibilities as provided in the Code embrace the fulfilment of contractual obligations, honouring financial obligations, respect for other's rights, compliance with Islamic legal principles and co-operation with legal authorities. All these responsibilities are meant to cater for personhood, i.e. human beings as a natural person. Muslim scholars have also explored the legal status of non-person, which the discussion now proceeds.

6 Non-person in Islam

The notion of non-person is not an alien term in Islamic discourse. The prevailing view is that it should not be misunderstood that a non-person being does not and will never obtain any legal status. For example, in

Islam, foetuses must be conferred certain human rights. This means a foetus is considered a person from the moment the ensoulment happens. The Quran has in many occasions touched on the rights of foetuses and the steps to safeguard their wellbeing.

In many scholastic characterisation of a person, biological considerations remain at the top of the list. The lack of individuality in a foetus also led some Western scholars to argue that despite the ensoulment, a foetus lacks full legal status. As the foetus is still growing, he lacks internal stability and numerical unity, and though he may feel pain, his senses are not fully developed yet, specifically its cognitive abilities. The ability for rational thinking is what distinguished a human from animals and other things. In a classic example, St. Thomas Aquinas defined a person as 'a subsistent individual of a rational nature' (Smith, 1983). In this context, there is a clear disparity in the line of thinking between Muslim scholars and Western natural thinkers when discussing about human beings.

Nevertheless, one theory which runs parallel to the Islamic definition of personhood, one that is avidly used by pro-life supporters, is the theory of potentiality. The theory presents the idea of (1) anything without a soul and has the potential to be something or (2) an 'agent' will be alive with soul after undergoing certain modifications or natural changes. The attention is on what the agent can do on its own rather than what can be done with it. This is called active potentiality, or in a living being's case natural potentiality, where if a foetus is left to its natural due course will eventually develop into a baby. For example, a clay, if no action or motion is asserted on it, will remain a piece of clay forever. On the other hand, a foetus, if left untouched in its due course, is a potential human and the destruction of a foetus, outside of its natural inclination, is like killing a person (Smith, 1983).

As for animals, according to Ibn Sina, they are considered as the creatures of Allah with soul. The only thing separating them from a person is the element of intellect or rational thinking. The element of intellect is a distinct characteristic that defines personhood, as it allows a person to acknowledge its own existence without the assistance of all five faculties of the body. An animal does not have such capabilities in which without their sense of smell and sight, they are not able to understand the reasons of their existence nor can they acknowledge themselves as being in existence (Mokhtar, 1994). Interestingly, this notion is parallel to the metaphysical definition of personhood proposed by Aquinas where a person is a 'complete individual entity which is able to exist by itself in that it possesses its own act of existing and in itself'.

7 Framing the Discussion

However intelligent, creative, efficient or legally accurate an AI is, legally and ethically it cannot represent, what more replaces, a human being. The granting of human personhood entails several consequences, most importantly in terms of rights and responsibilities. Despite the compelling normative arguments in favour of passive rights or from the angle of bundle of rights, with respect, those theories do not explore incidence of rights, privileges and responsibilities in its full ecosystem. In Islam, rights and responsibilities arise because of human interaction with others as well as his accountability to his ultimate Creator. Conferring rights to non-humans that owe no accountability to the Creator will be an exercise in futility. Ultimately, the core question to the exercise is to ask ourselves, honestly, for what purpose are we creating these new legal entities? If the objective is to empower human beings using AI tools and to make the AI accountable to their deeds and conduct, then the central question should be focused on these humans rather than the AI tools themselves.

Therefore, in the field of AI, if one were to argue that an AI can be granted personhood in Islam, the problem becomes, does AI have the capacity to be a *wakil* or perform Islamic contracts on behalf of someone? While other contemporary Muslim scholars agree that AI should be employed for low-level tasks such as smart contracts, this AI must be employed with specific guidelines (Nawi et al., 2021). Nonetheless, as there will be plenty of issues and discussions arising from granting AI the status of a person, a majority of the scholars agreed that an AI must not be considered a person on the basis of the Islamic jurisprudential maxim *Sadd al-Dhariah* approach, which is to prohibit any actions, ex ante, before bad consequences even occur (Nawi et al., 2021).

From all these discussions, the notion of legal personhood by Muslim scholars in *fiqhi* books bears more significance in the Islamic world in the form of legal capacity and ability to bear rights and obligations. This is unlike the recognition of the legal status of corporations for the purpose of financial responsibility akin to corporate responsibility. In Islamic traditional view, the significance of legal status is to determine culpability in criminal trials or abortion cases. It is for that reason, in a religious sense, one's personhood stems from the position of that person as Allah's servant and his life journey towards him. The whole corpus of rights and responsibilities, and all the consequential liabilities accruing therefrom, either in the form of penalty and retribution is to test humans so that they live their lives in full compliance with His laws.

In Islam the purpose of a personhood is to worship Him. This is as defined by the Islamic scholar Abu-Saud who identified the primary characteristics of personhood (Riddell, 2005). The first and foremost is to worship God, the second is so that mankind can be endowed with the obligations of being the vicegerent of Allah on earth. This obligation requires the ability of the human intellect as described by Ibn Sina and the drive and encouragement to fight for Allah. Man is best suited for this role as only man has the required faculties. In religious worldview, a human is created 'to cause growth on earth and make it more resourceful for his own benefit, welfare and prosperity' (Riddell, 2005).

Hence, it can be deduced that a person is only considered as a person if under Islamic law he will be answerable to Allah for his religious duties and he will be punished should he neglect these obligations.

In the context of responsibility, it has been raised whether the AIs as electronic agents can be conferred legal status under Islamic law. The argument is that these advanced computer systems that are capable of concluding transactions autonomously without the user's involvement be recognised so that the contracts are enforceable. If the electronic agents are considered as 'agents' on behalf of the human principals, then these electronic agents need legal status as well. The view is that if some form of recognition need be given to electronic agents, then the traditional interpretation of the concepts of '*dhimmah*' cannot be adopted (Almajid, 2010).

It is in this context that the Committee on Legal Affairs of the European Union made the following calls to the Commission in 2017 to:

> explore, analyse and consider the implications of all possible legal solutions, such as [...] creating a specific legal status for robots in the long run, so that at least the most sophisticated autonomous robots could be established as having the status of electronic persons responsible for making good any damage they may cause, and possibly applying electronic personality to case where robots make autonomous decisions or otherwise interact with third parties independently.

The call was followed by another EU in 2020 to the following:

> There are no technological, philosophical, nor legal reasons to deem machines as neither equal to human beings, nor belonging to an intermediate category to be distinguished between the two.

The fact that robots, or in the context of this chapter AI, are human made, not autonomous, cannot display self-determination, not independent defies the whole notion of personhood. The Report acknowledges the responsibility gap could be a form to detract the responsibility of the human beings behind the running of an AI.

Deriving from the Report, it is the exact lack of autonomy and purposeful action that deprives AI the status of legal person. Instead, AI reacts to certain predefined set of instructions in the form of algorithm and to undertake specific response as pre-programmed. What is required instead is a set of rules to determine the liability of activities conducted by AI as not doing so may lead to a 'liability gap', whereby the humans behind an AI are left scot-free. It is also possible that these humans may be accountable for the conducts of AI beyond their sanction.

Both scenarios are problematic as many legal actions require 'intention' or 'harm' which may not be precipitated by technical reaction dictated by programming codes (Novelli et al., 2021). In this case Novelli et al. suggested that a 'particular' legal status or even different legal statuses depending on the levels or performance and autonomy of AI as well as nature of the transactions and activities (Novelli et al., 2021). If the focus is more on responsibility and accountability and not full legal status as legal person, there may be compelling argument for Muslims and GCC countries to shift from the traditional conception of personhood. Through this shift, there will less strong legal obstacles to fully adopting AI in the GCC countries as there is no possibility of the 'liability gap' arising from the transactions and activities conducted using or by AI.

8 Conclusion

The whole discourse on conferring legal personhood to AI is premature. Many scholars have alluded to the fact that the AI systems in their current state are in no position to be considered as truly independent or autonomous that justifies such status. What is needed instead is clear exposition of potential civil and criminal liabilities arising from transactions or activities using AI platforms. The need for legal certainties on these legal issues is the exact rationale behind the framing of the EU AI Act.

Whilst this chapter tries to explore the possible arguments on legal personhood from Shariah perspectives, it must be acknowledged that this discussion is still preliminary. With the fast adoption of AI in the entire ecosystems of human life, a more serious, in-depth jurisprudential inquiry on this will be anticipated and much required in the future.

Acknowledgement This research is funded by the Malaysian Ministry of Higher Education under FRGS21-225-0834, entitled 'The Legal Framework for the Use of Artificial Intelligence in Legal Practice in Malaysia: Balancing Due Process and Access to Justice'.

References

998 N.Y.S.2d 248. (2014).

Afrouzi, A. E. (2020). Visa A.J. Kurki, A Theory of Legal Personhood. *Modern Law Review, 83*(6), 1354–1358.

Al Ibadi, A. S. D. (1974). *al-Milkiyya fi—al Shari'ah al-Islamiyyah: Tabi'aṭuha wa Wazifatuha wa Quyududa: Dirasah Muqaranah bi al-Qawanin wa an-Nuzum al-Wad'iyyah.* al Maktabah al Aqsa.

Al Majalla al Ahkam Al Adliyyah. (1302H). al-Maṭba'ah al-Adabiyyah. (n.d.).

Almajid, W. M. (2010). Can Electronic Agents Be Granted Legal Personality under Islamic Law? A Conceptual Rethink Is Imperative. *Arab Law Quarterly, 24*(4), 393–416. https://doi.org/10.1163/157302510X526733

Al-Zarqa, M. A. (1946). *Al-Figh al-Islami fi Thaubihi al-Jadid Al-Madkhal ila an-Nazariyyah al-Itizam al-Ammah fi al-Figh al-Islami* (Vol. 3). Damsyik.

Bar'i, A. S. A. (2022). Review of *Tatbiqat Althazakat Alistina'i Wa Rubut Min Manzur Alislam. Majallah Darul Iftaa' Almasriyyah, 14*(48), 88. https://doi.org/10.21608/dftaa.2022.231631

Bertolini, A. (2020). *Artificial Intelligence and Civil Liability.* https://www.europarl.europa.eu/thinktank/es/document/IPOL_STU(2020)621926

Gill, C. (1988). Personhood and Personality: The Four-Personae Theory in Cicero, De Officiis I. In *Oxford Studies in Ancient Philosophy: Volume VI.* Oxford University Press.

Hanafi, M. M., Kshetri, N., & Sharma, R. (2021). Economics of Artificial Intelligence in the Gulf Cooperation Council Countries. *Computing's Economics, 54*(12), 92–98. https://doi.org/10.1109/MC.2021.3113094

Hillier, C., & Koshul, B. (Eds.). (2017). *Muhammad Iqbal—Essays on the Reconstruction of Modern Muslim Thought.* Edinburgh University Press.

Kamali, M. H. (1993). Fundamental Rights of the Individual: An Analysis of Haqq (Right) in Islamic Law. *The American Journal of Islamic Social Sciences, 10*(3), 340–366. https://doi.org/10.35632/ajis.v10i3.2491

Kurki, A. J. V. (2019a). A Short History of the Right-Holding Person. In *A Theory of Legal Personhood, Oxford University Press*. Oxford University. https://doi.org/10.1093/oso/9780198844037.001.0001

Kurki, A. J. V. (2019b). The Legal Personhood of Artificial Intelligences. https://doi.org/10.1093/oso/9780198844037.003.0007

Latif, J. (2022). Rethinking Corporate Personhood in Consultation with Islam. *Journal of Markets & Morality, 25*(2), 353–364. https://link-gale-com.manchester.idm.oclc.org/apps/doc/A747784705/AONE?u=jrycal5&sid=bookmark-AONE&xid=22ee343b

Militsyna, K. (2022). Legal Personhood for Artificial Intelligence: Pro, Contra, Abstain? *Teisė, 122*(2022), 150–158. https://doi.org/10.15388/teise.2022.122.10

Mokhtar, M. K. (1994). The Treatise on the Knowledge About the Rational Soul and Its States by Ibn Sina: A Critical Edition and Annotated Translation. *Akademika, 44*, 45–71.

Naim, N. (2019). *An Examination of the Intellectual Property Regimes in the Gulf Co-Operation Council (GCC) States and a Series of Recommendations to Develop an Integrated Approach to Intellectual Property Rights*. https://bradscholars.brad.ac.uk/handle/10454/17386%0A; https://bradscholars.brad.ac.uk/bitstream/handle/10454/17386/naim,n.pdf?sequence=1

Naim, N. (2021). Critical Examination of the Intellectual Property Regimes in the Gulf Co-Operation Council (Gcc) States. *Indonesian Journal of International Law, 18*(4), 523–542. https://doi.org/10.17304/ijil.vol18.4.822

Nawi, A., et al. (2021). A Preliminary Survey of Muslim Experts' Views on Artificial Intelligence. *Islamiyyat, 43*(2), 3–16. https://doi.org/10.17576/islamiyyat-2021-4302-01

Novelli, C., Bongiovanni, G., & GiovanniSartor, G. (2021). A Conceptual Framework for Legal Personality and Its Application to AI. *Jurisprudence, 13*(2), 194–219. https://doi.org/10.1080/20403313.2021.2010936

Pagallo, U., (2018). Vital, Sophia, and Co.-The Quest for the Legal Personhood of Robots. *Information (Switzerland)*, 9. https://doi.org/10.3390/info9090230

*People ex rel. Nonhuman Rights Project, Inc. v. L*avery, No. 518336, 2014 WL 680276 (N.Y.) App. Div. Dec. 4, 2014.

Pratama, M. A., & Rizkiyah, E. L. (2022). A Theory of Legal Personhood by Visa A.J. Kurki. *Indonesian Journal of Law and Society, 3*(1), 157–166. https://academic.oup.com/medlaw/article/30/2/392/6588524

Price, D., & AlDebasi, A. (2017). The Golden Thread That Binds—The Shariah and Intellectual Property Protection. In *Protecting Intellectual Property in the Arabian Peninsula* (pp. 21–40). Routledge.

Raskulla, S. (2023). Hybrid Theory of Corporate Legal Personhood and Its Application to Artificial Intelligence. *SN Social Sciences, 3*(5), 1–14. https://doi.org/10.1007/s43545-023-00667-x

Riddell, P. (2005). Islam, Personhood and … Where Is God in All This? *Evangelical Quarterly, 77*(1), 47–63. https://doi.org/10.1163/27725472-07701005

Riddell, P. (2019). Islam and the Person: Historical and Contemporary Debates. *South Asian Journal of Religion and Philosophy, 1*(1), 38–51.

Rohman, A., Kusuma, A. R., & Firdausi, M. A. (2022). The Essence of 'Aql as Kamāl Al-Awwal in the View of Ibnu Sīnā and Its Relation to Education. *Dialogia, 20*(1), 176–207. https://doi.org/10.21154/dialogia.v20i1.3533

Saudi Data & AI Authority. (2023). AI Ethics Principles. https://sdaia.gov.sa/en/SDAIA/about/Documents/ai-principles.pdf

Smith, B. (1928). Legal Personality. *Yale Law Journal, Vol XXXVII*, No3 283.

Smith, P. A. (1983). The Beginning of Personhood: A Thomistic Perspective. *Laval Théologique et Philosophique, 39*(2), 195–214, p. 207. https://doi.org/10.7202/400029ar

Thaldar, D., & Naidoo, M. (2021). AI Inventorship: The Right Decision? *South African Journal of Science, 117*(11), 10–13. https://doi.org/10.17159/SAJS.2021/12509

Trahan, J. R. (2006). The Distinction between Persons & Things: An Historical Perspective. *Journal of Civil Law Studies, 1*.

Van Genderen, R. V. D. H. (2018). *Do We Need New Legal Personhood in the Age of Robots and AI?. Perspectives in Law, Business and Innovation*. https://doi.org/10.1007/978-981-13-2874-9_2

Wieacker, F. (1995). *A History of Private Law in Europe*. Clarendon Press.

Wise, S. (2015a). *Update on the Sandra Orangutan Case in Argentina*. NHRP Website https://www.nonhumanrights.org/blog/update-on-the-sandra-orangutan-case-in-argentina/

Wise, S. (2015b). *One Small Step for a Judge, One Giant Leap for the Nonhuman Rights Project*. NHRP Website http://www.nonhumanrightsproject.org/2015/08/04/thats-one-small-step-for-a-judge-onegiant-leap-for-the-nonhuman-rights-project/

Index

N. Naim et al. (eds.), *Intellectual Property and Innovation*, The Political Economy of the Middle East,
https://doi.org/10.1007/978-981-96-4020-1

The manufacturer's authorised representative in the EU is Springer Nature Customer Service Centre GmbH, Europaplatz 3, 69115 Heidelberg, Germany. If you have any concerns regarding our products, please contact ProductSafety@springernature.com

Printed and bound by CPI Group (UK) Ltd, Croydon, CR0 4YY
01/10/2026
02225854-0008